Rural Livelihoods in Chin

C000025738

In recent decades, China has undergone rapid economic growth, industrialisation and urbanisation concomitant with deep and extensive structural and social change, profoundly reshaping the country's development landscape and urban-rural relationships. This book applies livelihoods approaches to deepen our understanding of the changes and continuities related to rural livelihoods within the wider context of the political economy of development in post-socialist China, bridging the urban and rural scenarios and probing the local, national and global dynamics that have impacted on livelihood, in particular, its mobility, security and sustainability.

Presenting theoretically informêd and empirically grounded research by leading scholars from around the world, this book offers multidisciplinary perspectives on issues central to rural livelihoods, development, welfare and well-being. It documents and analyses the processes and consequences of change, focusing on the social protection of mobile livelihoods, particularly rural migrants' citizenship rights in the city, and the environmental, social and political aspects of sustainability in the countryside.

Rural Livelihoods in China contributes to the current scholarly and policy debates, and is among the first attempts to critically reflect on China's market transition and the associated pathways to change. It will be of interest to students of international development studies, China studies, social policy, public health, political science, and environmental studies at undergraduate and postgraduate levels, as well as academics, policy-makers and practitioners who are concerned with China's human and social development in general, and agriculture and rural livelihoods in particular.

Heather Xiaoquan Zhang is Senior Lecturer in Chinese Social Studies at the University of Leeds, UK.

Routledge Explorations in Development Studies

This Development Studies series features innovative and original research at the regional and global scale.

It promotes interdisciplinary scholarly works drawing on a wide spectrum of subject areas, in particular politics, health, economics, rural and urban studies, sociology, environment, anthropology, and conflict studies.

Topics of particular interest are globalization; emerging powers; children and youth; cities; education; media and communication; technology development; and climate change.

In terms of theory and method, rather than basing itself on any orthodoxy, the series draws broadly on the tool kit of the social sciences in general, emphasizing comparison, the analysis of the structure and processes, and the application of qualitative and quantitative methods.

Rural Livelihoods in China

Political economy in transition

Edited by Heather Xiaoquan Zhang

Routledge
Taylor & Francis Group

LONDON AND NEW YORK

First published 2015 by Routledge

2 Park Square, Milton Park, Abingdon, Oxfordshire OX14 4RN
711 Third Avenue, New York, NY 10017

Routledge is an imprint of the Taylor & Francis Group, an informa business

First issued in paperback 2017

British Library Cataloguing-in-Publication Data
A catalogue record for this book is available from the British Library

Library of Congress Cataloging-in-Publication Data
Rural livelihoods in China : political economy in transition / edited by
Heather Xiaoquan Zhang.
pages cm
Includes index.
1. Rural development–China. 2. Labor market–China. 3. Rural-urban
migration–China. 4. China–Rural conditions. 5. China–Economic
conditions. I. Zhang, Heather Xiaoquan.
HN740.Z9C66866 2015
307.1'2120951–dc23
2014036184

ISBN: 978-0-415-84467-3 (hbk)
ISBN: 978-0-8153-7975-1 (pbk)

Typeset in Goudy
by Cenveo Publisher Services

Contents

Figures

Tables

Contributors

Louis Augustin-Jean is a visiting scholar at the Hong Kong Polytechnic University. A specialist in economic sociology, his main research interests are agro-food markets, food habits and rural development in China and Hong Kong.

Bettina Gransow is Professor of Chinese Studies at Freie Universität Berlin, Germany, where she teaches at the Institute of East Asian Studies and the Otto Suhr Institute of Political Science. Her current research focus is on internal migration (voluntary and involuntary), migrants and health, and mega-city development.

Peter Ho is Chair Professor of Chinese Economy and Development at the Delft University of Technology, the Netherlands. He has published extensively on China's economic transition and environment, and has frequently acted as an advisor to members of the Chinese government and the Dutch Cabinet.

Nicholas Loubere is a PhD candidate in the White Rose East Asia Centre and the Department of East Asian Studies, University of Leeds, UK. His current research explores the role that rural financial services play in livelihood strategies, and local development practices and outcomes in rural China.

Chunling Pu is Professor and Dean of the College of Management of Xinjiang Agricultural University, China. Her research covers resource economics and agricultural economics.

Ngai Pun is Professor in the Department of Applied Social Sciences, Hong Kong Polytechnic University. Her research interests include labour, gender, social economy, China and globalisation.

Xiaoping Shi is Professor and Dean of the College of Public Administration and Professorial Research Fellow in the China Centre for Land Policy Research of Nanjing Agricultural University, China. His research covers development economics, and resource and environmental economics.

Graeme Smith is a research fellow in the College of Asia and the Pacific at the Australian National University, Australia. His research interests include the political economy of service delivery in rural China, as well as Chinese outbound investment, migration and development assistance in Pacific island countries.

Max Spoor is Professor of Development Studies at the International Institute of Social Studies, the Netherlands, Visiting Professor at IBEI Barcelona, Spain, and Guest Professor at Nanjing Agricultural University, China. His research focuses on transition economies such as Vietnam, China, and Central and Eastern Europe, with regard to rural and environmental issues, poverty and inequality.

Jac. A. A. Swart is Associate Professor in the Science and Society Group of the University of Groningen, the Netherlands. His work focuses on social and ethical aspects of the life sciences. He is a member of the Commission on Genetic Modification (COGEM), which advises the Dutch government on the environmental risks of biotechnology.

Ye Wang is a principal staff member in the Budget Division, Department of Finance, Ministry of Agriculture (MOA), China. She entered the Division of Special Funds, MOA, in 2005 and has researched agricultural policy and special funds since then. She completed her Master's thesis in Tsukuba University, Japan, in 2010.

Andrew Watson is Emeritus Professor at the University of Adelaide, Australia. His work discusses the issue of rural development in China and his recent focus has been China's social security system and its impact on farmers and migrants.

Yi Xu is a lecturer in the School of Sociology and Anthropology, Sun Yat-sen University, China. Her research interests include transnational labour rights activism, labour organising and industrial social work.

Dayuan Xue is Professor and Chief Scientist in the College of Life and Environmental Science, Minzu University of China. His academic and professional interests are related to biodiversity conservation, access and benefit sharing of genetic resources and associated indigenous knowledge, the regulation of GMOs, environmental economics, rural environmental management of protected areas and natural resources, and eco-farming.

Heather Xiaoquan Zhang is Senior Lecturer in Chinese Social Studies and Director of Postgraduate Studies, White Rose East Asia Centre, University of Leeds, UK. Her research interests include livelihood studies, rural-urban migration, social policy and citizenship, poverty, inequality and social exclusion, globalisation, gender, and health and well-being.

Jennifer H. Zhao is Professor of Agro-biotechnology and Biodiversity at the Chinese Academy of Agricultural Sciences, China. Her research focuses on plant genetic engineering and the social aspects of biotechnology and GMO research.

Abbreviations

ABC	Agricultural Bank of China
ACFTU	All-China Federation of Trade Unions
ADBC	Agricultural Development Bank of China
APEC	Asia-Pacific Economic Cooperation
ASEAN	Association of Southeast Asian Nations
ASEM	Asia-Europe Meeting
BEA	Bank of East Asia
BRCLAYP	Beijing Research Centre on Legal Aid for Young People
Bt Cotton	genetically modified cotton (*bacillis thuringiensis*)
Bt Rice	genetically modified rice
CAS	Chinese Academy of Sciences
CASS	Chinese Academy of Social Sciences
CBD	central business district
CBP	Cartagena biosafety protocol
CBRC	China Banking Regulatory Commission
CCP	Chinese Communist Party
CCPCC	Chinese Communist Party Central Committee
CEO	Chief Executive Officer
CFC	chlorofluorocarbon (freons)
CSTN	China Science and Technology Newsletter
DDT	dichlorodiphenyltrichloroethane
FPC	Funding the Poor Cooperative
GLF	Great Leap Forward
GM	genetically modified
GMO	genetically modified organism
HSBC	Hong Kong and Shanghai Banking Corporation
ILO	International Labour Organisation
ISAAA	International Service for the Acquisition of Agri-Biotech Applications
MCA	Ministry of Civil Affairs
MEP	Ministry of Environmental Protection
MFI	microfinance institution
MLC	microloan company

MLS	Minimum Living Standards
MOA	Ministry of Agriculture
MOF	Ministry of Finance
MOH	Ministry of Health
MoHRSS	Ministry of Human Resources and Social Security (before 2008, was MoLSS Ministry of Labour and Social Security)
MoLSS	Ministry of Labour and Social Security
MOST	Ministry of Science and Technology
NBSC	National Bureau of Statistics of China
NCMS	New Cooperative Medical Scheme
NEPA	National Environmental Protection Agency
NGO	non-governmental organisation
NPC	National People's Congress
NPO	non-profit organisation
OECD	Organisation for Economic Co-operation and Development
PAO	Poverty Alleviation Office
PBC	People's Bank of China
PI	"public intellectuals"
PLA	People's Liberation Army
PRC	People's Republic of China
PSBC	Postal Savings Bank of China
PSRB	Postal Savings and Remittance Bureau
RCC	rural credit cooperative
RCF	Rural Cooperative Foundation
RMCC	rural mutual credit cooperative
ROSCA	Rotating Savings and Credit Association
RTI	reproductive tract infection
SARS	severe acute respiratory syndrome
SAWS	State Administration of Work Safety
SEPA	State Environmental Protection Agency
SME	small and medium enterprise
SOE	state-owned enterprise
SSTC	State Science and Technology Commission
TVCM	township and village-run coal mine
TVE	township and village enterprise
UN	United Nations
UNDP	United Nations Development Programme
UNIDO-BINAS	United Nations Industrial Development Organisation – Biosafety Information Network and Advisory Service
USD	United States dollar
VTB	village and township bank
WHO	World Health Organisation
WTO	World Trade Organisation
XPCC	Xinjiang Production and Construction Corps
XUAR	Xinjiang Uyghur Autonomous Region

1   Introduction

Rural livelihood transformation and political economy in China

Heather Xiaoquan Zhang

Livelihood analysis and Chinese studies: exploring relevance and engaging with wider debates

This book aims to document and analyse the tremendous transformations of rural livelihoods, and the strategies, negotiations, contestations and struggles revolving around these livelihoods, their security, sustainability and their relationships with the "urban" in the wider context of the post-socialist Chinese political economy. The book as a whole also engages with some of the critical scholarly and policy debates over livelihood, its mobility and sustainability, and social development in China and beyond. Since the start of the market reforms in the late 1970s, rural livelihoods in China have undergone profound changes – from those gained primarily through grain farming to those characterised by highly diversified agricultural production, mixing grains with a variety of other crops, and with meat, aquaculture and dairy products; from those situated in the specific institutional arrangement of collective organisation of production to those drawing on small landholding family farming, and more recently, marked by an enlarged scale of production and cooperation resulting from increasing agricultural mechanisation and emerging farmers' cooperatives; from those largely in the mode of a subsistence agrarian economy to those diversifying into a plethora of farm, off-farm, non-farm activities and rural-urban migration. This transformative change is manifest in some key structural indicators. For example, the share of people employed in agriculture in the total national workforce declined significantly from 70.5 per cent in 1979 to 38 per cent in 2010 (Li *et al.* 2011: 12; Ye 2009: 118) and the proportion of the urban to the national total population, "the urbanisation rate", which is partly affected by rural-urban migration, increased from 17.9 per cent to 52.6 per cent between 1979 and 2012 (NBSC 2013; Ye 2009: 118). Rural off-farm and non-farm sectors, such as services and industries, have expanded rapidly. To take township and village enterprises (TVEs) as an example, their share in the country's gross value industrial output in 1980 was mere 9.8 per cent while by 2000 it had risen to 47 per cent (Chen 2004: 7), employing 142.7 million people in 2005 (Park 2008: 50) and accounting for about 36 per cent of the average annual income of farmers by 2007 (Chen *et al.* 2009: 210).[1] Today rural people engage in a wide range of socio-economic activities both in rural settings and across the increasingly blurred urban and rural scenarios, as partly characterised by the large-scale rural-urban migration that began in the early 1980s: more than 260 million migrant workers were employed in Chinese cities and towns in 2012 (State Council Migrant Workers Office 2013: 1). Many of these migrants have pursued translocal livelihoods within and across regions (against the structural restrictions embedded in the extant household registration [*hukou*] institution), and at the same time making an enormous contribution to the transformation of both the city (e.g. in respect of the largely urban-based economic growth) and the countryside (e.g. with regard to livelihood and income diversification, agricultural investment and poverty reduction), connecting rural-urban spaces, markets, societies and cultures in all the conceivable ways.

Meanwhile, the structural change witnessed during the past few decades entails important and profound relational (socio-economic) and allocational (income and resource distribution) dimensions, and ongoing struggles over these, both in the agrarian sector and between urban and rural societies, whose outcomes are being mediated and shaped by institutions and power to include also the politics of development policy interventions. While China's largely urban-centred economy has grown substantially, its agriculture and rural areas have become more marginalised than ever before and faced grave development challenges – typified in the so-called *san nong*[2] crisis – a crisis which was particularly severe between the 1990s and 2000s, and to an extent, still continues today. This is manifest, among other things, in constantly re-emerging rural poverty in both absolute and relative terms, widening inequalities between urban and rural areas, between coastal and inland regions and within the agrarian sector, in the often strained relationship between the local state and farmers, whose interests are frequently infringed upon in the form of, e.g. farmers' burdens caused by excessive taxes and fees, land requisitioning without appropriate compensation, environmental degradation and natural resource depletion, and in the exploitation and alienation of rural migrant workers in the city, and so forth (Li 2003; Lu 2005; Lü 1997; O'Brien and Li 2006; Sargeson 2013; State Council 2006; Taylor and Li 2012; Wang 2005; Wen 2004; Zhang *et al.* 2007). While more public actions have been taken since the early to mid-2000s to address the issues,[3] the policy measures, as argued by several chapters in this volume, have often missed their goals, resulting in "unintended outcomes". The latest national surveys conducted by leading Chinese think tanks show that the trend has not been effectively curbed. Inequality and wealth polarisation have continued their rapid rise and become the biggest socio-economic concern of all. Researchers from Beijing University recently report that nationally, family asset inequality measured by the Gini coefficient increased from 0.45 in 1995 to 0.55 in 2002, and further to 0.73 in 2012 with the top *1 per cent* of all families in China possessing more than *one third* of national wealth while the bottom *25 per cent* of families share only a minute *1 per cent* of national wealth (China Social Sciences Survey Centre 2014), positioning post-socialist China among the most unequal societies in the world with the largest wealth concentration in the hands of the few.

Analysts point out that regional and urban-rural inequalities still play a major role in this alarming polarisation – a conclusion supported by another authoritative source: A survey conducted by academics at the Chinese Academy of Social Sciences (CASS). The latest *Blue Book of China's Society*, published at the end of 2013, reported that the urban-rural income ratio between the richest and the poorest areas of the country exceeded 20:1 in 2012 (CASS 2013). Such macrodata help reveal a general trend and pattern, delineating a heavily lopsided development landscape in the country as a consequence of intense accumulation and expansion of capital and overall societal commodification in an inadequately regulated market economy. However, the exploration and documentation of the local scenarios in their historical, socio-cultural and political specificities, and the provision of deeper insights into and explanations of the complex causes and consequences of these processes, and their impact on people's livelihoods require detailed, contextualised, theoretically informed and empirically grounded research.

This collection contributes to the intellectual endeavour of this kind. Written by a group of leading researchers from across the world, who are concerned with China's agricultural and rural development, the chapters closely and critically examine some of the rural development challenges around the central theme of livelihoods in the larger context of China's political economy of development since the early 2000s. The recent decade and more have witnessed the rise of "livelihoods approaches", and the notion of "livelihoods" has become central to the thinking, practice and debate on agricultural and rural development worldwide (de Haan and Zoomers 2005; Scoones 2009). However, despite its increasing popularity elsewhere in the world, use of the approach and engagement with the wider debate in the China studies field have been limited, and the idea's potential (when combined with other development theories or concepts, as argued by Zhang and Loubere in Chapter 8 of this book)[4] to understand and explain China's rural development and agrarian change has been underexplored. This scenario may reflect, on the one hand, the ambiguity and vagueness in the English-Chinese translation of the term.[5] On the other, it may suggest a tendency in development studies and China studies alike to consider, explicitly or implicitly, China and its development experience as "exceptional" (particularly due to the perceived character of its state, its political system and the relations between the state and society). As a result, and with only a few exceptions,[6] development (as well as postdevelopment or poststructuralist) ideas, analytic concepts and critical social theories employed in other parts of the world (e.g. Latin America, South and Southeast Asia, Africa, as well as industrial societies, e.g. the USA, Europe), as Salmenkari (2013) incisively points out, tend to be considered inapplicable or irrelevant to the study of China. Where China is concerned, theoretical and analytical frameworks (which also inform policy thinking and practice) are still dominated by a kind of linear "development stages" thesis and binary framing at various levels (e.g. the "advanced" urban versus the "backward" rural, the "oppressive" state as opposed to a "submissive" society), which are essentially situated in the modernisation school of thought and its contemporary variants, e.g. neoliberalism, rational choice theory, hyper-globalism, and so forth (Wang 2011; Zhang and Sanders 2007).

Research methodologies guided by such frameworks have leaned overwhelmingly towards quantitative and statistical methods considered to be "objective", "value-free", "representative", and thus "scientific", as they are able to reveal a singular "universal truth". The attempts to quantify social data and to model on methods used in natural sciences are underpinned by positivist ontological and epistemological assumptions, which have become so predominant as to close down the possibility of even considering more balanced methodological approaches informed by plural or alternative theoretical paradigms.[7] Mainstream studies in the field frequently interpret the development processes and pathways that China has gone through in recent history as the "triumph" of "capitalist globalisation" driven by the "invisible hand" of the "free market" (Pun and Xu in Chapter 5 provide a powerful critique with their empirical case study of the relations of production between rural migrant labourers and their "invisible" employers in China's construction industry). Emerging development challenges like the *san nong* crisis have, accordingly, been framed in a way that the "legacy" of state socialism and "incomplete" marketisation or an inadequate degree of commodification are forever blamed as the culprit, with an underlying preconception of the market as a "level-playing field" allowing "equal" exchanges between "free" agents, and being able to increase efficiency and profits for economic growth. Thus, an unregulated "autonomous" market is considered the panacea, regardless of the vastly changed circumstances and the hugely different context now from nearly four decades ago. The market orthodoxy-informed "deepening reforms" agenda (i.e. further deregulation of and greater reliance on market forces) is often put forward by powerful and increasingly entrenched interests and elite "experts"[8] as the best solution to (rather than a main source of) China's development problems and challenges – old and new.[9] Such an interpretation is also based on many scholars' shared faith in the necessarily "progressive" nature of historical and societal change in China and globally, e.g. other "emerging economies" undergoing the presupposed unitary and "inevitable" *laissez-faire*, neoliberal historical transition, following "natural laws and regularities", and moving towards the "advanced stage" of greater global political, socio-cultural "convergence" with regard to the future of agriculture, development, globalisation and modernisation (Escobar 2010; Long and Liu 2009; Xu and Wang 2003; Zhang, Y. 2010).

Rural livelihoods in flux: a contested terrain

This collection of chapters, grounded on rigorous empirical, institutional and policy analyses, using diverse research methods, and from multi- and interdisciplinary perspectives, reflects on and interrogates, explicitly or implicitly, the modernist mega-narrative together with many of the taken-for-granted assumptions, and their informed sense of certainty, predictability, "necessity" and "inevitability" of historical change and social practice. As a whole, the chapters problematise, directly or indirectly, the prevailing discourse and linear conceptions of a singular modernity with regard to the Chinese experience in agricultural and rural development, urbanisation and industrialisation, and probe deeply the causes and consequences of the *san nong* crisis, as well as evaluating some of the recent institutional responses. Focusing on two interlocking and mutually constitutive themes resolved around livelihoods, i.e. first, mobility and second, sustainability, and other related and intersected sub-themes, e.g. the risk society, the developmental state (Jennifer Zhao and her co-authors in Chapter 6 investigate the ways in which genetically modified organisms [GMOs] and biotechnology, and their associated risks are governed in China, and whether China could be considered a "developmental risk society"), the chapters show, in different ways and through multi-scalar lenses, that China's agriculture and rural areas remain "backward" and are "lagging further and further behind" the country's metropolises (illustrated in part by the Gini coefficient and the urban-rural income discrepancy presented above) are not determined by "natural laws", e.g. the "survival of the fittest" evolutionary, market logic. Nor are these attributable to the "innate statics" and "inward-looking inclination", or "low quality" of the country people and their "agrarian traditions", as diagnosed by conventional modernisation theory. Rather, and engaging with the wider debate about livelihoods approaches,[10] the studies together show that the current predicament of Chinese agriculture and the plight of China's farmers, also including rural migrants who have worked in the city but have been systemically denied permanent settlement therein, or urban *hukou*,[11] and its associated rights and entitlements, are down to the workings of the political economy of post-socialist China – the kind of social closure and exclusion realised and maintained through larger institutional and systemic forces that have enabled the maximum extraction of surplus value (the various constitutive livelihood "capitals") from the countryside, the allocation of resources and the exercise of power at various levels in favour of the city, especially the urban-based elite. It is the continued "urban bias", to use Michael Lipton's (1977) classic thesis, coupled with the prevalent and protracted exploitation, alienation and commodification of migrant labour through urban and/or capital accumulation,[12] to use a Marxist conception, manifested and embedded in a series of national and local institutions, policies and social practices that have worked to the disadvantage of rural places, peoples, cultures and livelihoods.

It is recognised that one of the strengths of livelihood approaches is their potential or ability to bridge "perspectives across different fields of rural development scholarship and practice" (Scoones 2009: 171). This multi-perspective bridging analytical tool, however, has thus far primarily focused on livelihood-related agrarian change (especially in respect of local-level processes, practices and negotiations involving multiple and socially differentiated actors) on the rural scene. As a result, as Heather Xiaoquan Zhang (2007) points out, much less effort has been made to study "livelihoods on the move" or "mobile livelihoods" (see also Chapter 2 by Heather Zhang in this volume) and the struggles surrounding these livelihoods with a view that also connects the urban (e.g. migrant workers' urban experiences) with the rural (e.g. the locally understood meanings of such experiences for livelihoods, poverty or well-being at rural sites), and links the micro-level empirical observations with the political economy of development at the macro-level (e.g. the larger structural forces and broader social relations, such as those between capital and labour not only at particular urban sites but also in urban-based capital's penetration into rural scenes), as pointed out by Scoones (2009) and Bernstein (2010), among others. While a large body of literature on the migration–development nexus has shed light on migration as a household livelihood strategy, particularly emphasising the role of migrant remittances in diversifying livelihoods, managing farm risks, accumulating financial capital for investment and alleviating poverty in rural areas, or in the case of international migration, in countries of origin (Adams and Page 2003; Ratha 2013; Stark 1980, 1991), more recent research has started paying greater attention to the social cost of migrant workers' remittances in the China context (Murphy 2009), as well as to their utilisation by rural households: It is found that these monies have largely been spent on healthcare and/or children's education, pointing to an inadequate role of the Chinese state in rural welfare investment and public service provision (Huang and Zhan 2008). It is therefore argued by critics (e.g. Bakker 2010) that the euphoria about migrants' remittances as an automatic financial flow from the core to the peripheral regions – and thus a crucial developmental tool or even a panacea – fits well the neoliberal political philosophy and ideology, together with its prescribed market-based solutions to poverty, inequality and underdevelopment. Such a prevailing neoclassic/ neoliberal scholarly and policy discourse, the critiques maintain, marginalises the role of the state in strengthening the links between migration and development – broadly conceived as people-centred – through effective public policy interventions (ibid.). The chapters in Part I of this book, by focusing on public actions taken by the central and local state, including, e.g. social welfare institutions and practices for migrant workers and their families in Chinese cities, and social policy issues in the countryside, contribute to the wider scholarly and policy debate on the nexus between mobility, livelihood and development both within China and beyond.

The book's second interlocking theme, sustainability, is the focus of Part II and deals with the human and social dimensions of sustainability with regard to rural livelihoods and political economy, tackling issues ranging from food security and politics revolving around the sub-themes of the "risk society" and the "developmental state", to crop diversification adopted as the local development strategy for poverty reduction, the trajectory and contours of rural finance development and farmers' access to financial capital as a right to livelihood resources, rural bureaucratic restructuring, organisations and governance, and the design, implementation and effect of new policy interventions, especially the agricultural subsidy policy systematically introduced since the mid-to-late 2000s, as well as their interactions with wider institutional actors across sectors, locales and at various levels in rural China. Here, unlike conventional approaches whereby sustainable livelihoods are conceptualised and analysed more in relation to the different physical assets that rural people possess, the protection of the environment, as well as access to and management of natural resources (Chambers and Convey 1992; Ellis 2000), the chapters in Part II of this volume employ a broader understanding of sustainability and sustainable livelihoods incorporating also the social, human and political aspects as discussed above. As such, together they make a unique contribution – by examining the Chinese experiences and dynamics in this respect – to an evolving perspective accentuating social sustainability in the sustainable livelihoods and development scholarship (cf. Balaceanu *et al.* 2012; Hill *et al.* 2014; Lehtonen 2004), and to the related theoretical and policy debates nationally and globally.

The structure of the book

Bearing in mind the conceptual and thematic connections, policy issues and debates, as well as the development challenges relating to rural livelihoods and the political economy in China as the central concerns of this book, let us now turn to look at the topics of individual chapters, their main findings and arguments in the book's two parts.

A cluster of four chapters constitutes Part I. In Chapter 2, Heather Xiaoquan Zhang, drawing on extensive ethnographic fieldwork in Beijing and Tianjin, North China, engages with the debate about livelihoods approaches through investigating social welfare issues related to mobile livelihoods in Chinese cities. Zhang extends the livelihood approach to include Chinese migration studies, and expands the conventional focus of the framework (i.e. on economic opportunities) by incorporating a health and well-being perspective. Drawing on the work of Amartya Sen (1984, 1985, 1987, 1992), she conceives health as an essential "human capital", and examines migrants' health, in particular, work safety and occupational health. Zhang argues that for the more than 260 million migrant workers in China, maintaining good health is the major precondition for making a living for themselves and their families. Yet of China's workers, migrants are the most vulnerable to ill health and broken livelihoods, as they often face hazardous work and poor living conditions, and generally speaking, have no employment security, and are frequently excluded from healthcare services and other social insurance schemes. Undermined or destroyed ability to work, combined with high medical costs due to disenfranchisement, can push migrant workers and their families into deep poverty. The expanding academic literature on China's dynamic, massive rural-urban migration, however, has not seriously investigated the complex links between migration, health and livelihoods, their meanings for the welfare of migrants, and their implications for poverty reduction on China's urban and rural scenes. Zhang's research addresses this lacuna, and finds that migrant workers' social rights to health are a fiercely contested domain of citizenship, entailing aspects of exclusion, inclusion, and control and allocation of vital livelihood resources among different social groups at varied scales, with health and well-being outcomes being socially determined. She shows that despite the accelerated pace of legislation and consolidated efforts to reconstruct the welfare system in China in recent years, the new social security schemes have thus far, by and large, failed to protect migrant workers in a systematic manner. Connecting the urban and rural scenarios through closely examining the links between migration, health and livelihood security and sustainability, Zhang, in light of Scoones' (2009) critical commentary, suggests that if politics and power are central to livelihoods approaches, applying the approach to China's migration studies means paying greater attention to the more hidden historical and social processes and practices, whereby the rural surplus squeeze and the staggering rate of capital accumulation by the urban-based elite have been materialised, accelerated and intensified through the systemic denial of migrant workers' equal citizenship rights – perpetuating their "cheap labour" status, and narrowing the life chances of migratory individuals, families and communities. The implications of such massive disenfranchisement for poverty, social mobility, the emerging social stratification and the overall societal stability of Chinese society should be further explored in future research.

Continuing with migrants' social welfare as an issue central to livelihood and its security, in Chapter 3, Andrew Watson employs an institutional and policy analysis method, and conceptualises social protection as an essential part of livelihoods studies, on the basis that this helps people withstand external shocks, enhance their resilience and sustain capacity in the face of structural economic change. He illustrates this by investigating the emerging social security programmes for China's migrant workers with a focus on old-age security and retirement incomes. Watson applies an integrated and dynamic approach to examine the various pension schemes in breadth and depth. Concurring with Heather Xiaoquan Zhang (Chapter 2), Watson shows that migrant workers have become the key labour force in China's economic growth, but they have been largely excluded from the urban social welfare systems. This is partly due to the current character of the constitutive urban welfare schemes, which are based on a contributory social insurance model, are fragmented into local pools and are non-portable, thus seriously hindering obstacles to migrant workers' participation and ultimate pension benefit on retirement, given their insecure employment conditions and livelihood mobility. Watson further probes whether migrant workers are included in the rural pension schemes if the urban ones fail them, and finds that the new rural pension systems are very basic and separate from those in the city, where migrant workers have made huge contributions to its growth and prosperity. Looking closely at the urban and rural pension schemes in a holistic fashion, Watson argues that the current schemes of social protection and welfare support are geographically and socially differentiated, and in his particular case of old-age pension insurance, marked by the urban-rural divide, with the associated identities, rights and entitlements perpetuated by the *hukou* institution. This situation creates barriers to the movement of labour, which is especially important for rural migrants. At the same time, conflicting interests between levels of government and between different social groups mean that the political economy of policy development is complex, involving multiple actors and asymmetrical power across intersected social fields. Watson recommends that the construction of an integrated and flexible social welfare system for migrant workers should be prioritised as a public action response to the rapid changes and the concomitant challenges that large economic and political forces, e.g. urbanisation, industrialisation and globalisation, have wrought upon the lives and livelihoods of migrants, their families and communities.

Further deepening the thematic links between migration, health, livelihoods and poverty reduction (which are also dealt with in Chapter 2 by Heather Xiaoquan Zhang), Bettina Gransow in Chapter 4 conceives health as an essential asset for rural migrants in search of non-agricultural employment and higher incomes. Drawing on qualitative data, e.g. observations and in-depth interviews conducted in "urban villages" in Guangzhou, South China, Gransow traces the emergence of the "urban village" phenomenon, and concurs with the findings of other scholars (e.g. Wu *et al.* 2014) that "urban villages", while providing affordable housing for migrants and their families as "outsiders", are notorious for their cramped and poor living conditions, thus constitute potential risk factors for migrants' health. Gransow identifies a range of other work- or lifestyle-related health risks and threats – from both objective and subjective perspectives, and at the individual and institutional levels. While focusing on the strategies that individual migrants employ to cope with these health hazards, Gransow contextualises such strategies within the larger institutional environment and considers access to health insurance, information and healthcare services as an essential livelihood resource and entitlement. She finds that subjectively, rural migrants tend to downplay the health risks by emphasising the physical strength of their bodies. She then explains this subjective versus objective paradox through conceptualising migrants' self-perception and self-representation of their body – as strong and healthy – as a kind of psychological armour adopted to defend themselves against not only the hazardous aspects of their working and living conditions, but also an urban environment that is discriminatory and exclusionary, denying their basic social rights. This self-defensive, strong bodily image itself, Gransow argues, may paradoxically aggravate the vulnerability of migrants to ill-health. Gransow contends that migrant workers' individual strategies are unable to mitigate the health risks and sustain livelihoods unless government policies are changed to recognise and respond more effectively to the situation of migrants.

Studies on China's rural-urban migration in recent years have also witnessed a critical analytic turn with some scholars starting to go beyond market-based solutions to rural poverty via labour migration alone and probing deeply the relations of production and the myriad ways in which urban-based private capital (domestic and global) extracts maximum surplus value from migrant industrial workers, and the struggles by the latter for their basic labour rights, especially their delayed or default wages (though these wages are still below a "living wage", i.e. the level of pay which would allow for the reproduction of labour power).[13] In Chapter 5, Ngai Pun and Yi Xu, employing such a neo-Marxist perspective, contribute to the debate over the livelihood approach, particularly its need (as Bernstein [2010] and Scoones [2009] argue) to build multi-scalar links between the micro-, meso- and macro-processes, interactions and dynamics, and to address directly foundational issues of class, social relations and the broader political economy of development. Drawing on rich empirical data, including fieldwork observations and interviews with a range of key actors at both urban and rural sites across the country, Pun and Xu carefully unpack the complexities involved in the labour subcontracting system in the Chinese construction industry that has evolved in the post-socialist period. They demonstrate, conceptually and empirically, how changes in the political economy of the construction industry have given rise to the current labour subcontracting system characterised by a "double absence" – the absence of a boss and management, and the subsequent absence (i.e. invisibility) of a capital–labour relationship – and the ways that such a "double absence" has disguised the extreme exploitative relations of production, as well as perpetuated the phenomena of wage arrears and the struggle of migrant construction workers to pursue unpaid wages in various ways, sometimes involving violent collective action. Pun and Xu argue that underlying a narrative of "rightful resistance" (cf. O'Brien and Li 2006) – i.e. the use of morally or legally oriented language by migrant workers (e.g. "justice" and "law") in their everyday livelihood struggles – are what the authors term "incipient class actions" and collective resistance to capitalist exploitation embedded in social relations of production and reproduction in the free market.

Part II of the volume, comprising five additional chapters, turns to rural settings to consider issues related to the interconnected and intersected themes of livelihood and sustainability. In Chapter 6, Jennifer Zhao, Peter Ho, Dayuan Xue and Jac Swart engage with the debate from a novel interdisciplinary perspective, dealing with the regulation and management of the environmental uncertainties and risks associated with new agro-technologies, e.g. GMOs. They address the research question of whether China could be considered a "developmental risk society", by which the authors mean a "developmental state" (as China is sometimes conceived – see Chapter 8 by Heather Xiaoquan Zhang and Nicholas Loubere for further discussion), faced with a plethora of development challenges and dilemmas, in particular, the urgent need to safeguard food security for its large population on the one hand, and the uncertainties and risks relating to the new biotechnologies to produce food on the other, and thus could overlook or even disregard the risks and controversies surrounding such technologies, but rush to adopt them in favour of tackling the imminent issues and overall development – an approach which could have serious longer-term implications for ecological diversity, biosafety, and livelihood resilience and sustainability. Through a deep institutional analysis of the roles played by the key actors involved, including the central state, transnational biotech companies, non-governmental organisations (NGOs) and independent specialists, the authors argue that the answer to the question is, in effect, much more complex than a simple unilinear modernist or state–society binary perspective would offer.

They find that the pathways and processes of biotech development in China have involved substantial dynamics, negotiations and countervailing forces in society that balance the different – and often conflicting – interests of diverse social and political groups and actors. This socio-political constellation, the authors conclude, has allowed China to confront the "new risks" and deal with the livelihood dilemmas, albeit in a less consistent and coordinated manner.

In Chapter 7, Max Spoor, Xiaoping Shi and Chunling Pu apply a livelihood framework to explore the relationship between poverty and agricultural diversification in Xinjiang Uyghur Autonomous Region (XUAR), Northwest China, and to evaluate the recent policy interventions that have attempted to address issues of mono-crop dependency (particularly on cotton) and rural poverty in the region. Drawing on primary data gathered during household and village surveys in Awati County in southwestern Xinjiang, the authors find that limited livelihood choices other than farming and the lower level of crop diversification are largely responsible for the generally low farm income and relatively high poverty incidence therein. The chapter documents the ways in which recent government policies have responded to the challenge by encouraging greater agricultural diversification through, e.g. inter-cropping of fruits, nuts, vegetables, and so forth, with substantial state investment and provision of subsidies (which is the focus of Chapter 10 by Augustin-Jean and Wang). Evaluating these policy interventions in terms of their effect on local livelihoods, the authors show that these policies tend to be formulated in a top-down mass campaign style but lack careful weighing of the potential benefits against the constraints, e.g. water scarcity (which may affect longer-term environmental and livelihood sustainability) or the market for the new products. They argue that while crop diversification in XUAR could potentially sustain local livelihoods and alleviate poverty, such measures should be backed by policies of market development, and should take into full account the downside effects, e.g. increased competition (from domestic and international sources) and thus lower farm-gate prices. Combining more careful overall planning and active development of the market for the new products locally, regionally and nationally is suggested by the authors as a possible way forward.

The interlocking themes of livelihood and sustainability are further explored by Heather Xiaoquan Zhang and Nicholas Loubere in Chapter 8 through a close examination of the role that rural finance plays in local and national development in China. Zhang and Loubere, charting the trajectory of rural financial development, unravel the ways in which rural finance, during both the state socialist and post-socialist periods, has facilitated the outflow of rural financial resources to the urban sector to support urban-based industrialisation at the expense of local people's needs for credit, and for diverse financial services and products. Employing a critical perspective and focusing, in particular, on the more recent penetration of the so-called "microfinance industry" in rural China since the mid-2000s, Zhang and Loubere question the impact of the more neoliberal-oriented policies on the longer-term sustainability of rural livelihoods.

They argue that studies on rural finance in China, instead of being treated as "exceptional", need to engage with the global debates theoretically, methodologically and practically. The chapter argues that a strengthened livelihood approach (as proposed by Scoones 2009), combined with an actor-oriented perspective (cf. Long 2001; Long and Liu 2009), would serve as a valuable conceptual and methodological tool and be able to generate deeper knowledge and a more nuanced understanding of the intricate and dynamic interactions and relationships between rural finance, livelihoods and sustainable socio-economic development in China and beyond.

In Chapter 9, Graeme Smith examines what he terms the "soft centralisation" policy piloted in rural Anhui Province during the early-to-late 2000s (which is part of a larger central government administrative reform programme aimed at streamlining local bureaucracy and strengthening the organisational capacity of the Chinese state), and explores the policy's effects on the livelihoods of local officials and ordinary residents in the longer term. Drawing on detailed ethnographic data, Smith identifies two aspects that comprise this "soft centralisation" of local administration: the amalgamation of townships and villages as the lowest level of government, and the merger of specific township and county bureaus within a vertical-horizontal government organisational structure. Smith illustrates how the process of policy implementation was turned into a "battlefield" where a variety of actors involved (e.g. township and village heads, directors of offices/bureaus, frontline cadres and farmers) contested, negotiated, sometimes accommodated or even manipulated the policy, and manoeuvred to advance their own interests and make claims on the socio-economic and political resources during their redeployment. Policy outcomes were entangled with these livelihood struggles, and ultimately shaped by the dynamics and interactions between the actors differentially positioned in the existing administrative hierarchy, institutional structure and power relationship at various levels. Smith argues that these reform measures imposed from above by external actors created disincentives for frontline government workers, and undermined the originally designed goal of building a more effective bureaucracy at the level of local state, or "good governance". Recentralisation, hence, has resulted in many unintended consequences for the livelihoods of rural residents, particularly those in remote townships and villages. His case study of the implementation of the "soft centralisation" policy in Anhui evidences the theoretical insights offered by an actor-interface perspective that

> [I]f intervening parties ... fail to take seriously the ways in which people mobilise and use resources through existing social networks and cultural commitments, they run the risk of being rejected by, or distanced from, the life experiences and priorities of local [people].
>
> (Long and Liu 2009: 66)

Furthering the discussion on "unintended outcomes" of development policy interventions, Louis Augustin-Jean and Ye Wang, in the final contribution

(Chapter 10) of this collection, deal with a recent (but much under-researched) paradigm shift in policy and practice that has considerably impacted on rural livelihood and its sustainability, i.e. the provision of agricultural subsidies (in contrast to the previous surplus-extracting approach) under the broader central government guideline of "industry supporting agriculture", and in order to more effectively tackle the *san nong* issue. This new policy has been initiated also as a measure to safeguard food security (a topic tackled in Chapter 6 by Jennifer Zhao and her co-authors) in the face of the challenges posed by globalisation, concomitant with increasing competition as a result of the growing import of agricultural produce from industrial countries, whose agriculture enjoys strong government support (thus offering very competitive prices) in the form of subsidies and other measures backed by established institutional mechanisms and policy instruments (e.g. the EU Common Agricultural Policy introduced in the early 1960s). Augustin-Jean and Wang focus their analysis on the design and implementation of the "four subsidies" (*si butie*) policy, using Jilin as a case study. Paying close attention to the organisational dimension of policy implementation, they find that when a policy concerns two government ministries (in this case, the ministries of Finance and Agriculture), problems often arise because different organisational configurations (e.g. different modes of operation) and existing institutional obstacles (e.g. different objectives conceived by different government bodies) can hinder the negotiation process that is required to overcome bureaucratic rigidity. On the basis of a multi-scalar analysis of the "four subsidies" policy, Augustin-Jean and Wang argue that appropriate and effective policy-making aimed at strengthening the livelihoods of farmers should take into account the policy's "architecture", and allow for negotiation, flexibility and accommodation of the diverse operational practices of the different government administrative bodies, as well as the participation of local farmers, whose livelihood sustainability and welfare are the very goal of the development interventions in general, and the "four subsidies" policy in particular.

In short, this Introduction teases out and articulates the main theme and sub-themes of the book, i.e. livelihood, and its mobility and sustainability, and explores their relevance to contemporary Chinese studies. Employing a critical perspective, the chapter unravels some of the theoretical, ontological and methodological challenges that we face in understanding post-socialist Chinese experiences in agricultural and rural development. It argues that a genuine understanding of these experiences cannot be achieved without investigating the complexities and dynamics of the diverse aspects of rural livelihoods and the struggles around these livelihoods within the specific historical, political and socio-cultural context, and the political economy of development in China. In search of alternative analytical frameworks to the prevailing modernisation discourse, this chapter introduces the book as one of the first collective intellectual endeavours to confront the challenges in research, policy and practice, to engage with the wider debates and to interrogate the accepted wisdom of the modernist thesis.

Notes

1   The growth of the TVE sector has become stagnant since the late 1990s when most TVEs were privatised, transferring many collectively owned TVEs into private hands. There are a number of factors contributing to this scenario, including the increasing competition from urban-based larger industries with better technological knowledge, e.g. state-owned enterprises, joint ventures and foreign-owned companies, and the environmental damage and health risks caused by TVEs for local residents (Chen *et al.* 2009; Zhang L. 2007).

2   The term "*san nong*", or three "*nongs*" (in Chinese), stands for agriculture (*nongye*), the countryside (*nongcun*) and farmers (*nongmin*). Moreover, the use of "*san nong*" has different meanings in different contexts. For example, "*san nong*" sometimes refers to the problems related to the "three *nongs*", namely the "*san nong* issue", while on other occasions, it may simply mean the *san nong* sector.

3   The most noticeable policy measures include, e.g. the launch of the construction of the new countryside campaign in 2005, the national abolition of agricultural tax in 2006, the initiation of a broad "urban-rural integration" programme in 2007, the higher priority given to building a more comprehensive social welfare system in rural areas, and the greater support for agriculture through subsidies since 2008.

4   For example, with an actor-oriented theoretical perspective proposed and elaborated by Norman Long (2001), or a neo-Marxist class conception as argued by Henry Bernstein (2010).

5   When translated into Chinese, the term "livelihoods" often has varied meanings not necessarily in alignment with what is generally understood in "livelihood studies". It is sometimes translated as "*shengji*" (a means for a living), while at other times as "*minsheng*" ("well-being" or "welfare"). On still other occasions, it is translated as "*shenghuo*" ("life" or "subsistence"), e.g. the social assistance scheme "*zuidi shenghuo baozhang zhidu*" (equivalent to the low income benefits scheme, e.g. in the UK) is often translated into English as the "Minimum Livelihood Guarantee System".

6   Norman Long is one of the few influential social theorists, who have made pioneering and outstanding efforts to theorise and explain Chinese rural development and agrarian change from diverse theoretical lenses, and to bring China into the wider theoretical and policy debates. See, for example, Long (2010), Long and Liu (2009), Long *et al.* (2010).

7   See Michael Burawoy (2011) for a powerful critique of the positivist epistemological formulation in American sociology. Burawoy also points out that China studies, e.g. in the sociology discipline, have been heavily influenced by US positivist thinking and argumentation (ibid.: 400).

8   A deep analysis of the intricate process whereby knowledge, money and power are increasingly in alliance in present-day China – self-referencing and mutually justifying in an increasingly entrenched chain of vested interests – is beyond the scope of this work. That said, here I provide an illustrative example of the often self-proclaimed "public intellectuals" (PI, *gonggong zhishifenzi*). The PIs nowadays are becoming an essential part of the wealthy elite, using their embedded "knowledge" and influence to vigorously preach market fundamentalism often with self-serving hidden agendas. A case in point involves such a PI specialising in rural development. The PI volunteered to "go down" from Beijing to Guizhou in China's southwestern region in late 2013 to serve as a village official with the declared intention to take "new ideas" and "expert knowledge" to the remote "backward" area inhabited by the Buyi ethnic minority, and to "modernise" the village. The "innovative idea" is to turn the extremely beautiful but poor village into an "artist village" modelled on the expensive one located in suburban Beijing, where the wealthy PI resides. The "idea" is to persuade the villagers to contract out their "derelict" houses to external capital that the PI brings in through his business networks for redevelopment – transforming the village into a "Buyi Dayuan", i.e. a cluster of Buyi-style courtyards – to attract tourists. Meanwhile, modelled on the Beijing

village, the real target of the project is the rich, famous and powerful, including artists, celebrities and the business class, who are expected to visit and settle therein. The "deal" offered by the PI to the villagers for their houses is a *long-term rental contract* with a *30-year* tenure at the rate of *eight yuan/m²/year*, and for their unoccupied land (*kong di*) – *two yuan /m²/year for the same tenure*. Clearly local people's livelihoods and the long-term sustainability of these livelihoods are the least concerns of the PI. Evidently, as the external "expert", who offers voluntarily to "go down" there, the ulterior motive of the PI is to seek business opportunities and make a huge profit by taking advantage of the trusting villagers, and of the huge information asymmetry between the city-based elite and the local villagers with regard to the current and potential local land value. The proposal was, in the end, vetoed by the local authorities, which were then framed, on the Chinese Internet and on the social media, as "conservative" and "backward", lacking the "basic concept" of a "market economy" to "develop" their locales (*Sina News* 2013). For an insightful discussion of the increasing divide within the Chinese intelligentsia during the post-socialist period, see Y. Zhang (2008).

9 The wholesale privatisation of agricultural land, hard pushed by many elite "experts" both within and outside China in recent years, is a case in point. See Zhang and Donaldson (2013) for a detailed analysis of the debate on the issue and a counter-argument.

10 See de Haan and Zoomers (2005), and Scoones (2009) for in-depth analyses and critical reviews of the livelihoods perspectives and their related debates.

11 It should be noted that rural migrants who have stayed in the city for three months or more are counted as the "urban population" in the latest census of 2010. This "urban status" of migrants (who account for more than one-third of the "urban population"), however, has been uncoupled from urban *hukou*, whose non-monetary "added value" involves a whole package of born advantage and privilege, in particular, access to the labour market, public services and social welfare benefits – the most conspicuous aspects of urban-rural inequalities and the sources of persistent rural poverty. In other words, rural migrants' "urban status" in the official urbanisation statistics has not entailed equal citizenship rights with urban *hukou* holders. The "urbanisation rate" of nearly 53 per cent in 2012 (NBSC 2013) – an indicator of the level of industrialisation and development – is of little meaning from the perspective of welfare and well-being for all citizens as the ultimate development goal, and thus could well be described as, in Peter Laurence's (2010: 143) words, "development by numbers".

12 For detailed discussions on "urban accumulation", see Hirst and Zeitlin (1992), cited in L. Zhang (2007).

13 Li and Qi (2014) apply the combined social structure of accumulation theory and labour process theory to understand the puzzling contradictions caused by the large gap between the real wage (defined as the level of pay within the legally designated 8-hour work day for 5 days a week) and the living wage (which is the level of pay necessary for the reproduction of labour power), and to explain the astonishing pace of capital accumulation in post-socialist China. They identify two interlocking means by which existing urban-based labour institutions have maintained the rate of capital accumulation. The first is through making migrant workers depend on overtime work, and the second is through the rural economy. While their research provides deep insights into the first means, i.e. the ways that labour processes and labour institutions have jointly worked for rapid capital accumulation in the city, the second aspect remains unexplored, and hence requires closer scholarly scrutiny.

References

Adams Jr., Richard H. and John Page (2003), International migration, remittances and poverty in developing countries. World Bank Policy Research Working Paper No. 3179. Washington, DC: World Bank.

Bakker, Matt (2010) From "the whole enchilada" to financialisation: shifting discourses of migration management in North America. In Martin Geiger and Antoine Pécoud (eds), *The Politics of International Migration Management*. New York: Palgrave Macmillan, pp. 271–294.

Balaceanu, Cristina, Diana Apostol and Daniela Penu (2012), Sustainability and social justice. *Procedia: Social and Behavioural Sciences* 62: 677–681.

Bernstein, Henry (2010), Rural livelihoods and agrarian change: Bringing class back in. In Norman Long, Jingzhong Ye and Yihuan Wang (eds), *Rural Transformation and Ddevelopment: China in Context*. Cheltenham: Edward Elgar, pp. 79–109.

Burawoy, Michael (2011), The last positivist. *Contemporary Sociology* 40(4): 396–404.

CASS (Chinese Academy of Social Sciences) (2013), *Shehui lanpishu: 2014 nian zhongguo shehui xingshi fenxi yu yuce* [The Blue Book of China's society: society of China analysis and forecast 2014]. Beijing: China Social Sciences Academic Press. Available at: http://news.xinhuanet.com/legal/2013-12/27/c_125921145.htmews.xinhuanet.com/legal/2013-12/27/c_125921145.htm (accessed 15 June 2014).

Chambers, Robert and Gordon Conway (1992), Sustainable rural livelihoods: Practical concepts for the 21st century. Institute of Development Studies (IDS) discussion paper 296. Brighton: IDS.

Chen, Chih-Jou Jay (2004), *Transforming Rural China: How Local Institutions Shape Property Rights in China*. London: RoutledgeCurzon.

Chen, Xiwen, Yang Zhao, Jianbo Chen and Dan Luo (2009), *Zhongguo nongcun zhidu bianqian 60 nian* [Sixty years of change in China's rural systems]. Beijing: renmin chubanshe.

China Social Sciences Survey Centre, Beijing University (2014), *2014 nian zhongguo minsheng baogao* [Well-being development report of China 2014]. Beijing: Beijing University Press. Available at: http://news.sohu.com/20140726/n402746260.shtml (accessed 15 July 2014).

de Haan, Leo and Annelies Zoomers (2005), Exploring the frontier of livelihoods research. *Development and Change* 36(1): 27–47.

Ellis, Frank (2000), *Rural Livelihoods and Diversity in Developing Countries*. Oxford: Oxford University Press.

Escobar, Arturo (2010), Histories of development, predicaments of modernity: Thinking about globalisation from some critical development studies perspectives. In Norman Long, Jingzhong Ye and Yihuan Wang (eds), *Rural Transformation and Development: China in Context*. Cheltenham: Edward Elgar, pp. 25–53.

Hill, Peter S., Kent Buse, Claire E. Brolan and Gorik Ooms (2014), How can health remain central post-2015 in a sustainable development paradigm? *Globalisation and Health* 10(18): 1–5.

Hirst, Paul and Jonathan Zeitlin (1992), Flexible specialisation versus post-Fordism: Theory, evidence and policy implications. In Michael Storper and Allen J. Scott (eds), *Pathways to Industrialisation and Regional Development*. London: Routledge.

Huang, Ping and Shaohua Zhan (2008), Migrant workers' remittances and rural development in China. In Josh DeWind and Jennifer Holdaway (eds), *Migration and Development Within and Across Borders: Research and Policy Perspectives on Internal and International Migration*. Geneva and New York: International Organisation for Migration (IOM) and Social Science Research Council (SSRC), pp. 221–248.

Lawrence, Peter (2010), Development by numbers. *New Left Review* 62 (March–April): 143–153.

Lehtonen, Markku (2004), The environmental–social interface of sustainable development: Capabilities, social capital, institutions. *Ecological Economics* 49: 199–214.

Li, Peilin, Guangjin Chen, Wei Li, and Feng Tian (2011), A new phase of China's social development. In Xin Ru, Xueyi Lu, Peilin Li, Guangjin Chen, Wei Li and Xinxin Xu (eds), *Chinese Society: Analysis and Forecast (2011)*. Beijing: Social Sciences Academic Press, pp. 1–15.

Li, Xiande (2003), Rethinking the peasant burden: Evidence from a Chinese village. *The Journal of Peasant Studies* 30(3–4): 45–74.

Li, Zhongjin and Hao Qi (2014), Labour process and the social structure of accumulation in China. *Review of Radical Political Economics* online first view, June.

Lipton, Michael (1977), *Why Poor People Stay Poor: Urban Bias in World Development*. London: Temple Smith.

Long, Norman (2001), *Development Sociology: Actor Perspectives*. London: Routledge.

Long, Norman (2010), Introduction. In Norman Long, Jingzhong Ye and Yihuan Wang (eds), *Rural Transformation and Development: China in Context*. Cheltenham: Edward Elgar, pp. 1–22.

Long, Norman and Jinlong Liu (2009), The centrality of actors and interfaces in the understanding of new ruralities: A Chinese case study. In Heather Xiaoquan Zhang (guest ed.), special issue, Transforming rural China: Beyond the urban bias? *Journal of Current Chinese Affairs* 38(4): 63–84.

Long, Norman, Jingzhong Ye and Yihuan Wang (2010), *Rural Transformation and Development: China in Context*. Cheltenham: Edward Elgar.

Lu, Xueyi (2005), *San nong xinlun* [New perspectives on the three rural issues]. Beijing: Social Science Academic Press.

Lü, Xiaobo (1997), The politics of peasant burden in reform China. *The Journal of Peasant Studies* 25(1): 113–138.

Murphy, Rachel (2009), Migrant remittances in China: The distribution of economic benefits and social costs. In Rachel Murphy (ed.), *Labour Migration and Social Development in Contemporary China*. London: Routledge, pp. 47–74.

NBSC (National Bureau of Statistics of China) (2013), *2012 nian guomin jingji he shehui fazhan tongji gongbao* [2012 Statistical Bulletin of National Economic and Social Development]. Available at: http://news.xinhuanet.com/politics/2013-02/23/c_114772758.htm (accessed 15 August 2013).

O'Brien, Kevin J. and Lianjiang Li (2006), *Rightful Resistance in Rural China*. New York: Cambridge University Press.

Park, Albert (2008), Rural-urban inequality in China. In Shahid Yusuf and Tony Saich (eds), *China Urbanises: Consequences, Strategies and Policies*. Washington, DC: The World Bank, pp. 41–63.

Ratha, Dilip (2013), The impact of remittances on economic growth and poverty reduction. Migration Policy Institute policy brief No. 8. Washington, DC: Migration Policy Institute.

Salmenkari, Taru (2013), Theoretical poverty in the research on Chinese civil society. *Modern Asian Studies* 47(2): 682–711.

Sargeson, Sally (2013), Violence as development: Land expropriation and China's urbanisation. *The Journal of Peasant Studies* 40(6): 1063–1085.

Scoones, Ian (2009), Livelihoods perspectives and rural development. *The Journal of Peasant Studies* 36(1): 171–196.

Sen, Amartya (1984), *Resources, Values and Development*. Oxford: Basil Blackwell.

Sen, Amartya (1985), Well-being, agency and freedom. *The Journal of Philosophy* 132(4): 169–221.

Sen, Amartya (1987), The Standard of Living. The Tanner Lectures, Clare Hall, Cambridge: Cambridge University Press.

Sen, Amartya (1992), *Inequality Re-examined*. Cambridge, MA: Harvard University Press.

Sina News (2013), *Buyi dayuan jihua kong liuchan, yi yin difang guanchang luoji* [The Buyi-style courtyard redevelopment project might be aborted due to the "games" of local politics]. Available at: http://news.sina.com.cn/c/sd/2013-10-24/144428521666.shtml (accessed 29 December 2013).

Stark, Oded (1980), On the role of urban-to-rural remittances in rural development. *Journal of Development Studies* 16(3): 369–374.

Stark, Oded (1991), *The Migration of Labour*. Oxford: Blackwell.

State Council (2006), *Zhongguo nongmingong diaoyan baogao* [A research report on migrant workers in China]. Beijing: Zhongguo yanshi chubanshe.

State Council Migrant Workers' Office (2013), *Zhongguo nongmingong fazhan yanjiu* [Research on migrant workers' development in China]. Beijing: Zhongguo laodong shehui baozhang chubanshe.

Taylor, John G. and Xiaoyun Li (2012), China's changing poverty: A middle income country case study. *Journal of International Development* 24: 696–713.

Wang, Chunguang (2005), *Nongcun shehui fenhua yu nongmin fudan* [Rural social differentiation and farmers' burdens]. Beijing: Social Sciences Academic Press.

Wang, Hui (2011), *The Politics of Imagining Asia*, trans. Theodore Huters. Cambridge, MA: Harvard University Press.

Wen, Tiejun (2004), *San nong wenti yu shiji fansi* [The three rural issues and reflections of the century]. Beijing: Sanlian chubanshe.

Wu, Fulong, Fangzhu Zhang and Chris Webster (eds) (2014), *Rural Migrants in Urban China*. London: Routledge.

Xu, Baoqiang and Hui Wang (eds) (2003), *Fazhan de huanxiang* [Development illusions]. Beijing: Zhongyang bianyi chubanshe.

Ye, Xingqing (2009), China's urban-rural integration policies. In Heather Xiaoquan Zhang (guest ed.), special issue Transforming rural China: Beyond the urban bias? *Journal of Current Chinese Affairs* 4: 117–143.

Zhang, Qian Forrest and John A. Donaldson (2013), China's agrarian reform and the privatisation of land: A contrarian view. *Journal of Contemporary China* 22(80): 255–272.

Zhang, Heather Xiaoquan (2007), Conceptualising the links: Migration, health and sustainable livelihoods in China. In Heather Xiaoquan Zhang, Bin Wu and Richard Sanders (eds), *Marginalisation in China: Perspectives on Transition and Globalisation*. Aldershot: Ashgate, pp. 195–214.

Zhang, Heather Xiaoquan and Richard Sanders (2007), Introduction: Marginalisation and globalisation in transitional China. In Heather Xiaoquan Zhang, Bin Wu and Richard Sanders (eds), *Marginalisation in China: Perspectives on Transition and Globalisation*. Aldershot: Ashgate, pp. 1–11.

Zhang, Heather Xiaoquan, Bin Wu and Richard Sanders (eds) (2007) *Marginalisation in China: Perspectives on Transition and Globalisation*. Aldershot: Ashgate.

Zhang, Li (2007), Living and working at the margin: Rural migrant workers in China's transitional cities. In Heather Xiaoquan Zhang, Bin Wu and Richard Sanders (eds), *Marginalisation in China: Perspectives on Transition and Globalisation*. Aldershot: Ashgate, pp. 81–97.

Zhang, Yongle (2008), No forbidden zone in reading? Dushu and the Chinese intelligentsia. *New Left Review* 49: 5–26.

Zhang, Yongle (2010), The future of the past. *New Left Review* 62: 47–83.

Part I

Mobility and livelihoods

2 Migration, risk and livelihood struggles in China

Heather Xiaoquan Zhang

Introduction

In recent years, the need to rebuild social safety nets in China has attracted increasing attention from academics and policy-makers because the erosion of the traditional social support system and the state's long-term neglect of welfare investment have severely affected China's social development. The attempts to find solutions to this issue have gained momentum since the 2008 global financial crisis, which exposed the weakness of the Chinese system to protect its citizens under adverse global and domestic economic conditions. A growing body of research in English and Chinese has emerged on China's social welfare reforms, paying particular attention to the social protection of rural-urban migrants.[1] This has arisen in part from the very magnitude of rural-urban migration. Recent official estimates place the number of migrant workers in China's cities, including those in township and village enterprises (TVEs), at 225 million in 2008 (National Bureau of Statistics of China, hereafter NBSC 2009, cited in Chan 2010: 362), as well as around 300 million migrants' family members in urban or rural settings (Zheng and Huang-Li 2007: 18). Together they account for some 40 per cent of China's population of about 1.4 billion, suggesting that two-fifths of Chinese people are directly affected by issues related to migration. Moreover, there has been increasing media coverage of the horrific treatment of migrant workers by urban employers, labour brokers and contractors, the exploitation and social injustice that migrant workers experience, the growing numbers of organised labour protests by migrant workers in factories owned by domestic and global capital, and occasional extreme and desperate actions taken by migrants, including individual or collective suicidal attempts in public and organised violent protests as "weapons of the weak" (Chan and Pun 2009; Pun and Lu 2010a; see also Chapter 5 of this book).

Given the scale and seriousness of the migrant workers issue, and its economic, social and political ramifications, research in the field, despite a recent increase, is far from sufficient. Existing research published in English requires more micro-level fieldwork-based empirical evidence. The growing body of literature published in Chinese, while attaching greater importance to the issue, is either policy analysis that remains at the macro-level, or is dominated by quantitative survey methods (see Judd 2009). This approach, despite its merits, is unable to provide details of local processes and practices reflected in the voices and perceptions of the key actors involved, in particular, migrant workers as the agents of change. Nor does it allow nuanced analysis and deep insights into individual and collective experiences, negotiations and struggles around issues of livelihoods, mobility and social rights and entitlements – aspects that are equally vital to advance knowledge and inform policies.

Looking at the issue more broadly, and against the backdrop of a global concerted effort to meet the UN Millennium Development Goals, since the turn of the century, the international development community has placed high priority on the enhancement of social protection mechanisms and their role in poverty reduction. However, much of the debate tends to focus on the "poor" and the "poorest" (cf. Barrientos and Hulme 2008). The focus on the poor in research and policy-making has posed particular difficulties when analysing the large-scale rural-urban migration in China. Migrants, due to the mobile nature of their livelihoods, crossing geographical and administrative boundaries, are often missed by the various categories commonly used to define the "poor", such as the *urban* or *rural* poor, or the *absolute* or *relative* poor; we simply do not have a category of the "mobile poor". While the omission could have been tackled by livelihood research, which has gained increasing prominence since the mid-1990s, particularly with regard to its envisaged positive nexus between migration and livelihoods (de Haan 1999; Long 2008), this literature has thus far paid scant attention to the problems associated with migrants' social protection. Instead, the current debate on the theme tends to be overwhelmingly concerned with international migration (cf. Avato *et al.* 2010; McMichael and Gifford 2010; Sabates-Wheeler and MacAuslan 2007). Moreover, the relatively small (though growing) body of research on internal migration, livelihoods and development often overlooks the high risks involved in rural-urban migration, and the vulnerabilities of migrants to a wide range of hazards, and threats to their livelihoods, health and well-being.

This chapter seeks to contribute to the growing scholarship on migrants' social protection in China (see also Chapters 3 and 4 in this book) by focusing on their health issues through a livelihoods analysis. Drawing on extensive fieldwork conducted in Beijing and Tianjin between 2005 and 2009, it attempts to identify some of the major risks and threats to migrants' health, which is conceptualised as essential for livelihood, and its security and sustainability (Zhang 2007). The analysis of in-depth qualitative data collected through ethnographic fieldwork allows the marginalised voices of rural migrants expressing their experiences and perspectives to be heard. It enables a nuanced understanding of the structural barriers that migrants face regarding the full recognition and realisation of their equal citizenship, on the one hand, and their agency, negotiations and struggles around these issues, on the other. In the following, I first introduce the methodology and the analytical framework employed in the study. I then set the scene for the research by outlining the current state of affairs with regard to migrants' social protection. Focusing on work-related safety and occupational health as crucial elements of a wider set of multifaceted issues, I go on to examine the major health hazards for migrants, and the problems of access to healthcare that they face in urban settings. Throughout the chapter I also analyse migrants' strategies for dealing with these health challenges, as well as recent institutional responses. I conclude by summarising the key arguments and suggesting possible ways forward in policy and practice.

Methodology and analytical framework

The chapter draws on primary data from extensive ethnographic fieldwork conducted in 2005 in Beijing and Tianjin, northern China. Further field trips undertaken between 2006 and 2009 to these two cities and other cities in the South and Southeast provide supplementary data. The fieldwork investigated issues related to migration and health in urban settings, which is considered an important dimension of livelihood and its sustainability. It employed a number of qualitative research methods, including semi-structured and unstructured interviews and purposeful conversations with migrant workers, local non-governmental organisation (NGO) representatives, private entrepreneurs employing migrants, academics, nonparticipant observations, site visits, and documentary research, and so forth. More than 60 interviews were conducted, and those with migrant workers lasted between three to four hours in either single or separate sessions. These methods facilitated the gathering of detailed, in-depth data. Site visits to migrant workplaces were made where interviews, conversations and observations were conducted. These included construction sites, university campuses, factories and other locations where migrants performed diverse types of manual work; migrants' residences, including construction sites where unfinished buildings were used as temporary housing; and migrant communities on the outskirts of large cities. Secondary data were gathered during fieldwork, including original Chinese documents, and newspaper and internet materials. Such data help provide the broader political and socio-economic context and backdrop, where the actors' experiences and perspectives are situated. Such data also help us keep track of the latest developments in China's highly dynamic social policy landscape with regard to migrants' livelihoods and social protection.

It is worth noting that in using a range of qualitative research methods, this chapter, instead of providing a statistically representative description as is the case for many quantitative survey-based studies, aims to offer a contextualised understanding of the situated actors under specific socio-economic conditions and institutional settings, and provide deep insights into the complexities of micro-level socio-economic and policy processes, practices, negotiations and struggles surrounding the relevant issues. It emphasises agency, and offers a snapshot of how agency has simultaneously been exercised and constrained by wider social and political forces, as well as how structure and agency together have shaped the experiences, perspectives, and well-being outcomes of individuals and social groups.

The research employs a livelihood approach analytical framework. Livelihood studies, in contrast to the conventional negative conceptualisation of migration as caused by devastating events, such as natural disasters and civil strife, emphasise the positive links between migration and development in terms of livelihood diversification and poverty reduction, with a particular focus on the role of remittances (Cai 2003; Li 2001; Murphy 2002; UNDP 2009). In this approach, migration is considered a rural household strategy and a manifestation of individual agency (cf. Bebbington 2000; Ellis and Freeman 2004; Zhang et al. 2006). Despite this, livelihood studies have thus far largely focused on agricultural and rural settings, and have yet to pay sufficient attention to the livelihoods of rural migrants and their urban experiences (Zhang 2007). In this chapter, I extend the traditional focus of the livelihood approach by looking at the security and sustainability of mobile livelihoods, and the negotiations and struggles surrounding these against a complex backdrop of dramatic socioeconomic and political change in China's cities.

The research adopts the following definition of livelihood proposed by Ellis:

> A livelihood comprises the assets (natural, physical, human, financial and social capital), activities, and the *access* to these (mediated by *institutions* and *social relations*) that together determine the living gained by the individual or household.
>
> (2000: 10, my emphasis)

In applying this concept, however, the existing livelihood approach needs to be expanded to incorporate a health and well-being perspective by broadening an understanding of "human capital" (not just education as is generally interpreted but also health as an essential constitute of livelihood), of "sustainability" (not only environmental but also social), and of "access" (more than just to economic opportunities) (Zhang 2007). The chapter therefore is an initial attempt to apply the livelihood framework in this broader sense, paying particular attention to *access* to *institutions*, *resources* and *power* (such as *public goods*), and *legal* and *social justice*, in its investigation of the issues relating to migrants' health, and more broadly their citizenship rights.

Social protection of mobile livelihoods: the current state of affairs

Changing patterns and trends in China's rural-urban migration

Since its emergence in the mid-1980s, massive rural-urban migration in China has continued to grow in scale, and has therefore attracted the attention of academics and policy-makers both domestically and worldwide. In the early years, most migrants tended to be younger – typically in their early to late twenties (Davin 1999; Li 2004). Migration was initially a male-dominated phenomenon, with women "catching up" since the mid- to late 1990s (Du 2014;

Judd 2009; Pun 2005; Zhang 1999). It also tended to be seasonal and circular, and because of the restrictions of the household registration (*hukou*) system and the extreme difficulties in converting one's *hukou* status from the rural to the urban, only a better-off minority managed to settle permanently in the city (Chan and Buckingham 2008; Fan 2008). In the early to mid-1990s, most migrants were working in the non-state sector, and female migrants were frequently found in domestic and other service industries, as well as factories in joint ventures, foreign-owned companies, and so forth (Jacka 2005; Lee 1998; Sun 2009; Zhang 1999).

New trends in rural-urban migration in terms of the attributes of migrants, their marital and residential arrangements, and the sectors in which they are employed were observed during my 2005–2009 fieldwork. Among the most noticeable is age: about half of the migrant interviewees were older (late twenties to early sixties), and marital status: approximately two-thirds of the interviewees were married with diverse post-nuptial residential and child-rearing arrangements. These observations are in keeping with research findings based on statistically representative data. Yang and Hu (n.d.), drawing on a survey of 423 migrant workers in Beijing's Chaoyang District in late 2005, found that migrants' age ranged from 16 to 68 with an average age of 28.3, about half of them (49.2 per cent) were married, and more than 40 per cent were living with family members. The trend of family migration has become even more prominent in recent years. A national survey of eight large cities of migration management and service provision for migrant workers conducted by Nankai University in 2013 shows that nearly 89 per cent of migrant workers are married and live with their partners, and about 80 per cent have their children with them in the city (Du 2014: 8). Along with the increased age of the first generation of migrant workers is the emergence of the so-called "new generation of migrants" (*xinshengdai nongmingong*), who, born in the 1980s and 1990s, have either grown up in urban areas with their migratory parents or left the village after finishing secondary education (Hua 2010; Judd 2009). Unlike their parents, the younger generation "migrants" are more eager to settle and integrate themselves into the urban economy and society (CCP Central Committee and State Council 2010). All this has raised new issues and concerns with respect to employment, social inclusion and integration of migrants in the urban destination (Du 2014; Pun and Lu 2010b).

Migrant-concentrated residential areas on the outskirts of large cities like Beijing, Tianjin and Guangzhou have become much more established nowadays (Wang *et al.* 2010; Wu and Wu 2005). In addition to inter-provincial and inter-regional migration, there have been more short-distance migration, and commuting between downtown and suburban areas of large cities. During my fieldwork in Beijing and Hangzhou I observed that commuters included migrants working as taxi drivers (while in Tianjin laid-off workers from state-owned enterprises (SOEs) often took up taxi driving as a livelihood), as well as in other services and industries, such as retail, catering and construction.[2] With the deepening of the urban industrial restructuring since the second half of the 1990s, many state organisations have started employing non-locals (*chengshi wailai renkou*) as contract workers,[3] which has led to a growing number of migrants being employed on a temporary basis in the public sector, such as in universities, hospitals, SOEs or other governmental organisations, as cleaners, carers, kitchen assistants, and so forth (Anon. 2008). More recent policy changes and disparities in policy implementation with regard to migrants' social entitlements in the public and private sectors will be examined later.

While migrants are now much more varied in age and, in many cases, are older with a longer experience of migration, their average wage has remained low and failed to keep up with inflation or the rise of the average wage in the urban formal economy (Chan 2002; Ministry of Labour and Social Security Research Team 2006). Hua (2010: 194) shows that in 2006 the annual average wage of migrants was only 55.2 per cent of that earned by urban workers. In short, despite higher geographical mobility and frequent job changes, the occupational mobility of migrants, as observed in my fieldwork and consistent with other research findings (Li 2004; Lu 2004), is largely horizontal with respect to socio-economic status and associated remuneration. Moreover, rural-urban migration in China has started showing features similar to those observed in other developing countries and regions, such as Latin America, where migrants are frequently found living on the edge of large metropolises, establishing their own informal institutions, such as schools and medical clinics, and developing their communities separately from mainstream urban society.[4]

Welfare and social security for rural migrants: the unmet needs

Despite their huge numbers and longer stays in the city, China's rural migrants are now experiencing increased economic, social and political marginalisation, relative poverty and deprivation, which render them vulnerable to a wide range of risks and threats to their livelihood and its sustainability. Let us now examine how social security schemes in China are designed and developed, and whether they are able to tackle this vulnerability and protect migrants.

Generally speaking, China's social policy development since the onset of the market reforms has undergone two phases. In the first phase, which lasted until the early 2000s, the overwhelming emphasis was on economic growth. This, combined with the earlier experience of relatively high welfare provision but ineffective growth, resulted in a predominant perception that opposed social welfare to economic growth, manifest, e.g. in the typical "equity versus efficiency" antithesis (cf. Feng 2007; Gong *et al.* 2007). Guided by such thinking, state-promoted growth channelled most available resources into economic development while systematically minimising "unproductive" welfare expenditures. Stress was placed on "producing a larger pie" as opposed to the pre-reform policies accentuating egalitarian "redistribution". This "growth-led welfare model" or the "developmental welfare system" (White and Goodman 1998) – though highlighting the role of the state as the paramount institutional actor in managing economic growth and the market according to its perceived priorities as against the neoliberal state's hands-off approach – shares similar assumptions with neoliberalism with regard to social policy and welfare provision. Both models share a faith in the market's ability to automatically allocate resources in an optimal manner, and to redress inequality and uneven development through "trickle-down" (from the rich to the poor) and "spill-over" (from the urban core to the rural periphery) effects.

The consequence was a serious erosion of the social security system, prolonged neglect and under-investment in developing new welfare schemes, and a failure to protect Chinese citizens against the plethora of emerging uncertainties and risks associated with the market economy. For example, once a model of equitable healthcare provision for its large population in the developing world, China was rated 144th out of 191 countries in terms of healthcare performance, and 188th, or third from the bottom, with regard to the fairness of healthcare provision according to an assessment by the World Health Organisation (WHO) in 2000 (WHO 2000). The events surrounding the outbreak of severe acute respiratory syndrome (SARS) in spring–summer 2003, first in China and then beyond, suggested a growing public health crisis in the country (Duckett 2003, 2010). All this further exacerbated inequality, vulnerability and livelihood insecurity by the turn of the twenty-first century.

The second phase started following Hu Jintao and Wen Jiabao's assumption of office in 2003. Faced with mounting development challenges, and growing social tension and discontent, the new leadership, concerned with the political legitimacy of the ruling party, has begun paying greater attention to equity and social justice by giving higher priority to wider human development issues, in particular, building social safety nets and improving welfare. New discourses stressing "people-centred development" (*yiren weiben*), "building a harmonious society" (*goujian hexie shehui*), "urban-rural integration" (*chengxiang yitihua*), and so forth, have signalled a new emphasis on resource (re)distribution to address the problems of wealth polarisation and uneven development through central government fiscal support and improving public services. This phase has witnessed an accelerated pace of establishing, expanding and enhancing a wide range of social security programmes. These include new social insurance schemes with combined contributions from employers and employees, such as pension, healthcare, unemployment, maternity and work injury insurances; and means-tested social assistance programmes, such as the Minimum Living Standards (MLS) guarantee or *dibao*, medical assistance, housing subsidies, legal aid, disaster and social relief, social housing, and so forth.

This ongoing phase has been marked by greater importance attached to statutory social protection and the institutionalisation of the various welfare schemes. For instance, 2004 has been termed China's "social security year" with social security as a basic right of citizens formally incorporated in the country's Constitution. In the same year, the State Council published a White Paper entitled, "China's Social Security and Its Policy", detailing the state's responsibilities to support and improve a range of social insurance and welfare schemes under its evolving social security system (State Council 2004). The attempt to improve these schemes has been further strengthened since late 2008 in response to the serious challenges posed by the severe global financial crisis and the shocks it caused to China's economy, which has become heavily reliant on exports.[5] In October 2010, the Chinese government promulgated the Social Insurance Law (Central People's Government of the PRC 2010). Yet, despite the more determined efforts, most of the new social security programmes – embedded in the extant urban-rural dualism – remain urban-centred. Schemes such as work injury, unemployment and maternity insurances, minimum wages, and so forth, have been extended to the rural population in only a limited way.

While it is still too early to evaluate the actual effects of these policy initiatives, a closer look at the picture of the latest policy developments reveals some continuities with respect to livelihood security and social protection for rural migrants. In particular, migrants have not featured prominently in the new discourse, or in the institutional design of policy and practice, despite their large numbers and their status as one of the most vulnerable social groups in the country. This state of affairs is partially attributable to the institutionalised urban-rural divide in welfare production, financing and provision (in terms of quantity, quality and coverage), and to the dualistic citizenship embedded in, and reinforced by, the *hukou* system. It is also related to the mode of migrants' livelihoods, which involves frequent movement across geographical and administrative boundaries (hence posing challenges in the absence of universal entitlement and under the current practice of fragmented administration and management of welfare provision), and to the often bureaucratic and discriminatory attitudes of urban local officials and residents toward migrants.

I now turn to examine a specific aspect of social protection for mobile livelihoods, namely migrants' health, through first identifying the health risks as perceived by various actors concerned.

Risks and threats to migrants' health and livelihoods

Employing a livelihood framework in studying China's rural-urban migration from a well-being perspective suggests a focus on migrants' health, particularly in relation to *access*, as discussed above. This may initially point attention to migrants' access to healthcare services in urban settings, and, in effect, my 2005 fieldwork was originally designed to address this aspect of migrant well-being. The field study, however, turned out to be an unfolding process, during which new issues and sub-themes related to the core theme emerged and were identified. Accordingly the dimensions and scope of the investigation were adjusted and broadened. For example, my interviews with the director of a migrant NGO and the deputy director of a non-profit organisation (NPO) in Beijing revealed that there were a wide range of issues affecting migrants' health, some of which were acute and caused severe shocks due to their highly visible nature, while others were hidden or latent but could lead to potentially devastating impact on health and livelihoods. Moreover, *access* in the Chinese context should also take into account access to *institutional resources*, in particular those provided by the *state* such as *law* and *legal justice*.

Work safety and occupational health

The fieldwork interviews revealed that one of the most acute problems with regard to migrants' health was related to health and safety at work, particularly for those in high-risk occupations, such as construction, where 80 per cent of the workforce consists of migrants (State Council 2006a: 12), and mining, where migrants account for almost the entire workforce in township- and village-run coal mines (TVCMs) (Li 2005: 52). Employers' neglect of safety measures and of workers' training (in an attempt to minimise production costs) has led to low awareness of the risks, inadequate or no preventative measures, and frequent industrial accidents, causing injuries, disabilities and even deaths. These, together with occupational illnesses suffered by migrant workers, have seriously threatened their rights to health, livelihoods and, in some cases, life, and therefore are among the gravest health hazards and risks. In September 2008 alone, three disastrous mining accidents occurred; the most serious happening on 8 September in an iron ore mine in Shanxi Province, causing 265 fatalities (Xinhua Net 2008). On 20 September, a fire broke out in a coal mine in Heilongjiang Province, leading to the death of 31 miners (Anon. 2009). On 21 September, 37 miners died in an explosion at a coal mine in Henan Province (Beijing Youth 2008).

According to official statistics, nationwide fatalities and disabilities caused by industrial accidents of all sorts reached around 140,000 and 700,000 per year, respectively, and migrant workers are disproportionately represented among the victims (Zhao 2005: 5). Migrant workers are concentrated in the officially classified "highly dangerous enterprises" (*gaowei qiye*), including mining, construction and manufacturing using hazardous chemical materials (State Council 2006a). A report by the State Administration of Work Safety (SAWS) shows that in the first four months of 2004, there were 586 reported accidents in the construction industry nationally, causing 605 fatalities, of which around 90 per cent were migrant workers (Zhao 2005: 5). Fatalities in coal production alone reached over 6,000 per year on average from 1996 to 2005, of which about three-quarters occurred in migrant-concentrated TVCMs (Andrews-Speed 2007: 63).

While coal mine accidents and their fatalities have frequently made headlines in China and beyond, much less attention has been paid to occupational illness, which is also closely related to the mining industry. This health problem, albeit more hidden, is equally crippling. An SAWS report indicated that occupational illness has seen a continued increase in recent years with pneumoconiosis accounting for 83 per cent, or an accumulated 580,000 of the reported cases in 2002 (Figure 2.1) (Li 2005: 52, see also Chapter 4 of this book). Among those diagnosed, 140,000 had already died by 2002, and nearly half (250,000) were estimated to be suffering from coal mine pneumoconiosis. Moreover, a trend of decreasing age (i.e. younger age cohorts) of those suffering from pneumoconiosis has been identified in recent years. For example, those under the age of 40 who were diagnosed at work represented 8.1 per cent of the total diagnosed cases in 1997, while by 2002 this figure had risen to 11.2 per cent. Moreover, patients'

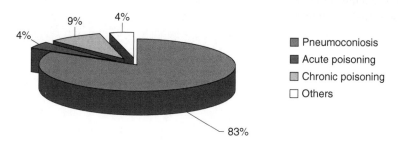

Figure 2.1 The proportions of major occupational illnesses in China, 2002.

Source: Based on data from Su (2005: 15).

average length of work as miners was shortened from 15 years before showing symptoms to three to five years (Li 2005: 52), suggesting migrant miners' intensified exposure to occupational health hazards, paucity of information on risks, and employers' (some public but mostly private mine owners) serious neglect of health, safety and protection measures. All this points to inadequacies in systematically regulating and supervising the mining industry, or enforcing health and safety regulations and laws. The consequence is livelihood unsustainability and increased vulnerability to poverty and destitution for migrant miners and their families.

It should be noted that the above statistics, collected by the Ministry of Health, were based only on the reported cases by large state-owned coal mines employing migrants as contract or temporary workers. Therefore, the situation could be far worse if those working in TVCMs were tested, reported and included. Based on this awareness, it is feared that occupational illness among migrant miners may emerge as a serious epidemic in many rural areas (Figure 2.1) (Li 2005), disabling people in their prime, crippling livelihoods, and exacerbating poverty for hundreds and thousands of individuals and families. The serious threat that this issue has posed to migrants' health and livelihoods is exemplified in the following case:

> Forty-two young farmers from Shanyang County, Shaanxi Province went to work in the Chen'er Gold Mine in Luonan County on a seasonal basis starting from the early 1990s. In the years that followed many became very ill showing shared symptoms of difficulty in breathing and some died of suffocation ... In 2000, advised by a fellow villager, the ex-miners visited a hospital in Xi'an, the provincial capital, to take a test. The result showed that they had caught pneumoconiosis while working in the gold mine ... By 2005, 13 of the ex-miners had died because the employer refused to pay any compensation and the miners couldn't afford proper treatment, and a few committed suicide after years of suffering and futile attempts at having their case redressed ... Among those already dead, the oldest was 39 and the youngest in their late 20s ... They died or lost the ability to work in their

prime, leaving behind their wives, elderly parents, and young children ... As a result, their surviving families are destitute.

(Interview with the deputy director of an NPO in Beijing, September 2005)

Concerns about occupational health were expressed by migrant workers during my interviews, in particular by those who worked in certain industries, such as construction and internal renovation (*zhuangxiu*). This is evidenced in the following account of a woman interviewee working in domestic service in Beijing, whose husband was an internal renovator:

Internal renovation work is harmful to his body. The work environment is heavily polluted. There is a lot of dust coming from stone, marble and hard floor materials. The dust is so heavy you can hardly see things around you, and this harms your lungs and eyes. In winter you can cover your mouth with a mask and wear glasses, but it's too hot to do so in summer and you're fully exposed. Also noise pollution is serious. It is so loud that if you talk to him while at work, he can hardly hear you. The third type comes from the poisonous materials used, such as industrial glues and paints; all of which have a strong unpleasant smell ... We don't know how to reduce the risks, except my husband doesn't intend to be in the trade for too long. Now he feels all right and wants to carry on working for another few years, and then change to a less harmful job.

(Interview with Wu, female, 28, August 2005)

A migrant construction worker in Beijing described his experience as follows:

I left my home village in Hebei Province 16 years ago ... Before I learned the skills of masonry and tiling (*wagong*), I initially worked as an unskilled labourer (*xiaogong*) in a construction company. My job was to apply cement to the outside walls of high buildings. It was very strenuous. I was only a teenager, but had to work for more than 10 hours every day. It was very dangerous too. We stood on the high scaffold and applied the heavy materials on the external walls. Accidents were quite common, and on average, completion of a construction project would claim one to two lives.

(Interview with Gu, male, 33, September 2005)

Institutions, social relations and power have shaped responses to such acute health hazards and risks as well as their outcomes. Individual migrant workers employ rather simple tactics, like the internal renovator who used a mask seasonally to deal with the heavy pollution, or the construction worker who changed jobs through learning a skill in order to reduce the risks associated with non-skilled work in the industry. Such tactics, though a manifestation of migrants' agency in self-managing and minimising exposure to risks, will not be able to systematically address the problem, and hence the protective effects are limited. When suffering from work injury-caused ill health, disabilities and poverty, or from serious stress – a potential threat to mental health – caused by other types of institutional deficiencies, including, for example, the prolonged delay or default on migrants' wages (see also Chapter 5 of this book),[6] migrants and their families could potentially seek justice and appropriate compensation through institutional channels, such as labour dispute resolution and arbitration (*laodong zhongcai*) organisations, the court, and the "petition" mechanism set up by the government.[7]

Access to the state and the law

When migrants' health is damaged and livelihoods are destroyed (in the case of work injury or ill health, disabilities or deaths caused by industrial accidents and occupational diseases), and their rights are violated (in the case of delayed or unpaid wages), they sometimes fight for their rights on the legal front. Theoretically, there are a number of formal avenues available for migrants to seek justice; however, in reality there are daunting obstacles in the way. This chapter does not aim to systematically analyse the relevant legislation, the labour dispute resolution system, or how these institutions have, in reality, discriminated against migrant workers and favoured employers and sometimes local authorities (i.e. the problems of the law and its enforcement). Suffice it to say that currently the procedure for addressing labour disputes, such as seeking insurance payments or compensation for work injuries, or for delayed or embezzled wages, that migrant workers must go through is extremely complex, time-consuming, financially prohibitive and practically ineffective. This was particularly emphasised in my interview with the deputy director of the NPO in Beijing:

> According to the Labour Law, in order to receive medical treatment and work injury insurance or compensation paid by the employer, a harmed migrant worker must first obtain an official work injury classification certificate (*gong-shang rending*). The application for this certificate, however, must be made by the employer within one month of the injury. If the employer doesn't apply, then the injured worker must apply within one year of the injury or in the case of occupational illness, of the designated hospital's diagnosis. Following this, the organisation in charge of the injury classification should make a decision within 60 days of receiving the application. In practice, however, if an injury occurs, the work safety department can fine the employer, and the social insurance department will also increase the insurance premium paid by the enterprise. Thus, the employer usually tries every means possible to conceal the injury and attempts to settle privately (*siliao*) by paying a little to the injured migrant rather than applying for the classification certificate on behalf of him or her ... In many cases, when a migrant is injured and hospitalised, the employer only contributes a little to the medical expenses before driving him or her out of the hospital [due to unpaid hospital fees]. No matter how serious the injury is, only a little money is paid by the employer with the aim of getting rid of the injured worker, and some employers even deny any labour relations with him or her.

Another problem lies in the fact that in order to obtain the injury classification certificate, the injured worker must produce evidence of the existence of employment relations. However, because of the delayed legislation
and underdevelopment of the labour contract system, many employers don't
sign contracts with migrant workers, and therefore the harmed migrant
worker cannot produce such evidence. As a result, they face great difficulty
in obtaining such a certificate. Without the classification certificate, the
labour arbitration committee won't accept the application of the injured
migrant for dispute resolution … In order to just obtain the classification
certificate, injured workers or their families must go through prolonged legal
and administrative procedures, frequently travelling between their home
villages and the city. Some cases lasted three or four years while others seven
or eight years. In the end, the injured migrants are effectively denied timely
medical treatment and appropriate compensation … Many migrants and
their families, on top of the injuries or disabilities they sustained, suffer from
extreme stress, financial hardship and destitution.

(Interview, September 2005)

Despite the enormous difficulties, some migrant workers have managed to get
their injuries redressed through seeking legal aid, a constituent of the social
assistance programmes introduced with the promulgation of the Legal Aid
Regulation in July 2003. Others have resorted to the law, using their limited
resources to hire a lawyer in their negotiations and struggles for a secure and
sustainable livelihood. A migrant interviewee working as a cleaner in a university in Beijing recounted his experience:

My son [who was also a migrant working in the university's catering centre]
was seriously injured at work early this year … I was very worried since he
was not yet 18. If he's made disabled, he'll lose the ability to work for the rest
of his life. I was so stressed that I haven't fully recovered yet. We're outsiders
here and don't know who we could go to for useful information. When we
were at home, we had friends and relatives to consult but in Beijing we've
got nobody to go to. One day, I happened to pass a legal service centre, so
I entered and asked for advice. Legal advice centres charge fees from 50 to
100 yuan per visit. But the lawyers told me that the catering centre had the
responsibility for my son's injury. I've consulted about 10 legal firms spending almost 1,000 yuan [nearly double his monthly net wage of 550 yuan]. My
lawyer lodged a lawsuit against the catering centre and they employed two
lawyers. In the end, the case was settled out of court through mediation and
the catering centre paid us 20,000 yuan in compensation.

(Interview with Yan, 48, September 2005)

These examples illustrate that migrant workers, instead of simply being victims
of discrimination and exploitation, are social actors who exercise agency through
actively seeking to redress the injustice that they experience. Despite the

unfavourable conditions and structural constraints they face, some do manage to obtain useful information formally or informally, and actively seek legal protection. In Mr Yan's case, failing to contribute to the social insurance (including work injury and medical insurance) that his son was entitled to, the employer violated the regulations and laws put in place by the central and Beijing municipal governments. During the interview, Mr Yan commented that health for a migrant worker was extremely important because without it one could not make a living and support one's family. The conceptual link between migration, health and livelihood was also shown in his fear that his son might lose "the ability to work" due to the injury. His experience also suggests that migrant workers' entitlements to social security and their rights to health and livelihoods are a fiercely contested domain of citizenship, entailing aspects of exclusion, inclusion, and control and allocation of economic, social and political resources. Despite the huge power and resource imbalance, migrants who are more aware and articulate about their rights, more active in seeking relevant information and, hence, more resourceful (like Mr Yan) can use the law to protect themselves in different ways. Individual and collective solidarity and mutual support in this regard were also demonstrated. For example, during the interview, Mr Yan pointed to a construction site on campus, saying that nowadays he kept newspapers carrying government documents on protecting migrant workers' rights, and often advised the migrant construction workers about using the law as a tool to demand timely pay or claim overdue wages.

Access to social insurance and entitlements

As mentioned above, social security as a citizen's basic social right was formally incorporated into China's Constitution in 2004. While new initiatives aimed at improving and strengthening a wide range of social protection programmes have been introduced, and new schemes especially targeting rural migrants have been designed and piloted, particularly since 2006 when the central government issued Document No. 5 on resolving the problems of migrant workers (State Council 2006b, see also Chapter 3 of this book), the state has yet to adequately accommodate the interests and needs of migrants. One major responsible factor lies in the institutional design: most schemes are still urban-centred: not only have they had limited extension to rural areas, but they have also excluded migrant workers in urban settings.

The unemployment insurance scheme only covers urban workers (*chengzhen zhigong*). The Regulations on Unemployment Insurance introduced at the beginning of 1999 exclude migrant workers from entitlements by defining the eligible as urban workers, namely permanent urban *hukou* holders (cf. State Council 1999). This exclusion is reinforced by other government regulations at the central and local levels. For example, the Methods of Application for and Distribution of Unemployment Benefits issued by the Ministry of Labour and Social Security (MoLSS, which changed its name to the Ministry of Human Resources and Social Security [MoHRSS] in late 2008) at the beginning of 2001 reiterate several conditions of eligibility for unemployment benefits, including city and town workers (see the official definition above), evidence of the termination of a formal labour contract, and evidence that both the employer and the employee have contributed to the unemployment insurance scheme for at least one year, and so forth (MoLSS 2001). As discussed above, such conditions effectively exclude migrant workers from the scheme. These regulations also ignore the fact that most migrant workers have experienced periodic unemployment in the city and thus have a need for support, a fact that I found during my fieldwork and that has been documented by other researchers. Yang and Hu (n.d.), in their 2005 survey of migrants in Beijing, reported that 40 per cent of the respondents experienced unemployment lasting longer than a month. Maternity insurance, which provides a range of benefits, including paid maternity and paternity leave following child birth (90 days for women, 10 days for men), prenatal health checks, reimbursement of hospital delivery fees, and so forth, is confined entirely to urban *hukou* holders (Anon. 2008). This is in keeping with my fieldwork findings that none of the female migrant interviewees was aware of this scheme, to say nothing of being covered by it.

The MLS or *dibao*, a means-tested social assistance scheme providing support for low-income individuals and families, only targeted people in poverty with urban *hukou* until late 2007 when it was extended to rural areas.[8] In either setting, however, the "mobile poor" have not been taken into account. The minimum wage, despite the recent implementation and enforcement efforts through establishing the Minimum Wage Regulation in December 2003 (MoLSS 2004), has limited coverage of migrant workers. Du and Pan's (2009) investigation into China's minimum wage shows that while there has been significant progress in adjusting and implementing a minimum wage across the country since 2004, coverage of migrant workers as of 2005 was only about one-fifth of the surveyed samples, with coverage of males nearly double that of females. They consider the design of the scheme to be problematic, in that it is predominantly based on monthly minimum wages (varying by region) rather than hourly rates, disregarding the fact that migrants work many more hours per day and more work days per week than local urban workers. It is also recognised that even the one-fifth figure could be an overestimation of the actual coverage rate given the fact that China's statistical reporting system frequently excludes employment and wage information in the informal economy, where most migrant workers, particularly females, are employed (Du and Pan 2009).

For the few schemes that should include migrant workers according to specific government policies and regulations, such as work injury insurance, basic medical insurance and pensions, compliance by employers is highly uneven. My fieldwork revealed that in Beijing and Tianjin, particularly since 2004, the city governments have placed greater emphasis on employers abiding by the law and extending such insurance schemes to migrant workers, which is also evidenced in the city authorities' websites (cf. Beijing Municipal Government 2006; Tianjin Municipal Government 2006). My fieldwork interviews, however, revealed considerable discrepancies between public and private sector employers in this regard, with the former more willing to comply. My interviewees working in the public sector, including hospitals and universities, were aware of the major social insurance schemes, particularly medical and pension insurance, and said that these had been recently extended to cover them. Data from quantitative surveys conducted in Beijing further confirm this. Lu and Qin (2007: 132) reported that SOEs in the city topped the performance ranking of all the seven social protection indicators for migrant workers in their 2005 survey. In the informal economy dominated by private capital, where the majority of my interviewees worked, migrant workers were rarely aware of the insurance schemes. Furthermore, enforcement of the relevant laws and regulations was ineffective and coverage was patchy at best.

Institutionalised and widespread discrimination against migrants underpinned by the dual urban-rural labour market and the *hukou* system, deep-rooted socio-cultural prejudice against rural people (reinforced further by the negative representation in the media through, e.g. stereotyping and scapegoating migrants for exacerbating social problems in urban areas such as increased crime and unemployment), unequal social power, and limited political representation[9] have all combined to further undermine migrant workers' statutory rights and livelihoods. Moreover, more powerful, vested interests formed through a close alliance between global and domestic capital, and between capital and local political power, are at play, as their profits and revenues are derived, to a considerable extent, from migrant workers' "cheap labour" at the expense of their decent wages and social welfare rights (see also Chapter 5 of this volume). This, together with a continued policy priority placed by many local authorities on economic growth through attracting more external investments with cheap labour as a "comparative advantage" (Dong 2008), has further disadvantaged and disempowered migrant workers. One example is provided by a private entrepreneur in Tianjin who employed about 20 migrant workers. He said in the interview that following the enactment of the government's Regulation on Work Injury Insurance at the beginning of 2004, the city government required all private businesses to contribute to employees' social insurance regardless of their *hukou* status. If an employer was found to be non-compliant, his or her business licence would be revoked. This, combined with an earlier experience of a worker being injured in an accident, made the entrepreneur especially serious about complying with the new rule. He visited one government department after another in an attempt to pay the insurance for his migrant employees, but wherever he went he was told that he was in the wrong department. In the end, he was "like a ball kicked back and forth (*ti piqiu*) and no department really cared". Finally he told an official that he had to buy insurance for his migrant workers, otherwise he would risk losing his business licence. To his surprise, the official replied, "They're outsiders; why bother? Nobody will check and you can forget it and go home!"

Bureaucratic irresponsibility, institutional apathy and inertia can also hinder institutional innovation, targeted design, multi-sector collaboration and creative action required to protect mobile livelihoods. The latest official emphasis is on urban-rural integration, particularly in social welfare provisioning, as a necessary step to render obsolete the *hukou* regime by hollowing out its essential function of dividing urban and rural societies through unequal citizenship, social entitlements and rights, as well as the differentiated provision of and access to welfare resources. This initiative has been piloted since 2007 in Chengdu and Chongqing followed by other large cities, including Beijing, Shanghai and Tianjin in their suburban areas, i.e. rural counties. In addition, in 2009, it was reported that 13 provincial authorities were considering abolishing the *hukou* system by allowing all citizens to register as "residents" (*jumin*) regardless of their origins (Hua 2010: 190).[10] Such initiatives would, hopefully, facilitate the inclusion of migrant workers in the still-evolving social security system and the ultimate integration of migrants and their families into urban local communities. Yet, despite the policy dynamics in recent years, the needs of the mobile population have not been systematically targeted or seriously considered in the new initiatives and practices. The voices and perspectives of migrant workers are barely heard, their interests and rights severely under-represented socially and politically, and thus are hardly incorporated into the new schemes during both the upper-level design and local implementation. There has often been a largely unchallenged widespread assumption about migrants' "identity" (as rural) and "belonging" (to the countryside) with regard to spatial and social rights and entitlements, as well as a dominant neoliberal discourse of "free choice" (e.g. in relation to the substandard working and housing conditions of migrant workers, their "opt out" of the urban-centred social insurance schemes), which serve (socially and politically) to justify both the continued denial of migrants' rights to the city and the many exclusionary policies and practices.

In my interviews with migrant workers employed in the public sector, some expressed the concern that even though they were now entitled to join certain welfare schemes, they were unsure about how they could eventually benefit given that the current schemes were not portable, and thus unsuitable to their mode of livelihoods (see also Chapter 3 of this volume). Moreover, they expressed a lack of trust in the bureaucracy, as echoed in Mr Yan's concerns:

> Since the beginning of this year I've joined a few insurance schemes, including medical, unemployment and pension insurance. Each month 43.3 yuan is deducted from my monthly wage of 598 yuan and the employer contributes to these too. However, except for the medical insurance, for which I've been given an insurance booklet (*yiliao baoxian ben*), I don't have any proof (*ziju*) of the other schemes. I've asked my employer, but was told that nobody had been provided with such proof and all my contributions were recorded in my personnel file kept by the university ... The explanation hasn't convinced me though ... It's like going to the bank to withdraw money – we have to present our account booklets (*cunzhe*), but we don't have any proof for the social insurance that we've contributed to, so I'm not so reassured and don't feel secure. Joining the medical insurance scheme guarantees healthcare for us migrants and I'm quite happy with the new policy. However, this is a good

thing in principle but I don't know whether it really works when we need it. I also don't have an account number or any other evidence for the pension insurance – how could I withdraw a pension when I retire? Also, since the home of a migrant worker like myself is not in Beijing, how can I get my pension when I return to my home village after retirement? ... In my home village, villagers are reluctant to join the rural New Cooperative Medical Scheme [NCMS] mainly because the scheme is often useless when you really need it. If you fall seriously ill and need help, then you'd find nobody is actually in charge. You go from the lowest- to the highest-level authorities but nobody takes the responsibility of covering your medical expenses ... I wish the government could do something more about this.

(Interview with Yan, September 2005)

While the NCMS has expanded considerably since 2007 with substantial fiscal support from the central and provincial governments, and the urban medical insurance scheme has extended, since 2008, from covering only urban workers and employees (*chengshi zhigong*) to include all "urban residents" (*chengshi jumin*) – both are urban *hukou* holders, however, the situation where migrants frequently fall into the gap in coverage between the urban and rural spaces has not been fundamentally altered in most Chinese cities. This shows that translating access and equity into practice is still often based on a lack of understanding or even indifference to the needs of the mobile population, which in turn aggravates their exploitation, inequality and social exclusion. The process of recognising and dealing with migrant workers' needs has too often been hindered by segregated and fragmented programmes differentiated by the sector where migrants work and subject to the vagaries of local political will and budgetary conditions, and to implementation by people embedded in socio-cultural prejudice, neoliberal ideology, or lacking awareness, sensitivity or a sense of responsibility. In the end, the uneven process of extending the social security schemes to migrant workers in the city has largely become one of making the mobile population fit the system, rather than the other way around. It is therefore important to develop a more effective, integrated and accountable public administration system to design, initiate, deliver and implement the social welfare policies for the mobile population, on top of the imperative task of fundamentally challenging an emerging neoliberal ideology that has attempted to individualise the social disadvantage and exclusion experienced by migrant workers in Chinese cities, which also underpins an increasingly dominant discourse on migrants' identity, belonging and the associated rights and entitlements.

Conclusion

This chapter addresses the problem of migrants' social protection by focusing on the linkage between health and livelihoods in China. It aims to contribute to a growing body of research on the evolution and development of China's social policy and welfare schemes particularly targeting rural migrants, who, for the past three decades and more, have made possible China's rapid and sustained economic growth, unprecedented urbanisation and societal transformation, while disproportionally sharing in few of the benefits. Drawing on extensive fieldwork conducted in Beijing, Tianjin and other cities between 2005 and 2009, and applying a livelihood framework combined with a well-being perspective, the chapter demonstrates that in spite of the accelerated pace of legislation, and the consolidated efforts to reconstruct the social safety net and welfare system in China since the early 2000s, the emerging institutional frameworks entailing a range of social security schemes have thus far, by and large, failed to cover migrant workers in a systematic manner. Migrant workers continue to face high risks and threats to their health as an essential component of livelihood. Citizenship in the sense of economic and social rights, despite its more recent expansion through official reinterpretation, and new legislation and amendments to existing laws, is still dualistic and exclusionary – defined, applied and acknowledged differentially along the dividing lines of, among other things, individuals' geographical origin, *hukou* status and their livelihood modes.

Migration, health and livelihood security and sustainability, as related to social rights and citizenship, constitute a set of complex and multifaceted issues, and this research focuses its attention on the specific aspect of migrants' work safety and occupational health. Combining in-depth ethnographic fieldwork and a livelihood analysis, the chapter presents the marginalised voices of migrant workers, and a deeper insight into their lived experiences in terms of health, livelihoods and life worlds. It emphasises *access*, directing attention to issues related to institutions, social relations and power that have shaped, controlled and frequently constrained migrants' access to vital resources, including formal institutions such as the state, law and public goods. The chapter argues that migrant workers are social actors, and they exercise agency through negotiating, managing and dealing with health risks, and by nurturing and developing informal mutual support mechanisms and institutions (such as kinship- and friendship-based networks, and informal medical clinics), by employing individually devised tactics and strategies, and by mobilising the limited resources at their disposal. It further shows that livelihood struggles are sometimes fought on the legal battlefields when mobile livelihoods are seriously damaged. Despite this, however, such individual efforts are unable to systematically tackle the structural deficiencies that generate vulnerabilities, increase risks, undermine entitlements, deny statutory rights of migrant workers to institutional social protection and, in many cases, lead to ill-health, broken livelihoods, poverty and destitution.

This chapter argues that the social welfare of the mobile population is essentially a matter of equity and social justice, and points to an urgent need to address more effectively the issues identified, namely the health and well-being of migrants. This is a challenging programme requiring multi-sectoral, multi-ministerial collaboration, and a well-coordinated holistic approach engaging diverse actors and stakeholders, such as the central and local state, civil society, migrant workers, and urban, rural and migrant communities. That the majority of migrant workers are gaining their livelihoods in the informal sector together with their relatively high physical/geographical mobility also poses special challenges when designing, initiating, implementing, enforcing and managing the social security schemes and funds for this group. Migrant workers bore the brunt of the massive impact caused by the global financial crisis on China's economy and labour market: it was estimated that in early 2009 about 12 million migrants – 8.5 per cent of the entire migrant workforce – had to return to rural areas after losing their urban jobs (Mo *et al.* 2009: 38). I myself observed this in late 2008 during a field trip to Tianjin, where empty residential courtyards in its peri-urban districts (previously rented out to migrants and their families and now marked with "To let" signs) evidenced the precariousness, vulnerability and insecurity of mobile livelihoods under such external shocks. Since then a much more dynamic landscape has emerged in the development of China's social security system to protect migrants, in part as a response to the great challenges posed by the global financial crisis. While new experiments and initiatives have been introduced in coastal cities and different regions of the country, as analysed by several researchers (Hua 2010; Watson 2009; see also Chapter 3 of this book),[11] the effects of these and the extent of institutional innovation are still too early to assess. The issues raised in this chapter, therefore, call for more empirical and particularly qualitative in-depth research to improve the evidence base for policy-making, as well as for more inclusive (of migrant workers in particular through, among other things, their greater political representation) and forceful institutional responses to the challenges.

Acknowledgements

I would like to thank the British Academy and the Sino-British Fellowship Trust for supporting the fieldwork of the research project, "Migration and Sustainable Livelihoods: An Investigation into Health and Well-Being of Rural Migrants in Transitional China" (SG-40617, 2005–2006). This chapter is an updated version of an article entitled, "Protecting Mobile Livelihoods: Actors' Responses to the Emerging Health Challenges in Beijing and Tianjin", *Modern China* 38(4): 446–78.

Notes

1   Recent research has investigated the problem from different perspectives. Murphy's volume (2009) analysed a range of issues in relation to migration and social development in China, including migrants' housing, children's schooling, and NGOs working with migrants; Chan (2010) and Tao (2009) linked migrant social security problems to the *hukou* reform; Hu *et al.* (2008) highlighted the main concerns with migrants' health in present-day China. At a theoretical level, Huang's (2009) insightful analysis looked at China's expanding informal economy, where most rural migrants find employment, and the theoretical and ideological underpinnings of its omission from official statistics, as well as its policy implications. Solinger (1999) carried out pioneering work on rural migrants' citizenship in China. Among the recent work published in Chinese, the most influential include the State Council's (2006a) comprehensive research report

on the migrant worker issue, and subsequent publications on the various aspects of migrants' social security (cf. Deng and Liu 2008; Zheng and Huang-Li 2007).

2 Variations in local policies often explain the different occupational patterns for different social groups. For example, taxi-driving, when profitable, is reserved for residents with urban *hukou* status, especially SOE laid-off workers. This is the case in Tianjin where most taxi drivers own their cars, bought at prices substantially subsidised by the municipal government, and a business licence, making taxi-driving a profitable, sought-after business. Tianjin City Government regulations explicitly barred non-local *hukou* holders from entering the occupation (interviews with taxi drivers, 2008). When taxis are owned and business licences are monopolised by big private companies, which charge taxi drivers outrageous fees, turning taxi-driving into a hard-to-sustain livelihood, as is the case in Beijing, Hangzhou and many other cities (interviews with taxi drivers, 2005–2009), it then became an occupation dominated by commuting migrants and "outsiders". The latter scenario is also due to differentiated social entitlements, e.g. taxi companies in these cities prefer employing "outsiders" since they are not expected to pay full social insurance contributions for non-local *hukou* holders (interviews with taxi drivers, 2005–2009; Anon. n.d.; Lu 2009).

3 Until quite recently public sector employers were not expected to contribute to the social security schemes for temporary workers.

4 Housing difficulties faced by migrants in large cities have only recently been recognised by the Chinese government as indicated in the China Development Report 2008/2009, where it is recommended that China's urban planning should take account of and incorporate the housing needs of migrants to prevent the emergence of the shanty town phenomenon (China Development Research Foundation 2009).

5 Between March 2008 and March 2009 China's exports decreased by about 48 percentage points, leading to the non-materialisation of about 9.5 million export-related jobs expected otherwise. In addition, many people lost their jobs, particularly those employed in small and medium enterprises more vulnerable to external shocks. Between October 2008 and January 2009, the total decrease in jobs reached 8.1 per cent nationwide (Mo *et al.* 2009: 37–8).

6 According to incomplete statistics collected by the All China Federation of Trade Unions, by November 2004, overdue pay to migrant workers reached around 100 billion yuan nationally. A survey of 8,000 migrant workers conducted by the Beijing Research Centre on Legal Aid for Young People (BRCLAYP) at the end of 2003 showed that nearly half (48.1 per cent) had experienced unpaid wages, of whom about one-third (30.6 per cent) lost 100–1,000 yuan, 15.7 per cent lost 1,000–5,000 yuan, and 1.6 per cent lost more than 5,000 yuan (BRCLAYP 2005). Given that migrants' average monthly wage was 600–1,500 yuan, this problem constituted a serious stressor and threat to migrants' economic and psychological well-being (cf. Wong *et al.* 2008). While resolving this problem has been repeatedly emphasised by the central government in, for example, its No. 1 Document issued at the beginning of each year since 2003, it continues to recur (Wu 2006).

7 The petition mechanism refers to *xinfang* or *shangfang* (letters and visits). Individuals write petition letters or go in person to upper-level authorities to make a complaint and seek justice when other institutional channels fail, and then, if they are not satisfied, they appeal to still higher authorities until (if petitioners are tenacious enough) they reach the ultimate authority – the State Council's Office for Dealing with Petitions (*Guowuyuan xinfang bangongshi*).

8 This scheme was introduced in parts of rural China in 2004 with nationwide expansion following the issuing in August 2007 of the State Council's Circular on Establishing a National Rural MLS Guarantee System (State Council 2007). Yet again, mirroring China's great regional and urban-rural inequalities, the level of *dibao* provision has

been hugely different between the city and the countryside, and between the coastal and inland regions. In the first half of 2007, the national monthly rural per capita *dibao* benefit was 70 yuan as against its urban counterpart of 182.4 yuan (NBSC 2008: 196). In 2008, the monthly rural per capita *dibao* in suburban Shanghai on the southeastern seaboard was 263 yuan – almost seven times as much as the 38 yuan per capita *dibao* in rural Gansu in the northwest (Wang *et al.* 2010: 114).

9 Despite the massive scale of rural-urban migration – the estimated number of rural migrants working in Chinese towns and cities has reached 260 million, accounting for one-third of the entire urban labour force, representation of migrants in China's political system has been extremely low and hugely disproportionate. For instance, there had been no one on the National People's Congress (NPC – China's Parliament) representing migrant workers until 2008 when just three migrant workers were elected to the 11th National People's Congress held that year. At the 12th National People's Congress convened in 2013, the number of migrant worker representatives rose to 31, and this has been hailed as progress by the mainstream media (cf. Baidu 2012; Xinhua Net 2013) ignoring the fact that the figure is from a large pool of about 3,000 NPC representatives. In other words, even with this increase, the political representation of the 260 million migrant workers (who, together with their families, account for *one-quarter to one-third of China's total population* of 1.3 billion) in the NPC in 2013 was only about 1 per cent.

10 These local plans, however, have triggered heated academic and policy debates, with powerful and vested interests fiercely opposing such a radical measure. It has also caused apprehension that without the control of the *hukou* system, "chaos" would break out in China's cities (cf. Tao and Du 2009).

11 Hua (2010: 199–200) classifies existing local practices into three different "models", namely, (1) the "integrated urban model", in which migrant workers join urban social security schemes, experimented with in Beijing, Guangdong, etc.; (2) the "specially designed model", whereby social security schemes are tailored to the needs of migrant workers, experimented with in Shanghai, Chengdu, etc.; and (3) the "integrated rural model", whereby migrants join rural social security schemes, piloted in parts of Jiangsu where rural industries are relatively developed.

References

Andrews-Speed, Philip (2007), Marginalisation in the Chinese energy sector: The case of township and village coal mines. In Heather Xiaoquan Zhang, Bin Wu and Richard Sanders (eds), *Marginalisation in China: Perspectives on Transition and Globalisation*. Aldershot: Ashgate, pp. 55–80.

Anon. (n.d.), *Shui gei women kai chuzu? chuzuche siji chenfulu* [Who would be driving the taxis? The vicissitudes of taxi drivers]. Available at: http://news.163.com/special/0001139T/taxi060209.html (accessed 12 February 2011).

Anon. (2008), *Fei Beijing hukou jiao shengyu baoxian youyong ma?* [Is there any use for us as non-Beijing *hukou* holders to contribute to maternal insurance?] Available at: http://zhidao.baidu.com/question/76210314.html?fr=qrl&cid=204&index=5 (accessed 14 February 2011).

Anon. (2009), *Jinnian lai Heilongjiang meikuang shigu zhuangkuang* [The status of mine accidents in Heilongjiang Province in recent years]. Available at: www.bjhgsy.cn/view77.asp?id=2471 (accessed 10 October 2010).

Avato, Johanna, Johannes Koettl and Rachel Sabates-Wheeler (2010), Social security regimes, global estimates, and good practices: The status of social protection for international migrants. *World Development* 38(4): 455–466.

Baidu (2012) *Di 12 jie quanguo renmin daibiao dahui you duoshao daibiao?* [How many representatives are there for the 12th National People's Congress?] Available at: http://zhidao.baidu.com/question/474893542.html (accessed 23 December 2013).

Barrientos, Armando and David Hulme (eds) (2008), *Social Protection for the Poor and Poorest*. Basingstoke: Palgrave.

Bebbington, Anthony (2000), Reencountering development: Livelihood transitions and place transformations in the Andes. *Annals of the Association of American Geographers* 90(3): 495–520.

Beijing Municipal Government (2006), *Shi laodong he shehui baozhang ju luoshi zhongyang jingshen jiang nongmingong naru gongshang baoxian* [Implementing the central government's policy, Beijing Labour and Social Security Bureau includes migrant workers in the work injury insurance scheme]. Available at: www.beijing.gov.cn/zfzx/fg/zcxx/t359117.htm (accessed 5 July 2010).

Beijing Research Centre on Legal Aid for Young People (BRCLAYP) (2005), *Zhongguo nongmingong wei quan chengben diaocha baogao* [Research report on the cost of protecting the rights of migrant workers in China]. Beijing: BRCLAYP.

Beijing Youth (2008), *Dengfeng kuangnan 37 ren yunan* [Thirty-seven miners died in Dengfeng coal mine disaster]. Available at: http://bjyouth.ynet.com/article.jsp?oid=43442281 (accessed 10 June 2010).

Cai, Qian (2003), Migrant remittances and family ties: A case study in China. *International Journal of Population Geography* 9(6): 471–483.

CCP (Chinese Communist Party) Central Committee and State Council (2010), *2010 nian zhongyang yihao wenjian* [The 2010 central government No. 1 document]. Available at: http://news.qq.com/a/20100131/001379.htm (accessed 28 May 2011).

Central People's Government of the PRC (People's Republic of China) (2010), *Zhonghua renmin gongheguo shehui baoxian fa* [The Social Insurance Law of the PRC]. Available at: www.gov.cn/flfg/2010-10/28/content_1732964.htm (accessed 15 April 2011).

Chan, Anita (2002), Globalisation and China's "race to the bottom" in labour standards. *George Ernest Morrison Lecture on Ethnography*. Contemporary China Centre, National University of Australia. Available at: www.eSocialSciences.com/data/articles/Document126102006590.7598383.pdf (accessed 25 January 2010).

Chan, Chris King-Chi and Pun Ngai (2009), The making of a new working class? A study of collective actions of migrant workers in south China. *The China Quarterly* 198: 287–303.

Chan, Kam Wing (2010), The household registration system and migrant labour in China: Notes on a debate. *Population and Development Review* 36(2): 357–364.

Chan, Kam Wing and Will Buckingham (2008), Is China abolishing the *hukou* system? *The China Quarterly* 195: 582–606.

China Development Research Foundation (2009), *China Development Report 2008/2009*. Beijing: Zhongguo fazhan chubanshe.

Davin, Delia (1999), *Internal Migration in Contemporary China*. Basingstoke: Macmillan.

de Haan, Arjan (1999), Livelihoods and poverty: The role of migration – a critical review of the migration literature. *Journal of Development Studies* 36(2): 1–47.

Deng, Dasong and Changping Liu (eds) (2008), *2007–2008 Zhongguo shehui baozhang gaige yu fazhan baogao* [2007–2008 report on China's social security reform and development]. Beijing: Renmin chubanshe.

Dong, Yuexian (2008), *Jianli nongmingong shehui baozhang zhidu de tantao* [An exploration of establishing a social security system for migrant workers]. Available at: http://wenku.baidu.com/view/f6b8e7fdc8d376eeaeaa3188.html (accessed 20 May 2011).

Du, Ping (2014), *Jiatinghua qianyi yu nongmingong dingju yiyuan tanxi* [Research on family migration and the willingness of migratory families to settle in the city in China]. Paper presented at the Chinese Sociological Association annual conference, Wuhan University, Wuhan, 10–13 July.

Du, Yang and Weiguang Pan (2009), Minimum wage regulation in China and its applications to migrant workers in the urban labour market. *China and World Economy* 17(2): 79–93.

Duckett, Jane (2003), An opportunity for China's health system? *China Review* 25: 5–7.

Duckett, Jane (2010), *The Chinese State's Retreat from Health: Policy and the Politics of Retrenchment.* London: Routledge.

Ellis, Frank (2000), *Rural Livelihoods and Diversity in Developing Countries.* Oxford: Oxford University Press.

Ellis, Frank and H. Ade Freeman (2004), Rural livelihoods and poverty reduction strategies in four African countries. *Journal of Development Studies* 40(4): 1–30.

Fan, C. Cindy (2008), *China on the Move: Migration, the State, and the Household.* London: Routledge.

Feng, Zhiqiang (2007), Marginalisation and health provision in transitional China. In Heather Xiaoquan Zhang, Bin Wu and Richard Sanders (eds), *Marginalisation in China: Perspectives on Transition and Globalisation.* Aldershot: Ashgate, pp. 99–117.

Gong, Sen, Alan Walker, and Guang Shi (2007), From Chinese model to U.S. symptoms: The paradox of China's health system. *International Journal of Health Services* 37(4): 651–672.

Hu, Xiaojiang, Sarah Cook and Miguel A. Salazar (2008), Internal migration and health in China. *The Lancet* 372(Nov.): 1717–1719.

Hua, Yingfang (2010), *Nongmingong shehui baozhang wenti* [The migrant workers' social security issue]. In Jiagui Chen and Yanzhong Wang (eds), *Zhongguo shehui baozhang fanzhan baogao (2010) No. 4* [China's social security system development report [2010] No. 4]. Beijing: Shehui kexue wenxian chubanshe, pp. 190–216.

Huang, Philip C.C. (2009), China's neglected informal economy: Reality and theory. *Modern China* 35(4): 405–438.

Jacka, Tamara (2005), Finding a place: Negotiations of modernisation and globalisation among rural women in Beijing. *Critical Asian Studies* 37(1): 51–74.

Judd, Ellen R. (2009), Starting again in rural west China: Stories of rural women across generations. *Gender and Development* 17(3): 441–451.

Lee, Ching Kwan (1998), *Gender and the South China Miracle.* Berkeley, CA: University of California Press.

Li, Qiang (2001), *Zhongguo waichu nongmingong jiqi huikuan zhi yanjiu* [A study of remittances by rural-urban migrants in China]. *Shehuixue yanjiu* 4: 64–76.

Li, Qiang (2004), *Nongmingong yu zhongguo shehui fenceng* [Migrant workers and social stratification in China]. Beijing: Shehui kexue wenxian chubanshe.

Li, Yuhuan (2005), *Guanzhu meikuang chenfeibing, baohu nongmingong jiankang quanyi* [Paying closer attention to pneumoconiosis, protecting migrant workers' rights to health]. In Zhen Li (ed.), *Gongshang zhe* [Victims at work]. Beijing: Shehui kexue wenxian chubanshe, pp. 51–55.

Long, Norman (2008), Translocal livelihoods, networks of family and community, and remittances in central Peru. In Josh DeWind and Jennifer Holdaway (eds), *Migration and Development Within and Across Borders: Research and Policy Perspectives on Internal and International Migration.* Geneva: International Organization for Migration and Social Sciences Research Council, pp. 39–70.

Lu, Bo (2009), *Beijing chuzuche gongsi quanshi pengzhang shi* [A history of the expansion of Beijing taxi companies' power and influence]. Available at: www.xici.net/b1126347/d89143997.htm (accessed 28 September 2011).

Lu, Quan and Li Qin (2007), *Beijingshi nongmingong wenti yu shehui baohu* [The migrant workers' issue and their social protection in Beijing]. In Gongcheng Zheng and Ruolian Huang-Li (eds), *Zhongguo nongmingong wenti yu shehui baohu* [Rural-urban migrant workers in China: Issues and social protection], two volumes. Beijing: Renmin chubanshe, pp. 119–152.

Lu, Xueyi (ed.) (2004), *Dangdai zhongguo shehui liudong* [Social mobility in contemporary China]. Beijing: Shehui kexue wenxian chubanshe.

McMichael, Celia and Sandra Gifford (2010), Narratives of sexual health risk and protection amongst young people from refugee backgrounds in Melbourne, Australia. *Culture, Health and Sexuality* 12(3): 263–277.

Ministry of Labour and Social Security Research Team (2006), *Nongmingong gongzi he laodong baohu wenti yanjiu baogao* [A research report on the issue of migrant workers' wages and social protection]. In State Council of the PRC (ed.), *Zhongguo nongmingong diaoyan baogao* [A research report on migrant workers in China]. Beijing: Zhongguo yanshi chubanshe, pp. 201–217.

Mo, Rong, Liwei Zhao, and Lan Chen (2009), *2009 nian: guoji jinrong weiji xia de jiuye xingshi he zhengce* [2009: the employment situation and relevant policies under the global financial crisis]. In Xin Ru, Xueyi Lu, Peilin Li, Guangjin Chen, Wei Li and Xinxin Xu (eds), *2010 nian zhongguo shehui xingshi fenxi yu yuce* [Society of China: analysis and forecast, 2010]. Beijing: Shehui kexue wenxian chubanshe, pp. 31–48.

MoLSS (Ministry of Labour and Social Security) (2001), *Shiye baoxianjin shenling fafang banfa* [Methods of application for and distribution of unemployment benefits]. Available at: http://trs.molss.gov.cn/was40/mainframe.htm (accessed 19 March 2010).

MoLSS (2004), *Zuidi gongzi guiding* [Minimum wage regulations]. Available at: www.molss.gov.cn/gb/ywzn/2006-02/15/content_106799.htm (accessed 12 December 2010).

Murphy, Rachel (2002), *How Migrant Labour Is Changing Rural China*. Cambridge: Cambridge University Press.

Murphy, Rachel (ed.) (2009), *Labour Migration and Social Development in Contemporary China*. London: Routledge.

NBSC (National Bureau of Statistics of China) (2008), *Zhongguo tongji zhaiyao 2008* [China statistical index, 2008]. Beijing: Zhongguo tongji chubanshe.

NBSC (2009), *2008 nianmo quanguo nongmingong zongliang wei 22,542 wanren* [Total migrant workers reached 225.42 million nationwide at the end of 2008]. Available at: www.stats.gov.cn (accessed 18 November 2010).

Pun, Ngai (2005), *Made in China: Women Factory Workers in a Global Workplace*. Durham, NC: Duke University Press.

Pun, Ngai and Huilin Lu (2010a), A culture of violence: The labour subcontracting system and collective action by construction workers in post-socialist China. *The China Journal* 64: 143–158.

Pun, Ngai and Huilin Lu (2010b), Unfinished proletarianisation: Self, anger, and class action among the second generation of peasant-workers in present-day China. *Modern China* 36(5): 493–519.

Sabates-Wheeler, Rachel and Ian MacAuslan (2007), Migration and social protection: Exposing problems of access. *Development* 50(4): 26–32.

Solinger, Dorothy (1999), *Contesting Citizenship in Urban China: Peasant Migrants, the State, and the Logic of the Market*. Berkeley, CA: University of California Press.

State Council of the PRC (1999), *Shiye baoxian tiaoli* [Regulations on unemployment insurance]. Beijing: Falü chubanshe.

State Council of the PRC (2004), China's social security and its policy. Available at: http://china.org.cn/e-white/20040907/ (accessed 26 August 2010).

State Council of the PRC (2006a), *Zhongguo nongmingong diaoyan baogao* [A research report on migrant workers in China]. Beijing: Zhongguo yanshi chubanshe.

State Council of the PRC (2006b), *Guowuyuan guanyu jiejue nongmingong wenti de ruogan yijian* [The State Council's several proposals on resolving the issue of migrant workers]. Available at: www.gov.cn/jrzg/2006-03/27/content_237644.htm (accessed 22 February 2011).

State Council of the PRC (2007), *Guowuyuan guanyu zai quanguo jianli nongcun zuidi shenghuo banzhang zhidu de tongzhi* [The State Council's circular on establishing a national rural minimum living standards guarantee system]. Available at: www.gov.cn/zwgk/2007-08/14/content_716621.htm (accessed 27 March 2011).

Su, Zhi (2005), *Woguo nongmingong zhiye jiankang xianzhuang jiqi baozhang* [The current state of occupational health and protection for migrant workers in China]. In Zhen Li (ed.), *Gongshang zhe* [Victims at work]. Beijing: Shehui kexue wenxian chubanshe, pp. 11–25.

Sun, Wanning (2009), *Maid in China: Media, Mobility, and a New Semiotic of Power.* London: Routledge.

Tao, Ran (2009), Hukou reform and social security for migrant workers in China. In Rachel Murphy (ed.), *Labour Migration and Social Development in Contemporary China.* London: Routledge, pp. 73–95.

Tao, Weihua and Juan Du (2009), *Zhuanjia ji bian shifou ying yibu quxiao huji zhidu* [Experts debate heatedly about whether the *hukou* system should be abolished immediately]. Available at: http://news.sina.com.cn/c/sd/2009-08-13/165418428964_6.shtml (accessed 20 October 2011).

Tianjin Municipal Government (2006), *Tianjinshi renmin zhengfu wenjian No. 78: guanyu guanche "Guowuyuan guanyu jiejue nongmingong wenti de ruogan yijian" de shishi yijian* [Tianjin Municipal People's Government document No. 78: Recommendations on implementing and enforcing "The State Council's several proposals on resolving the issue of migrant workers"]. Available at: www.tj.gov.cn/zwgk/wjgz/szfwj/200710/t20071006_27699.htm (accessed 19 November 2010).

UNDP (United Nations Development Programme) (2009), *Human Development Report 2009: Overcoming Barriers: Human Mobility and Development.* New York: UNDP.

Wang, Yanzhong, Xia Wei, Yuqi Long, Dasheng Shan and Fenglei Jiang (2010), *Fazhan zhong de zhongguo nongcun shehui baozhang zhidu* [China's evolving rural social security system]. In Jiagui Chen and Yanzhong Wang (eds), *Zhongguo shehui baozhang fanzhan baogao 2010 No. 4* [China's social security system development report, 2010, No. 4]. Beijing: Shehui kexue wenxian chubanshe, pp. 105–160.

Wang, Yaping, Yanglin Wang and Jiansheng Wu (2010), Housing for migrant workers in rapidly urbanising regions: A study of the Chinese model in Shenzhen. *Housing Studies* 25(1): 83–100.

Watson, Andrew (2009), Social security for China's migrant workers: Providing for old age. *Journal of Current Chinese Affairs* 4: 85–115.

White, Gordon and Roger Goodman (eds) (1998), *The East Asian Welfare Model: Welfare Orientalism and the State.* London: Routledge.

WHO (World Health Organisation) (2000), *The World Health Report 2000 – Health Systems: Improving Performance*. Available at: www.who.int/whr/2000/en (accessed 9 January 2011).

Wong, Daniel Keung Fu, Xuesong He, Grace Leung, Ying Lau, and Yingli Chang (2008), Mental health of migrant workers in China: Prevalence and correlates. *Social Psychiatry and Psychiatric Epidemiology* 43: 483–489.

Wu, Jingjing (2006), *Woguo zhuajin cong genben shang jiejue tuoqian kekou nongmingong gongzi wenti* [China is determined to fundamentally resolve the problem of delayed or unpaid wages to migrant workers]. Available at: http://news.sina.com.cn/c/2006-03-27/17318541839s.shtml (accessed 10 March 2011).

Wu, Mingwei and Xiao Wu (2005), *Woguo chengshihua beijing xiade liudong renkou juju xingtai yanjiu – yi jiangsusheng weili* [A study of the patterns of migrants' residential arrangements in the context of China's urbanisation: The case of Jiangsu Province]. Nanjing: Dongnandaxue chubanshe.

Xinhua Net (2008), *Shanxi renshi tiaozheng nengfou niuzhuan kuangnan pin fa jumian?* [Can the situation of frequent mine disasters be reversed through provincial personnel change in Shanxi?]. Available at: www.sx.xinhuanet.com/ztjn/2008-09/16/content_14403126.htm (accessed 18 May 2011).

Xinhua Net (2013) *Cong san dao 31: Zhongguo nongmingong quanguo renda daibiao renshu dafu tisheng* [From three to 31: The number of migrant worker representatives in the National People's Congress has sharply increased]. Available at: http://news.xinhuanet.com/politics/2013-03/04/c_114878972.htm (accessed 23 December 2013).

Yang, Guihong and Jianguo Hu (n.d.), *Nongmingong chengshi shenghuo shehui baozhang de shizheng yanjiu* [An empirical study of migrant workers' social security in the city]. Available at: www.sociology.cass.cn/gqdcyyjzx/xsjl/P020060705448030155879.pdf (accessed 26 December 2010).

Zhang, Heather Xiaoquan (1999), Female migration and urban labour markets in Tianjin. *Development and Change* 30(1): 21–41.

Zhang, Heather Xiaoquan (2007), Conceptualising the links: Migration, health and sustainable livelihoods in China. In Heather Xiaoquan Zhang, Bin Wu and Richard Sanders (eds), *Marginalisation in China: Perspectives on Transition and Globalisation*. Aldershot: Ashgate, pp. 195–214.

Zhang, Heather Xiaoquan, P. Mick Kelly, Catherine Locke, Alexandra Winkels and W. Neil Adger (2006), Migration in a transitional economy: Beyond the planned and spontaneous dichotomy in Vietnam. *Geoforum* 37(6): 1066–1081.

Zhao, Tiechui (2005), *Guanzhu nongmingong, cujin anquan shengchan zhuangkuang de wending haozhuan* [Paying close attention to migrant workers' occupational health and steadily improving work safety conditions]. In Zhen Li (ed.), *Gongshang zhe* [Victims at work]. Beijing: Shehui kexue wenxian chubanshe, pp. 3–9.

Zheng, Gongcheng and Ruolian Huang-Li (eds) (2007), *Zhongguo nongmingong wenti yu shehui baohu* [Rural-urban migrant workers in China: Issues and social protection], two vols. Beijing: Renmin chubanshe.

3 Social protection and livelihoods

Providing old-age social insurance for migrant workers in China

Andrew Watson

Introduction

Since the early 1990s, the livelihoods perspective has become one of the most dominant ways of thinking about solving issues of development and rural poverty. As Ian Scoones' (2009) review of the history and uses of the concept has shown, promoting livelihoods as a model for rural development seeks to link human capabilities, activities and assets together as part of an integrated system that generates incomes and development. Livelihoods can be seen in terms of different types of occupations or sectors and in terms of different social groups. They can also be understood as part of a dynamic process that constantly evolves in response to shifting community and institutional frameworks, environmental changes and the political economy of the global economy. Scoones' study underlines how the concept has become central to the work of many development agencies: it is used to define their strategic approach to rural development programmes and is formalised into the design of aid projects. At its core, the livelihoods perspective argues that creating sustainable means of generating a living is the key to rural development and the eradication of poverty.

To a large extent, this perspective tends to put issues of social protection to one side. Social welfare and social safety nets are seen as mechanisms to address failure, rather than a means of promoting livelihoods. As argued by Cook *et al.* (2003), however, it is important to recognise social protection as *developmental*. Whether provided by the state, the community, the family, or the individual, social protection provides a framework within which poor, vulnerable and disadvantaged groups can withstand shocks, build resilience and sustain their livelihoods. In other words, social protection policies for such things as health, unemployment, work injury, maternity and old age, should be seen as part of a livelihoods approach: they are mechanisms that are fundamental to ensuring the sustainability of livelihoods over a full lifetime.

This chapter reviews the development of old-age social insurance policies for China's rural-to-urban migrant workers (hereafter migrant workers). It sees this as an urgent challenge in sustaining their livelihoods. Heather Xiaoquan Zhang (2007) has made a parallel case in respect of the provision of health services for these migrants. The focus here is the provision of old-age retirement incomes.

In the following, I shall first discuss two major challenges facing the provision of old-age livelihoods for migrant workers in China. Subsequent sections will discuss the characteristics of China's migrant workers and the implications for designing old-age insurance schemes, China's current social security system and the place of rural-to-urban migrant workers within it, the attempts to develop policies for migrant worker old-age insurance, and the new rural pension plan and its implications for migrants. The conclusion will discuss the obstacles facing the development of an effective scheme and the consequences for migrant workers' livelihoods.

Two major challenges to the provision of migrants' old-age insurance

The emergence of the migrant workers as a major force in the Chinese economy during the 1980s can be seen as a model example of how pro-livelihoods policies can promote rural development and reduce poverty. The original rural reforms after 1978 had three main elements: (1) land was contracted to households; (2) farmers were enabled to plan their own production provided they met their obligatory tax and grain sales targets; and (3) surplus products could be sold on local free markets. The incentives created by these changes had consequences for livelihoods that went well beyond the original goals of increasing agricultural production. They encouraged farmers to raise their labour efficiency, to diversify production in order to supply the markets and, most importantly, to shift their labour to higher value-added off-farm employment in manufacturing, marketing and services, including migration to urban areas. The end result has been both a transformation of the structure of the Chinese economy and a significant growth in rural incomes. Since the 1980s, therefore, the migrant workers have made a huge contribution to China's rural development, economic restructuring and growth. They have realised China's comparative advantage in labour-intensive manufacturing. They have promoted the export of manufactures. They have provided the workforce for the development of infrastructure. They have stimulated the growth of the service sector. They have been the source of growth in rural incomes. And they have promoted urbanisation. Migration has been one of key factors contributing to prosperity in China's urban and coastal areas and to the maintenance of a strong, internationally-competitive economy.

Despite their huge economic contributions, however, migrant workers and their families have borne all the risks of this development themselves. The operation of China's household registration system (*hukou*) introduced during the planned economy era (Zhang 1983) forms a major barrier facing the provision of social protection and especially old-age insurance for migrant workers. This system defines people's social identity by their registered place of birth and residence. Introduced in the 1950s as a mechanism to control the movement of people, particularly from rural to urban areas, the result has been the creation of a dual structure, with a sharp division between rural and urban societies and people. The two populations became subject to different administrative, social and economic management systems, and the labour force was segmented (Cai 1990). China's migrant workers can thus be defined as people with rural *hukou* who move to work in cities or in non-agricultural township and village enterprises (TVEs). Their income is derived outside agriculture and they live for extended periods in cities and towns away from their native villages, but their *hukou* status means that they still retain an identity linked to their home village and to their contracted land.

Even though its role in restricting population movement has declined under the reforms because the market economy increasingly demands a flexible and mobile labour force, *hukou* remains a major factor in social policy. The migrants' rural *hukou* means that they cannot gain access to the same social services and social security as urban residents. China's decentralised fiscal and administrative system delivers public and social services through the local government where one is registered. Migrants are therefore expected to access health, education and other welfare services in their home villages. Except where reform experiments are under way, they are excluded from services in urban areas where they live and work. This exclusion is a key factor in the lack of social equity in the current system, and the provision of equal access for migrant old-age social insurance thus requires fundamental changes to the operation of the *hukou* system. A second key factor that underlines the importance of this issue is China's rapid demographic transition towards an aging society. The momentum created by China's fertility and mortality rates will have this inevitable outcome, even if population policies were to change soon. According to the United Nations (2009, hereafter UN), the proportion of China's population aged 60 and above reached over 12 per cent in 2010, will approach 17 per cent by 2020 and will be nearly 28 per cent by 2040. While there may be debate about the accuracy of the figures and Zhao and Guo (2007) suggest they may underestimate the rate of aging, the reality is that when the current population of migrant workers, whose average age is around 29, retires, the proportion of the working-age population able to support them will be declining. The migrant workers currently make up the largest proportion of the youthful working-age population of China. If appropriate policies are not adopted now to prepare for their aging, their low wages and lack of insurance, the erosion of traditional rural family and social support systems, and the reduced number of rural young mean that they will face challenges in maintaining their livelihoods in their old age. While they may retain their contractual rights to land use, those rights are not an economic asset that can be realised and, in any case, the land system itself may also be open to change over the next 30 years.

The implications of this for old-age social security policy have been explored by Jackson and Howe (2004), and it is clear that if China does not start to prepare to meet the anticipated needs of the migrant workers now, it will face a major crisis in providing for their livelihoods when they retire. The need to develop a stable and effective old-age income policy for migrant workers while they are still young, working and able to contribute is thus a major challenge. From a livelihoods perspective, the issue is one of income smoothing. Part of current income needs to be saved and invested to provide for future consumption and stable livelihoods in old age. The problem is how to design a system that corresponds to migrant needs.

The nature of migrant workers and their needs[1]

Given their mobility and the absence of a reliable means to count them, estimates of the total number of migrant workers vary, but according to the official figures, there are now around 269 million (National Bureau of Statistics of China 2014, hereafter NBSC), of whom some 166 million are working away from their home district (77 million in other provinces and 89 million in their own provinces, and about 35 million of them moving with their families) and nearly 103 million are in rural enterprises in their local areas. These workers make up around two-thirds of China's non-agricultural labour force, and they are the dominant proportion of the total workforce in many sectors such as construction (90 per cent), mining and extraction (80 per cent), textiles (60 per cent) and services (50 per cent) (Han 2009). Their incomes and remittances have been a major factor in the reduction of rural poverty, and by 2006 off-farm sources in aggregate accounted for around one-third of rural per capita incomes (NBSC 2006: 369). This combination of their overall economic role and their contribution to rural incomes underlines the way in which policies with pro-livelihoods outcomes can have a dramatic impact on development processes.

The high mobility of the migrant workers, their flexibility in responding to shifts in the urban and rural economies, and the changes in their composition and behaviour over the period since the early 1980s, all mean that there are statistical variations in defining their key characteristics. There have been many large and small surveys, each with differences in the details reported according to definitions and sampling. Though the statistics vary, these surveys have identified a number of common attributes (see, for example, Cai and Bai 2006; Cai and Du 2007; Cui 2008; Han 2009; Hua 2010; Meng *et al.* 2010; NBSC 2014).

- They are approximately two-thirds male and one-third female, with some clear gendered divisions of labour in the job market, for example, males in construction and heavy work, females in textiles and electronics.
- The average age is around 29, and job opportunities decline after age 40.
- Their employment tends to be in "dirty, demanding and dangerous" occupations, which threatens their health and the length of their working life.
- They tend to move between jobs and cities frequently in search of higher wages, though the rate of mobility slows down, the longer they have been working outside their home village.
- Large numbers are in informal employment, and many do not have formal labour contracts.
- Migrant wages are around half or less those of urban wages, with females lower than males.

- They are increasingly drawn from among the better-educated farmers. Around two-thirds have junior secondary school education and a little over 10 per cent are senior secondary graduates.
- About 20 per cent of them settle permanently in urban areas. Some of these have technical or management roles and increasingly see themselves as urban. Around 60 per cent are more mobile. They spend most of the year outside the villages, but may return for festivals or busy farming periods. They move between employers and locations fairly regularly. Another 20 per cent are seasonal workers, who retain an important role as agricultural labour and only "migrate" during the slack agricultural seasons.
- Generational changes have taken place in the nature of the migrants. The first wave in the 1980s was essentially strong but unskilled rural labour, taking any work in order to earn more income than they could get farming, with many staying locally and retaining strong rural links. Subsequent waves have travelled further and become more educated. In recent years, many have left their villages directly after graduating from school and have never worked on the farm. They no longer see themselves as farmers. They are less willing to take on dirty and heavy work such as construction, and their consumption patterns and life styles are increasingly urban in character.
- A proportion of these migrant workers eventually return to their original counties or provinces to settle in local towns and to set up small businesses or seek employment in local enterprises.

As noted above, despite their major role in total employment, the average monthly income of migrant workers remains well below the average urban wage. Furthermore, their wages remained almost static from the 1980s until the early 2000s (Li 2005). It is only since 2009 that their wages have begun to grow significantly (NBSC 2014). China's development model has thus relied heavily on maintaining the supply of cheap labour. Furthermore, through its formal institutional barriers the operation of the *hukou* system works to sustain the low level of migrant income and benefits (Chan 2010). Migrant workers' rural *hukou* means that employers are under no obligation to treat them the same as urban residents.

Until the late 2008 economic downturn brought about by the global financial crisis, there were signs that the supply of rural labour, especially in the 16–40 age group, which was most in demand, was beginning to dry up and this was leading to a rise in wages. Some Chinese researchers, such as Fang Cai at the Chinese Academy of Social Sciences (CASS), argue that this heralds the approach of the Lewisian turning point at which the supply of surplus rural labour dries up, the cost differential between urban and rural labour declines, and a shift to greater capital intensity becomes necessary (Cai and Du 2007). This issue is, however, debated. Chan (2010), for example, argues that, while it is true that the supply of young rural labour is tending to decline, there is still a large pool of available rural labour. The current situation tends to reflect the distortions created by the *hukou* system and the biases in the employment demand, rather than a full uptake of surplus rural labour.

According to the National Rural Fixed-Point Survey, national average migrant monthly wages rose from 781 yuan to 953 yuan between 2003 and 2006. Of these, the wages of males rose from 855 yuan to 1,048 yuan and of females from 632 yuan to 711 yuan (Zhao and Wu 2007). In 2006, over half earned less than 800 yuan and one third between 200 yuan and 600 yuan. The 2009 survey (NBSC 2010) reported that the average wage in 2009 was 1,417 yuan, with some 39 per cent earning less than 1,200 yuan and 34 per cent earning between 1,200 yuan and 1,600 yuan. These monthly figures should be compared with urban per capita annual disposable income in 2009 of 17,175 yuan and rural annual disposable per capita income of 5,153 yuan (*China Daily* 2010). The 2013 survey (NBSC 2014) indicates that since 2009 there has been steady growth in migrant wages up to 2,609 yuan in 2013. While the accuracy of these wage data can be questioned, their relative sizes underline that migrant workers earn much less than their urban counterparts and that their remittances are important for those left behind in the villages. They are also likely to have to work longer hours for their wage. A final important aspect of their income is that, unlike urban residents, whose income levels rise gradually over their employment life and peak towards the end, migrant wages tend to rise to a peak early and then decline over time, as the migrant's physical strength declines (Zhang 2008).

Low wage levels and early peaking have important implications for migrant expectations and for their capacity to build assets for their old age. Their lower wage levels make it difficult for them to contribute to old-age insurance, when they are given access, and they cannot save at the same rate as urban residents. Moreover, when they are young and their income is highest, remittances to their family, preparations for marriage and other needs tend to take priority. As they age, they have fewer resources to prepare for retirement compared to urban people. The high cost of urban old-age insurance compared to their low incomes is recognised as one of the strongest disincentives for migrant participation (Beijing Normal University 2010: 27). On the other hand, a lower contribution rate would mean a lower income in old age. For women, the issue is particularly serious. Apart from the fact that they are lower paid and are generally in the more informal employment sectors, they also tend to have more breaks from work for child-bearing and family duties and are thus less able to make the regular contributions that are needed. Their accumulation will thus be less than that of males, but they will tend to live longer and be poorer in their old age. The cost of urban old-age insurance is thus a significant issue facing all migrants, and especially women.

In sum, the major characteristics of migrant workers are:

- relative youth;
- high geographical and job mobility;
- informal employment;
- low income;
- gender disparity in incomes, with females tending to have even lower incomes and even more informal employment;

- an income structure that peaks early and tails off as they get older;
- a trend towards having better levels of education; and
- a trend towards becoming more settled in cities.

The design of old-age social security programmes for migrants needs to address these characteristics and to respond to the nature of the demand that they create.

Apart from these structural constraints of mobility, types of employment and income levels, the migrants' own preferences and expectations must also be considered when designing old-age insurance systems to meet their needs (He and Hua 2008; Zhao *et al.* 2006: 306–314). The migrants are predominantly young and healthy and do not have a long-term perspective on their needs in old age. They are also not familiar with concepts of insurance against risk or of rights to a social security system. Furthermore, even if they are aware, they are hesitant to assert their rights at the risk of losing their employment. In addition, since their income is low and they do not own many assets, they are not willing to sacrifice part of their wages to what is still an unknown and uncertain scheme. For most of them, the key goals are to send money home to their family, to help build a new family house in their home village and to prepare for their own wedding and family. They tend to assume that they will have to look after themselves when they are old. These attitudes are not surprising, but as they age, the need to consider their future income becomes more important. According to official figures, in 2009, some 11.9 per cent of migrant workers were aged 40–50 and a further 4.2 per cent were over 50 (NBSC 2010). The issue of their needs in old age is thus becoming increasingly pronounced. Furthermore, migrant priorities are changing as the migrant generations evolve. Those who are settling in cities for longer and becoming more urban are increasingly aware of the need to consider their social security. Yingfang Hua reports a study in 2005 by the Ministry of Human Resources and Social Security (hereafter MoHRSS, which was called the Ministry of Labour and Social Security (MoLSS) until 2008) which found that up to one third of migrants were willing to participate in urban old-age insurance schemes if they could (Hua 2010: 8). A similar result was found by a research team from Beijing Normal University (2010: 31), which also noted that the trend was highest among the younger and more educated migrants.

For many migrants, however, especially those who have moved to the cities with family members, urban *housing* may be more important than old-age insurance. Urban housing regulations and the nature of the housing market mean it is hard for them to get access to affordable housing and to urban housing schemes (Lin and Zhu 2008; Zhang and Ge 2007). *Education* for migrant children in cities is another priority (Gao 2009). A further need is *healthcare*. Their employment in dirty and dangerous jobs and their long working hours put their health at risk. Many have to rely on informal medical treatment, but they tend to seek better healthcare for their children. For female migrants, *maternity insurance* is also an issue. Without it, they face a challenge to their work and health. They have to go back home to give birth, or they have to rely on cheap, informal, and sometimes unsafe services.

Alongside this is the perception of risk. A commitment to long-term participation in old-age insurance schemes requires a sense of trust in the quality of management and security of the funds and awareness that the value of one's benefits are being preserved and improved. If policies keep changing, if fund management is not stable and transparent, if people fear corruption and misuse of funds, and if there is a broad awareness that many funds are in deficit, then it is not surprising that migrants are suspicious. They will need to feel confident that all the contributions they are making are accumulating and that they have a growing stake in the system. Regular reporting on their account and reassurance about its growing value are needed to build such incentives. In the absence of transparent reporting systems, it is not surprising that they are not enthusiastic.

Given these characteristics and the context of the *hukou* system, it is not surprising that a lot of discussion of migrant problems focuses on the issue of exclusion.[2] As discussed above, the current social security system is structured around a person's place of registration. The migrants are excluded from urban services and, assuming that all citizens should have a right to equal access, the answer to the problems can be found in breaking down the barriers and allowing migrants equal access to urban schemes. While this is a fundamental issue to be resolved, it is important to recognise that other factors also need to be taken into account. Based on work on local urbanisation in small towns and cities, on the multi-directional flows of migrants between cities and to and from their rural origins, and on their double identities as both urban and rural people, Yu Zhu argues that the policy response to migrants social security needs should also include flexibility and diversity (Zhu 2002, 2004, 2007; Zhu and Chen 2010). Migrants may not see themselves as part of a one-way movement from the countryside to the cities. For various reasons, they may prefer to circulate between cities and ultimately to return to their original home areas. They may see migration as part of a household strategy in which the goal is to achieve the best outcomes for the family as a whole. In other words, given their diverse life goals and circumstances, they need some choice in terms of participation in urban or rural schemes and in terms of portability and links between systems. Media reports of migrants' unwillingness to relinquish their rural registration when given the opportunity also tend to support this view (Moxley 2010). While exclusion created by the *hukou* system is a key factor shaping this situation, issues such as migrant demographic characteristics, employment options, long-term goals and household-level decision-making also need to be considered. While an equitable system for all citizens should be the ultimate goal, policy design should recognise this reality and provide wider choice and flexibility. With this in mind, we can now turn to examine the existing barriers to the development of migrant old-age insurance.

China's old-age social security system and the barriers facing migrants

Broadly speaking, retirement incomes can be provided by individuals in the form of savings and assets built up during their working life, by the state in the form of pensions paid from government revenue, by the employer in the form of a pension or annuity, or by a combination of savings by the individual, the employer and the state in the form of old-age insurance. Most societies rely on a combination of these approaches, and the general trend in developed market economies is to design systems around three pillars (OECD 2008; Hu and Stewart 2009):

1 A basic state pension that is funded from government revenue.
2 A compulsory individual account old-age insurance scheme that is funded by employer contributions alone or by employer and employee contributions over the working life of the individual.
3 A voluntary scheme whereby individuals also contribute to funds that are saved for their old age.

In China's case, however, the system as a whole is still in the process of reform and development, and the position of migrant workers within it remains uncertain. Urban schemes have been developing rapidly since 1995, but rural schemes lag behind and provide a much lower level of benefits.[3] The *first* pillar of an old-age pension provided from fiscal revenue does not exist. There is, however, a minimum income guarantee provided through the Ministry of Civil Affairs (hereafter MCA) as a form of social assistance for those who have no other sources of income. This is targeted at those in poverty but not specifically old people. It is funded from fiscal revenue and calculated according to family income. If a family's per capita income is below the locally-set minimum, the supplement is paid. The system is most developed in urban areas, and it is being implemented in rural areas at a much lower level of payment. The *second* pillar primarily consists of the basic urban old-age insurance scheme managed by the MoHRSS through its subordinate public service unit, the Social Insurance Administration. This is a contributory scheme for all those in formal employment. Alongside this are the various defined benefit schemes for cadres and public servants that are paid directly from government revenue and at a much higher level than that of the social insurance schemes for enterprise employees.[4] In a number of cities, especially in the richer areas, there are also emerging contributory insurance schemes designed for urban residents who are not employed. In some cases, these are also open to rural people living in suburban counties under the urban administration. Finally, as discussed below, a universal rural scheme has been introduced, beginning in 2010. This involves both a government subsidy and contributions. It is still developing, and the level of benefits largely depends on the level of development of the local economy. The *third* pillar is left to the individual and to the emerging system of enterprise annuity schemes.

The adoption of this type of structure was a necessity, given the erosion of the socialist planned economy and the closure of many state-owned enterprises (SOEs). It underlined that the old defined benefit schemes for urban SOE workers under the centrally planned economy was unsustainable, with some

20–30 per cent of state enterprise wage costs being used to pay the pensions of retired employees, no accumulated provision to fund pensions, and the ratio of pensions to wages increasing disproportionately (Zhao *et al.* 2006). The government could no longer guarantee a fixed percentage of an individual's final wage as a pension, and it was necessary to look for ways to ensure that individuals could smooth income over time to provide for their old age and also build assets on which they could depend in later life. The prospect of an aging population underlined the urgency of the change, given the growing number of people dependent on pensions and old-age insurance.

China's current urban social insurance schemes depend on contributions from the employer and the employee. These are fixed as a percentage of the wage. Currently employer contributions for urban employees for all types of insurance and housing provision are set at around the equivalent of 43 per cent of the wage. The health, maternity, work injury and unemployment benefits are short-term and relate to needs as they arise. The insurance is provided by employers for the period of employment, and the benefits are paid as required by the regulations. By its nature, however, the old-age scheme is on-going over the lifetime of the individual. It requires contributions to be recorded and accumulated in a fund, careful management of funds to preserve and improve value, secure systems to manage information databases over many decades, and a method for the payment of benefits. For each participant, the process might last up to 60 or more years, from the time of joining to the time of death.

The design of the basic old-age insurance for urban workers in China is straightforward, though the implementation is complex and there is considerable regional variation in the application of the basic design. Employers and employees respectively contribute at a rate of 20 per cent and 8 per cent of the wage. The employer contribution goes to the local social pool and the individual contribution goes to the individual account. Individuals are able to retire after reaching the requisite age (55 for women and 60 for men) and, provided they have contributed to the local scheme for 15 years or more, they are eligible to register for a monthly pension. That pension comes in two parts: the social pool and the individual account. The social pool part is meant to provide a replacement ratio of about 60 per cent of the local social average wage after a minimum of 15 years' contributions, with the last five being continuous in the pool area. This pension level is therefore not based on the actual wage of the individual but on a local average. This average pension is adjusted over time to take account of local wage increases. The individual account part of the pension is calculated according to the amount of accumulation in the individual account and is paid at a monthly rate of 1/139th of the total accumulation (i.e. it assumes an actuarial life of 139 months after retirement. This actuarial figure is also open to adjustment.) As noted above, employees in government agencies, public welfare units and similar institutions still receive the old planned economy-defined benefits pensions and do not participate in these schemes (though there is now considerable discussion of reforming the system for public welfare units). As set out in the regulations, the policies for urban social security and old-age insurance are intended to cover all workers in urban employment, including migrants. Moreover, as discussed below, in places with large concentrations of migrants, such as Shenzhen and Dongguan in Guangdong, migrants have been enrolled in the urban schemes. However, in operation, the system has a number of special characteristics that add to its complexity and also act as barriers to the participation of migrant workers.

First, the national scheme is not managed as a single integrated system but as a set of parallel local pools (*tongchouqu*). Each local pool consists of the contributions from the employer and is managed as a local fund. Each fund can have its own specific features, and there is no single standard national computer system used to manage them. Local governments can make adjustments to adapt the national standards to local conditions, so that levels of contributions and benefits will also vary. Although efforts are under way to raise the level of pooling and a growing number of provinces are implementing some transitional forms of provincial-level pooling, currently, there are some 2,000 pools across China, and most of them are at city or county level. This means that the transfer of contributions and benefits between cities and regions is complicated and difficult, even for urban residents. It is much more so for migrant workers, who might move between jobs and regions within a single year and certainly would do so many times over the course of their working lifetime. In recognition of this, the government has adopted new procedures for the transfer of social security registration in December 2009 (State Council 2009a).

Second, the pools also tend to be structured around the hierarchical level of registration of the employer. Thus, the Guangdong Province Social Security Bureau deals with the employees of enterprises registered at provincial level, while the Guangzhou City Bureau deals with those of enterprises registered at the city level, and so on down through the system. The concept of locality thus combines both a notion of place and of administrative hierarchy, and both of these can have an impact on benefit levels. Unifying this is also a challenge for the reform agenda.

Third, participation requires a formal employer who registers the employee in the scheme. After registration, the monthly contributions from the employer and employee are calculated by the social security department and collected from the employer, who deducts the employee amount from the wage. Collections are either through the tax office or through the social security agency, which places them in a special account. This generally operates through the fiscal offices and is subject to strict management rules in an effort to ensure the security of the funds. Self-employed urban people can also register and make contributions.

Fourth, as described above, the contributions from employers and from individuals are treated differently. The employer contribution is seen as part of the common social pool (*shehui tongchou*) and the individual contributions are seen as part of an individual account (*geren zhanghu*). Both are used to pay the final benefits, but they are recorded and managed differently.

Fifth, when the system was introduced in 1996, no provision was made for existing retirees or for those approaching the end of their working life.

These people were eligible for payments from the funds since they had carry-over entitlements from the SOE system, but they had not made contributions over their working lifetime or, in the case of those close to retirement when the reforms were introduced, had only contributed for a few years. In other words, the new scheme inherited large unfunded liabilities from the pre-existing system. Wang Dewen (2005) divides the scheme participants into three categories: (1) the "old" (those already retired in 1997 who continue to draw pensions from the funds but have never made any contributions); (2) the "new" (those contributing to the new schemes from the beginning); and (3) the "middle" (those in mid-career who are part of the transition with some unfunded and some funded years). The result is that there are many people with "empty accounts", and the payment of benefits from the funds far exceeds the level of contributions. Many funds are in deficit and are supported by transfers from fiscal revenues (Zhao *et al.* 2006: 55). Wang (2005: 8) quoted estimates that the national deficit was 2.5 trillion yuan and likely to grow to 6 trillion over the next 30 years. According to a 2009 newspaper report, the individual account part of the system had a deficit of 1.4 trillion yuan, despite having a contributing membership of 210 million people (Guo 2009). While the reliability of these figures may be questioned, the huge estimates underline the scale of the problem. Apart from these foreseen deficits, the risks from poor fund management or corruption add to the uncertainties. Clearly, many existing schemes are currently not fully funded and will require substantial fiscal inputs for many years.

This combination of high costs relative to incomes, local pools and barriers to portability, the lack of formal employment contracts for most migrants, the fact that enterprise contributions form the basis for the local social pool, and the overall shortfall in fund accumulation vis-à-vis benefit payment obligations have acted as powerful barriers to the integration of migrants into the existing systems. Their job mobility, their frequent inter-regional movement and their employment in the informal sector have made participation in the urban schemes even more complicated. Furthermore, it is difficult for migrants to guarantee that they will be able to make 15 years' worth of contributions to a single fund (including the required five consecutive years of contributions in the final years of employment) and thereby qualify for a local retirement benefit in a single social pool area.

In places where they have been encouraged or allowed to join the urban schemes, the fact that they regularly change jobs or move between regions has made continuity in contributions difficult. Until recently, the lack of compatibility between pools and the absence of mechanisms to transfer funds were major challenges. As a result, most pools with migrant participants allowed them to withdraw their account when they moved elsewhere. When they did so, however, they could only withdraw their contributions to their individual account. Until the 2009 procedures on transfers were published, there were no mechanisms for the transfer of pool funds, and they lost their claim on the employer's social contribution made on their behalf. In effect, retaining employer contributions for migrant workers in the local pool improved the local balance and reduced the funding shortfall. As a result, migrants have had low motivation to participate in the urban scheme, which merely represents an enforced saving of a proportion of their wages until they change jobs. The new procedures for transfers are intended to resolve this problem, but many technical issues of implementation remain to be resolved. Unless these issues are resolved and mechanisms found to bring migrant workers into old-age insurance schemes, they face the prospect of little or no old-age retirement income in future. Given this situation and the challenge it presents for both social justice and social stability, it is not surprising that the provision of migrant worker old-age insurance has become a government priority.

The policy response

Faced by the many complex issues and challenges discussed in the preceding sections, since the 1990s, many local governments have experimented with the provision of social security and old-age insurance for migrant workers (Han 2009; Hua 2010; Liu and Xu 2008). Places like Dongguan in Guangdong, which are heavily reliant on migrant labour, began to allow migrants to participate in the urban schemes during the mid-1990s or even earlier.[5] Other cities with large numbers of migrants, such as Wuxi in Jiangsu, also began to allow migrants to join the urban schemes during the late 1990s.[6] During the early 2000s, these experiments spread to places like Shanghai and other cities and provinces, some of which introduced schemes specially designed for migrants. The early focus was on health and work injury insurance, but this was gradually extended to old-age insurance, either through participation in the urban schemes or through specific programmes. In 2002, Shanghai, for example, established a single integrated scheme to provide all five types of insurance[7] for migrants, separate from the urban resident insurance schemes (Shanghai People's Government 2002). Employer contributions were set at a total of 12.5 per cent of wages. Furthermore, the old-age insurance was established by issuing annual certificates through the China Life Insurance Company (*Zhongguo renshou*). In this scheme, once migrants had accumulated 15 years' worth of certificates, they become eligible for an annuity paid from the insurance company. Overall, these local schemes fell into three main categories:

1   those that brought migrants into the urban schemes;
2   those that set up special schemes for migrants; and
3   those that placed migrants in rural schemes.

These experiments took place against the background of increasing emphasis on migrant issues by the Chinese leadership. A series of government policy documents after 2003 addressed migrant employment, welfare, education and training. Then in 2006, Document No. 5 (State Council 2006) provided a comprehensive review of all migrant problems and declared the central government's commitment to help solve them. In respect of old-age insurance, this document set out the basic principles for policy development. These were (Article 19):

> *Explore a scheme for old-age insurance that suits the characteristics of migrant workers.* Focus research on a migrant worker old-age insurance scheme that has a low rate of contributions, broad coverage, is transferable, and can link to existing old-age insurance systems. Where conditions are suitable, migrant workers in stable employment can be brought directly into the basic old-age insurance for urban employees. Employers of migrants already participating in urban schemes should continue to pay contributions for them. The Labour and Social Security Departments must urgently determine methods for transferring and linking migrant worker old-age insurance across regions.
>
> (State Council 2006)

Since Document No. 5 was issued, migrants have been increasingly seen as a group that needs policy support, rather than a group to be excluded from local social welfare services. The problem, however, has been how to develop policies in practice that match their particular characteristics. The key challenges are:

- Job mobility: migrants regularly change their employment. This requires constant registering and re-registering by employers, with changes to the employment list every month.
- Regional mobility: migrants move frequently between provinces and cities and also between local rural enterprises in their home province and enterprises in other regions.
- Migrants are more likely to find informal employment than work with a formal employment contract.
- Female migrants tend to have greater job mobility, greater levels of informal employment, and more inconsistent employment records because of child-rearing and family responsibilities.
- Migrants lack incentives and faith in the long-term benefits they are supposed to receive from existing schemes and are therefore reluctant to contribute or withdraw when they move.
- Employers are often unwilling to accept the higher labour costs of paying contributions to migrant workers' old-age insurance.
- Migrants' income levels are low and the costs of participating in urban schemes (8 per cent of wages) are high.
- Migrants find it difficult to fulfil contribution requirements of existing urban schemes, such as contributing for 15 years and having continuous contributions for the last 5 years of employment.
- Designing schemes to match these features require flexible, accurate and integrated information management systems to cater for frequent movement and changes, and mechanisms to ensure that fund contributions are preserved in the various pools, combined together and transferred to the

place of final residence when the individual retires and starts to draw retirement benefits.

Drawing on the lessons of the various local experiments in dealing with these issues, during 2008 the MoHRSS drafted a "Procedure for migrant worker participation in basic old-age insurance" (*Nongmingong canjia jiben yanglao baoxian banfa*) and in February 2009 issued a discussion draft for public comment (MoHRSS 2009). The draft was made available for public comment until July 2009, with the goal of revising it to a final version during the second half of 2009. At the same time, since the issue of portability applies not only to migrants but to workers moving between cities, the Ministry also addressed the issue of transfer of social insurance registration for urban workers with a "Draft temporary procedure on the transfer of basic old-age insurance registration for urban enterprise employees" (*Chengzhen qiye zhigong jiben yanglao baoxian guanxi zhuanyi jiexu zhanxing banfa*). In June 2009, Vice-Minister Hu Xiaoyi of the MoHRSS reported that many comments had been received and that, while much complex technical work needed to be done on the implementation procedures, he anticipated final revised drafts would be issued by the end of the year (Hu 2009).

The discussion draft put forward the following main policy principles (MoHRSS 2009):

1   The procedures would be compulsory and apply to all migrants in urban employment with formal contracts.
2   The contribution rate would be an amount equivalent to 12 per cent of the wage by the employers and between 4 and 8 per cent by the migrant worker (according to the individual's preference). Employer contributions would go to the social pool and individual contributions to the individual account.
3   Migrants already enrolled in urban schemes would be allowed to adjust their contribution rates to the new levels if they wished.
4   Withdrawals would not be allowed when migrants changed jobs. Instead the migrants would be issued with a contribution certificate by the local social security agency. They would then re-join the scheme in their new place of employment and present the certificate issued by the previous agency. The two social security agencies concerned would complete the transfer of the registration, and the new contributions to the scheme would accumulate in the new fund. The funds and records of those who did not go to new employment would be sealed in their original place of employment. Interest would continue to accumulate in the sealed fund according to the national regulations.
5   After 15 or more years of contributions, the migrant would qualify for benefits. The migrant would apply to the social insurance agency at their place of final employment, which would verify and issue the retirement benefit, including both the social pool and the individual contribution. This required designing arrangements to transfer funds from the earlier social pools to the final one. Those not completing 15 years might have their

benefits transferred to a rural scheme or might make a lump-sum withdrawal of their individual contributions.

6   A unified national information database for old-age insurance contributions by migrants would be established and a lifetime national social insurance card would be issued, bearing a specific identity card number. The migrants would have access to their insurance contribution record from any social insurance office.

In sum, the basic outline of the proposed new scheme required: (1) compulsory participation with no withdrawals; (2) reducing the entry threshold for migrants; (3) maintaining sealed accounts in local pools when migrants moved; (4) establishing a national database for migrant records; and (5) a mechanism for pooling lifetime contributions at the place of final residence. While these proposals are straightforward, they require substantial adjustments to the existing local practices and also the development of new standardised national procedures for fund and database management. Given the large variations currently existing in local schemes, the implementation of the new policy faced a number of challenges and risks. These included:

- the potential for continued discrimination against migrant workers by consolidating their status through a separate old-age insurance system;
- the risk of undermining the rights of migrant workers already in stable employment and participating in urban schemes who considered themselves urbanised and did not want to change;
- the need to manage the transition from existing schemes for migrants in ways that did not lose established rights;
- the possibility that establishing two levels of contributions would potentially encourage employers to favour cheaper migrant labour and create discrimination against urban employees;
- the need for transparent and reliable management and information systems that provided clear incentives to encourage migrant workers to join;
- the development of fund management and fund security in ways that ensured contributions both preserve and increase value;
- the complexity of fund control and account management problems if each migrant worker's contributions were dispersed among local pools;
- the need to establish a national standardised information database system which could handle large amounts of data at a unified national level.

The creation of a separate structure for migrant workers with different contribution standards from other schemes also risked creating obstacles to the long-term goal of unifying the national system. While the development of a national migrant worker system might provide lessons for the integration of a comprehensive national scheme, it would also result in the further fragmentation of the current structure with the parallel existence of separate schemes for urban enterprise employees, urban public servants, urban non-employed residents, migrant workers, and township and village workers. Even as this draft procedure was under review, however, the context for policy development was made more complicated by Document 32, 2009, which announced a new old-age pension scheme for rural residents (State Council 2009b). The publication of this new plan, which is discussed in more detail below, immediately raised a challenge for the proposed migrant-worker old-age insurance scheme. Migrants might move regularly between rural and urban employment and might also have the choice of belonging to either scheme. Furthermore, if they eventually decide to return to rural areas in their retirement, there would be problems in determining how their urban-based insurance should be linked with or converted into the proposed rural system. The fragmented structure of old-age insurance schemes thus risked further complication.

In the face of these problems and new developments, the proposed separate scheme for migrants was reassessed, and the decision was taken to require migrants to participate in the basic urban scheme and to reaffirm their rights to transfer their pension entitlements between cities when they moved. On 28 December 2009, the State Council issued the final version of the "Procedure for Migrant Worker Participation in Basic Old-age Insurance" and the "Interim Measures on the Transfer and Continuation of Urban Employee Basic Old-age Insurance Relationships" (State Council 2009a). The first of these reaffirmed that migrants would be required to join the urban scheme but pay a reduced rate of contribution, and the second set out the procedures for the portability of old-age insurance registration for both urban employees and migrant workers, but in a concession to local funds decreed that only a proportion of the social pool funds would be transferred (the equivalent of 12 per cent of wages rather than the full 20 per cent). While this was meant to address the issue of workforce mobility, it still left unsolved the many constraints facing migrant worker participation discussed above. It also raised many urgent practical questions related to database management, fund management, procedures for transfers and so forth. As a result, during 2010 policy development focussed on developing the practical procedures for implementing the new policy goals for migrants, the transition to the new national standard scheme for the various provincial and urban experimental policies, and the implications for migrant workers of the new rural pension plan. From the point of view of the migrants, the co-existence of urban and rural schemes now presents them with choices that reflect their double identity and also risks related to how they might preserve the value of contributions and entitlements in the urban scheme when transferred to the rural one. The following section therefore discusses the new rural scheme and its implications in more detail.

The impact of the new rural pension plan

Until 1978, social security in the Chinese countryside was provided through the People's Communes. These provided collective welfare services, including those for the elderly, of which the most celebrated was the "five guarantees" (food, clothing, medicines, housing, and burial) (Dixon 1981). With the collapse of the communes, these collective mechanisms declined, and it became necessary to build new forms of rural social security. Inevitably this resulted in a large range of local experiments and innovations (Luo and Lü 2006; Song 2008; Zhao *et al.* 2002). These initial efforts were localised and only covered a small proportion of the rural elderly. After 1992 in the wake of a series of policy guidelines from the central government, a number of provinces and localities introduced contributory old-age insurance programmes for farmers, managed through the MCA (Fujian Province Rural Social Insurance Administration Centre 2010; Institute of Economics, Chinese Academy of Social Sciences 2010; Luo and Lü 2006: 120–141). Collectively known as the "old rural pension plan", these schemes were hampered by total reliance on individual contributions, low rates of return, poor and fragmented administration, mixed government and commercial operation, and high risks. It was estimated that by the end of 1997 they covered around 80 million farmers. After 2000, efforts were made to reorganise these programmes and improve their management, but little progress was made.

Given the absence of an effective social security system for the rural elderly and the declining role of family support systems, especially with decreasing family size and young people taking up work as migrants, the need to take action was becoming increasingly urgent. After 2007, therefore, the central government re-emphasised the need to develop a rural pension system (Institute of Economics, Chinese Academy of Social Sciences 2010: 353). The 17th Congress of the Chinese Communist Party (CCP) in 2007 called for a plan "exploring the establishment of a rural old-age insurance system", and the Third Plenum of the CCP's 17th Congress in October 2008 proposed building "a new rural pension system requiring a combination of individual contributions, collective subsidies and government subsidies". This latter statement for the first time established the principle of direct government financial support for the rural scheme. Eventually a new national system was formally announced in August 2009, with trial implementation to begin in 10 per cent of counties in 2010 and national coverage to be achieved by 2020 (State Council 2009b).

The new scheme is intended to provide a minimum monthly cash pension of 55 yuan to all rural residents, male and female, over the age of 60. This basic pension is guaranteed by government and funded by a combination of contributions from the central, provincial and collective levels. In addition, individual farmers can voluntarily contribute an annual payment into the scheme. If they do so, when they reach pensionable age they would receive an additional monthly amount calculated at the actuarial rate of 1/139th of the total funds in their individual contribution account (i.e. the system uses the same actuarial estimate as the urban individual account system and assumes an average life expectancy of 139 months on retirement). The pension thus has two components: the basic pension and the individual account. All farmers aged 16 and over who do not belong to urban schemes are eligible to join in their home villages. In effect, this rules out migrant workers who are formally enrolled in urban schemes, but leaves open the issue of what happens to migrants who might rotate between the two locations. The State Council guidelines also laid down the rules for the management of the funds and the principles for the payment of the benefits. The main features of this scheme are straightforward, and the payment of the government subsidy from the state budget marks an important innovation in social security payments. There is also gender equity in terms of both males and females receiving equal payments. While the total amount of 55 yuan per month per person is not huge, it is in cash. In poor areas of China there are clear benefits for an old married couple to receive 110 yuan cash income every month. Furthermore, the total can be expected to rise over time and, as discussed below, is already paid at higher levels in richer areas.

The trial implementation during 2010 introduced a number of local policy variations.[8] The government subsidy was designed to be provided 100 per cent from the central government in the poor western provinces and 50 per cent from the centre and 50 per cent from the provincial governments in the richer east. In the eastern provinces, there were further variations. For example, in Fujian, the provincial government established several ways of providing the 50 per cent local component of the subsidy. In poor counties, the province put up 30 per cent and required the counties to supply the remaining 20 per cent. In intermediate level counties, the ratio became 10 per cent provincial and 40 per cent county. Rich counties had to provide the full 50 per cent themselves. In addition, some rich counties then added an additional amount on the top again so that the monthly pension might be 10 yuan higher than the national guideline. A further variation was in the contributory amount to be paid by farmers. The guidelines proposed five levels from 100 to 500 yuan per person per year. Fujian allowed 12 levels from 100 to 1,200 yuan. Furthermore, to encourage farmers to join, Fujian also proposed paying a 30 yuan state subsidy to the individual account of farmers who started at the basic level, though once again, the proportion of this paid by the provincial and local governments varied. Administrative villages may also contribute an amount if they have the resources. In effect, therefore, it is possible for the basic pension in rich areas to be higher than the norm and for richer farmers to accumulate more in their account. These examples underline the potential for large regional variations in contributions and benefits to emerge in the system.

The implementation of the trial programme also highlighted some of the difficulties and teething problems.[9] Issues included:

- identifying all the people who are eligible (some elderly people do not have ID cards or good records of age);
- keeping records up-to-date so that new entrants and exits through death can be accurately recorded each month;
- having staff available at the basic level to manage the scheme;
- ensuring that the elderly people had bank accounts through which the pension could be paid in a situation where many elderly people are barely literate and villages do not have a local financial institution;

- persuading young farmers to join (there is the possibility that young farmers will not join at all or only join late in life. Some may not be able to make regular contributions, and contributions may only be made for males and not for females);
- in some parts of China a system of "binding" was introduced that required young family members to join the scheme and make contributions to their own account before their elderly parents could qualify for pension payment – in effect, this changed a voluntary scheme into a compulsory one.

Inevitably, there will be a large number of practical issues of this kind as the scheme is rolled out. Overall, however, it represents a step forward for rural welfare and the rural elderly, as well as a means of beginning to redress the inequities between urban and rural levels of social protection.

As noted above, however, the introduction of the new rural pension plan also creates a challenge for migrant workers and for the design of old-age insurance schemes for them. They now face a range of old-age insurance choices, depending on their place of origin and the places to which they move. They may be in a position to join the local rural pension in their home village, to enrol in local insurance schemes for township and village employees, to enrol in any remaining special schemes for migrants in some cities and/or to join the basic urban scheme. They may also shift between these as their employment changes. The fragmentation of the schemes and the uncertainty about the differences in final outcomes for each of them make a clear choice difficult. Furthermore, over time it is likely that the various schemes will gradually merge and that the entitlements and benefits will be transferred. Migrants might try to join the rural scheme and look forward to enjoying the benefits of the government subsidy, while not making contributions from their current income to urban accounts. If they move back to the countryside, they may hope to transfer all of the benefits they accrue in urban areas back with them, where the lower cost of living would work to their advantage. There may even be the possibility that the system will eventually allow them to draw benefits from each of the stages of their working life proportionately to the time spent, rather than trying to transfer funds across systems as they change their work. This complexity underlines the dual identity of migrants studied by Yu Zhu (2007) and the need to allow for flexibility and diversity as migrants work through their options.

From the administrative point of view, maintaining reliable and accurate records of highly-mobile migrants is difficult and will require improved and integrated computerised management and information systems. Keeping track of contributions to individual accounts and to social pools in different locations adds another layer of complexity. Calculating the ratios for the transfer of entitlements and benefits between schemes which operate with different standards is also very difficult. Moving the funds to follow the person between the pools would also require special arrangements. Ultimately, the need to move gradually towards a standard, integrated national scheme for all citizens, regardless of where they live and work is obvious, despite the many obstacles facing such a transition. This discussion of the impact of the rural pension plan is impressionistic. It does, however, underline that the range of migrant preferences and behaviour needs to be taken fully into account if a successful set of social security policies are to be developed for them.

The net result of this complex set of challenges is that migrant worker participation rates in social insurance have been very slow to rise. Despite the amount of policy innovation, between 2009 and 2013 migrant worker old-age insurance participation only grew from 7.6 per cent to 15.7 per cent (NBSC 2014). The ratio of the other types of insurance also remained very low.

Conclusion

As discussed at the outset, creating sustainable livelihoods for migrant workers requires making preparations for their old age. The long-term horizon of old-age insurance schemes also makes it essential that this should begin as soon as possible. This chapter has outlined the systemic and contextual challenges facing the development of these schemes. It argues that, while an integrated national system for all citizens would solve many problems, it is necessary to recognise the diverse needs of migrants. Achieving an integrated system, however, faces many challenges. Apart from the many structural and practical problems discussed above, there are also significant conflicts of interest.

Local governments, for example, are broadly keen to encourage the employment of migrant workers, since they promote the development of the local economy. They provide cheap labour for the construction of infrastructure and housing. They do work that local residents are unwilling to take on. There are also some incentives for local governments to encourage migrants to join the existing urban schemes since they help maximise the local social pool for old-age insurance, though this may change as mechanisms for transfers are improved. The new transfer regulation acknowledges this, to some extent, by only allowing for the transfer of 60 per cent of the employer contribution to the social pool. On the other hand, local governments may equally be hesitant to enforce migrant registration in urban schemes since that would increase labour costs through raising employer social welfare payments. They may feel that this increase in production costs might have the negative effect of reducing local attractiveness, deterring investment and slowing down local economic growth. In places heavily dependent on migrant labour, the need to attract migrants through social security provision may outweigh these concerns, but the issue is not straightforward.

The focus on local economic priorities also illustrates the potential for conflicts of interest between different regional governments and different levels of government. Governments in the poorer migrant-sending regions have a legitimate concern that they might have to make provision for older migrants returning to their home areas, while contributions made to social pools on their behalf remain in the areas in which they worked. Governments in the urban destinations might take the position that they are unwilling to subsidise social security in distant areas not part of their local economy. Fiscal departments are concerned that they face risks in making provisions for old people with no old-age insurance accumulation of their own. The tensions between central government fiscal responsibilities and local government efforts to maximise local benefits may also play a role. Until a national unified scheme for all forms of old-age insurance is developed, the potential for such frictions will always exist.

For employers, paying social security contributions for migrants means an increase in costs and many surveys report a tendency to under-report the number of migrant labour employees or to avoid reporting altogether. Furthermore, the constant movement of migrants means that employers continuously have to adjust the name list of migrant employees that they report to the social security bureaus each month. They thus have a strong incentive to avoid participation for their employees and to prefer schemes that have a lower contribution rate for migrants. It is also likely that this issue will vary between different types of employers and different sectors. Finally, there is also conflict between the interests of local residents and people from outside. As is common throughout the world, there are stereotypical perceptions of migrants as poorly educated, "uncouth" and "low quality". In the minds of local residents, they are associated with social disorder and crime, with dirtiness, and with pressures on urban services. Their rural background and regional accents make them clearly distinguishable. The systemic discrimination of the *hukou* system is thus reinforced by social and cultural discrimination and prejudice (Li 2004: 217–239; Lu 2004: 306–337). Given this context, it is not surprising that local authorities and residents feel that the local social security pool belongs within the local economy and to them. They tend to resent the idea that the migrants from outside, despite their contributions, might have a right to part of it and take it away.

In sum, the development and implementation of social security schemes for migrant workers are a contested issue. While central policy is promoting greater social equity and innovations to help the migrants, the legacy of existing systems, the demands and power of local interests and the nature of social stratification combine to create obstacles to their realisation. They also ensure that the implementation of policy will be influenced by the way these conflicting forces play out. Nevertheless, old-age social protection for migrant workers remains a pressing challenge for the long-term livelihoods of the migrant population, for the resolution of urgent issues created by the aging society, to promote further economic reform in the labour market, and to rebalance China's development model towards greater sustainability, human security and people-centeredness. The developmental and livelihood dimension of social security needs to be recognised as an integral part of the next stage of China's development.

Notes

1 This and the following two sections are based on Watson (2009), with amendments and additions.

2 The issue can be seen as one of exclusion/inclusion or of equal citizenship.
3 Information on the following schemes can be found on the website of the MoHRSS and its provincial and urban departments. A useful overview of the broad policy issues can be found in Wang (2001).
4 Chen (2008) provides a useful review of the history and current state of public servant pensions. He summarises the system as being generous, paid from the budget, pay-as-you-go with no accumulation and indexed for wage increases. In 2004, public servant average annual pensions were 15,932 yuan compared to 7,831 yuan for enterprise employees (p. 60). In 2006, the then Ministry of Labour issued revised regulations to clarify the standards and, for example, public servants retiring after 35 years service would get a replacement ratio of 95 per cent of their final salary (Ministry of Labour and Social Security 2006).
5 Interview, Dongguan Social Security Bureau, 28 April 2009.
6 Interview, Wuxi Social Security Bureau, 25 November 2009.
7 The five basic insurances are old age, unemployment, health, work injury and maternity.
8 Interview, Fujian Social Insurance Centre, 29 March 2010.
9 Interview, Fujian Social Insurance Centre, 29 March 2010.

References

Beijing Normal University, School of Social Development and Public Policy Research Team (2010), *Nongmingong jiuye shouru moshi jiqi dui yanglao baoxian sheji yingxiang de yanjiu* [Research on the employment and income model of migrant workers and their impact on the design of old-age insurance]. In Ministry of Human Resources and Social Security (MoHRSS), *Nongmingong yanglao baoxian yanjiu chengguo huibian* [Collection of research results on old-age insurance for migrant workers], reports on the China-Australia Governance Programme project, internal publication, September, pp. 24–70.

Cai, Fang (1990), *Zhongguo de eryuan jingji yu laodongli zhuanyi* [China's dual economy and the transfer of labour]. Beijing: Zhongguo renmin daxue chubanshe.

Cai, Fang and Nansheng Bai (eds) (2006), *Zhongguo zhuangui shiqi laodongli liudong* [Labour migration in transitional China]. Beijing: Shehui kexue wenxian chubanshe.

Cai, Fang and Yang Du (eds) (2007), *Renkou yu laodong lüpi shu 2007* [2007 Green book on population and labour]. Beijing: Shehui kexue wenxian chubanshe.

Chan, Kam Wing (2010), A China paradox: Migrant labor shortage amidst rural labor supply abundance. *Eurasian Geography and Economics* 51(4): 513–530.

Chen, Jianhui (2008), *Gongwuyuan yanglao baoxian zhidu gaige yanjiu* [Research on the reform of the system of old-age insurance for public servants]. *Fuzhou Daxue Xuebao*, 2: 59–62.

China Daily (2010), China's rural, urban income gap widens. 22 January 2010. Available in: www.chinadaily.com.cn/bizchina/2010-01/22/content_9361049.htm (accessed 31 December 2010).

Cook, Sarah, Naila Kabeer and Gary Suwannarat (2003), *Social Protection in Asia*. New Delhi: Har-Anand Publications.

Cui, Chuanyi (2008), *Nongmin jincheng jiuye yu shiminhua de zhidu chuangxin* [Farmers coming to town to work and system innovation for transformation into urban citizens]. Taiyuan: Shanxi chubanshe jituan.

Dixon, John (1981), *The Chinese Welfare System 1949–1979*. New York: Praeger.

Fujian Province Rural Social Insurance Administration Centre (2010), *Xinxing nongcun shehui yanglao baoxian zhidu jianshe ji fazhan* [The establishment and development of the new rural old-age insurance system]. In MoHRSS, *Nongmingong yanglao baoxian yanjiu chengguo huibian* [Collection of research results on old-age insurance for migrant workers], reports on the China-Australia Governance Programme project, internal publication, September, pp. 306–318.

Gao, Wenshu (2009), An analysis of left-behind and migrant children's education. In Fang Cai (ed.), *Renkou yu laodong lüpi shu 2009* [2009 Green book on population and labour]. Beijing: Shehui kexue wenxian chubanshe, pp. 175–191.

Guo, Jinhui (2009), *Zhuanjia cheng yanglao baoxian geren zhanghu kongzhang 1.4 wan yi, 13 sheng zuoshi* [Experts reckon that the "empty" individual accounts in the old-age insurance total 1.4 trillion yuan: 13 provinces have already worked to fill the gap]. *Diyi Caijing Ribao*, 21 May.

Han, Jun (2009), *Zhongguo nongmingong zhanlüe yu zhengce wenti zonghe yanjiu baogao* [Comprehensive research report on strategic and policy issues for China's migrant workers]. In Jun Han (ed.) *Diaocha Zhongguo nongcun* [Surveying the Chinese country-side]. Beijing: Zhongguo fazhan chubanshe, pp. 449–534.

He, Ping and Yingfang Hua (eds) (2008), *Feizhenggui jiuye qunti shehui baozhang wenti yanjiu* [Research on the question of social security for groups in informal employment]. Beijing: Zhongguo laodong shehui baozhang chubanshe.

Hu, Xiaoyi (2009), *Xiabannian dinghui chutai shishi chengzhen zhigong nongmingong yanglao baoxian banfa* [In the latter half of the year, we will certainly issue the regulations for old-age insurance for urban employees and migrant workers]. Available at: www.gov.cn/zxft/ft177/content_1337560.htm (accessed 11 June 2009).

Hu, Yu-Wei and Fiona Stewart (2009), Licensing regulation and the supervisory structure of private pensions: International experience and implications for China. *OECD Working Papers on Insurance and Private Pensions*, No. 33, 2009. Available at: www.sourceoecd.org/10.1787/227280580833 (accessed 3 January 2011).

Hua, Yinfang (2010), *Nongmingong shehui baozhang xiangmu jixian baogao* [Baseline study for social security for migrant workers project]. In MoHRSS, *Nongmingong yanglao baoxian yanjiu chengguo huibian* [Collection of research results on old-age insurance for migrant workers], reports on the China-Australia Governance Programme project, internal publication, September, pp. 1–23.

Institute of Economics, Chinese Academy of Social Sciences (2010), *Xinxing nongcun shehui yanglao baoxian yu nongcun nüxing de xuqiu yanjiu* [Research on the new rural social old-age insurance and the needs of rural women]. In MoHRSS, *Nongmingong yanglao baoxian yanjiu chengguo huibian* [Collection of research results on old-age insurance for migrant workers], reports on the China-Australia Governance Programme project, internal publication, September, pp. 352–372.

Jackson, Richard and Neil Howe (2004), *The Graying of the Middle Kingdom: The Demographics and Economics of Retirement Policy in China*. Washington, DC: Center for Strategic and International Studies, April.

Li, Dehong (2005), *Beijing Chenbao*, January 27, cited in Kam Wing Chan (2009), Introduction. In Fang Cai and Yang Du (eds) *The China Population and Labor Yearbook*, vol. 1: *The Approaching Lewis Turning Point and Its Policy Implications*. Dordrecht: Brill, pp. xix–xli.

Li, Qiang (2004), *Nongmingong yu zhongguo shehui fenceng* [Migrant workers and social stratification in China]. Beijing: Shehui kexue wenxian chubanshe.

Lin, Liyue and Yu Zhu (2008), *Liangxi zhuangtai xia liudong renkou de juzhu zhuangtai jiqi zhiyue yinsu: yi Fujiansheng weili* [The housing situation of the floating population in the context of having two locations and the constraints: The example of Fujian Province]. *Renkou Yanjiu* 32(3): 48–56.

Liu, Chuanjiang and Jianling Xu (eds) (2008), *Zhongguo nongminggong shiminhua jincheng yanjiu* [Research on the process of urban transformation of China's migrant workers]. Beijing: Renmin Chubanshe, pp. 221–227.

Lu, Xueyi (ed.) (2004), *Dangdai Zhongguo shehui liudong* [Social mobility in contemporary China]. Beijing: Shehui kexue wenxian chubanshe.

Luo, Zhixian and Jie Lü (eds) (2006), *Nongcun shehui: yanglao baoxian shouce* [Rural society: Handbook on old-age insurance]. Beijing: Zhongguo shehui chubanshe.

Meng, Xin, Chris Manning, Shi Li, and Tadjuddin Noer Effendi (2010), *The Great Migration: Rural-urban Migration in China and Indonesia*. London: Edward Elgar.

Ministry of Human Resources and Social Security (MoHRSS) (2009), *Nongmingong canjia jiben yanglao baoxian banfa* [Procedure for migrant workers' participation in basic old-age insurance]. Available at: www.gov.cn/gzdt/2009-02/05/content_1222469.htm (accessed 3 January 2011).

Ministry of Labour and Social Security (2006), *Guanyu jiguan shiye danwei lituixiu renyuan jifa lituixiu feideng wenti de shishi banfa* [Implementation procedures for the calculation and issues of retirement payments and related issues for retired personnel from official organs and public service units]. Document 60, 20 June. Available at http://hi.baidu.com/a0909/blog/item/0f05fc1f2e5cc763f624e4fd.html (accessed 6 April 2011).

Moxley, Mitch (2010), China's city workers prefer rural roots. *Asia Times* (online edition), 1 December. Available at: www.atimes.com/atimes/China/LL01Ad01.html (accessed 13 Dec 2010).

NBSC (National Bureau of Statistics of China) (2006), *Zhongguo tongji nianjian 2006 nian* [China statistical yearbook 2006]. Beijing: Zhongguo tongji chubanshe.

NBSC (National Bureau of Statistics of China) (2010), *2009 nian nongmingong lince diaocha baogao* [Report on the 2009 monitoring survey of migrant workers]. Rural Department, 19 March. Available at: http://wenku.baidu.com/view/065bc38a6529647d27285255.html (accessed 30 August 2010).

NBSC (National Bureau of Statistics of China) (2014), *2013 nian nongmingong lince diaocha baogao* [Report on the 2013 monitoring survey of migrant workers]. Rural Department, 12 May. Available at: www.stats.gov.cn/tjsj/zxfb/201405/t20140512_551585.html (accessed 29 July 2014).

Organisation for Economic Co-operation and Development (OECD) (2008), *Pensions at a Glance: Asia Pacific Edition*. Available at: www.oecd.org/dataoecd/33/53/41966940.pdf (accessed 16 November 2009).

Scoones, Ian (2009), Livelihoods perspectives and rural development. *The Journal of Peasant Studies* 36(1): 171–196.

Shanghai People's Government (2002), *Shanghaishi wailai congye renyuan zonghe baoxian zanxing banfa* [Shanghai City temporary procedures for comprehensive insurance for employees from outside]. 22 July. Available at: www.shanghai.gov.cn/shanghai/node2314/node3124/node3125/node3129/userobject6ai1130.html (accessed 8 April 2011).

Song, Hongyuan (ed.) (2008), *Zhongguo nongcun gaige sanshi nian* [Thirty years of rural reform in China]. Beijing: Zhongguo nongye chubanshe.

State Council (2006), *Guanyu jiejue nongmingong wenti de ruogan yijian* [Some proposals for resolving the problems of migrant workers]. Document No. 5, 31 January.

State Council (2009a), *Nongmingong canjia jiben yanglao baoxian banfa* [Procedure for migrant workers' participation in basic old-age insurance] and *Chengzhen qiye zhigong jiben yanglao baoxian guanxi zhuanyi jiexu zhanxing banfa* [Interim measures on the transfer and continuation of urban employee basic old-age insurance relationships]. 28 December. Available at: http://hi.baidu.com/zhou1995888/blog/item/76402699794156036e068cd5.html (accessed 3 January 2011).

State Council (2009b), *Guanyu kaizhan xinxing nongcun shehui yanglao baoxian shidian de zhidao yijian* [Guidance on the trial sites for the new rural social old-age insurance]. Document No. 32, 1 September. Available at: www.gov.cn/zwgk/2009-09/04/content_1409216.htm (accessed 4 January 2011).

United Nations (UN) (2009), *World Population Prospects: The 2008 Revision*. Available at: http://esa.un.org/unpp/p2k0data.asp (accessed 29 December 2010).

Wang, Dewen (2005), China's urban and rural old age security system: Challenges and options. In Centre for Human Resources Research, Research Division of Labour and Human Capital, Institute of Population and Labour Economics, Chinese Academy of Social Sciences, Working Paper Series No. 53, October, p. 7.

Wang, Mengkui (2001), *Zhongguo shehui baozhang tizhi gaige* [Reform of China's social security system]. Beijing: Zhongguo fazhan chubanshe.

Watson, Andrew (2009), Social security for China's migrant workers: Providing for old age. *Journal of Current Chinese Affairs* 38(4): 85–115.

Zhang, Heather Xiaoquan (2007), Conceptualising the links: Migration, health and sustainable livelihoods in China. In Heather Xiaoquan Zhang, Bin Wu, and Richard Sanders (eds) *Marginalisation in China: Perspectives on Transition and Globalisation.* Aldershot: Ashgate, pp. 195–214.

Zhang, Qingwu (1983), *Hukou dengji changshi* [Basic facts on the *hukou* system]. Beijing: Falü chubanshe. Trans. Michael Dutton (1988), *Chinese Economic Studies* 22(1).

Zhang, Xiulan (2008), The costs of migration: A life stage perspective. Presentation at the India China Institute, The New School, 27 March.

Zhang, Xiulan and Ying Ge (2007), *Housing and Health Care Deprivations of Migrant Populations in China: A Report to the Asia Development Bank.* December. Manila: Asia Development Bank.

Zhao, Changbao and Zhigang Wu (2007), *Nongmingong gongzi shouru wenti* [Migrant worker wages and incomes]. In Fang Cai and Yang Du (eds) *2007 nian renkou yu laodong lüpi shu* [2007 Green Book on population and labour]. Beijing: Shehui kexue wenxian chubanshe, pp. 22–34.

Zhao, Renwei, Desheng Lai, and Wei Zhong (2006), *Zhongguo de jingji zhuanxing he shehui baozhang gaige* [The transformation of the Chinese economy and the reform of social security]. Beijing: Beijing shifandaxue chubanshe.

Zhao, Ruizheng, Aili Wang and Ling Ren (2002), *Zhongguo nongmin yanglao baozhang zhilu* [The road to old age security for China's farmers]. Harbin: Heilongjiang renmin chubanshe.

Zhao, Zhongwei and Fei Guo (eds) (2007), Introduction. In Zhongwei Zhao and Fei Guo (eds) *Transition and Challenge: China's Population at the Beginning of the 21st Century.* Oxford: Oxford University Press, pp. 1–18.

Zhu, Yu (2002), Beyond large-city-centred urbanisation: *In situ* transformation of rural areas in Fujian province. *Asia Pacific Viewpoint* 43(1): 9–22.

Zhu, Yu (2004), Changing urbanization processes and *in situ* rural-urban transformation: Reflections on China's settlement definitions. In Tony Champion and Graeme Hugo (eds) *New Forms of Urbanization: Beyond the Urban-Rural Dichotomy.* Aldershot: Ashgate, pp. 207–228.

Zhu, Yu (2007), China's floating population and their settlement intention in the cities: Beyond the hukou reform. *Habitat International* 31: 65–76.

Zhu, Yu and Wenzhe Chen (2010), The settlement intention of China's floating population in the cities: Recent changes and multifaceted individual-level determinants. *Population, Space and Place* 16(4): 253–267.

4 Sustaining livelihoods in urban villages

Health risks and health strategies among rural-to-urban migrants in China: the case of Guangzhou

Bettina Gransow

Introduction

Good health is an important asset for rural-to-urban migrant workers in China who are predominantly hired as unskilled or semi-skilled labour. Generally speaking, the migrant population is younger and healthier than the average population at the origin and destination, but the high numbers of work-related accidents and occupational diseases suffered by migrants as a result of working in the city cast doubt on how many of them could stay healthy (and for how long) after taking up particularly dirty, dangerous and tiring occupations with a lack of access to proper healthcare and/or health insurance. Despite the serious nature of this issue, for quite some time the health of migrants in China was ignored in national and local politics, as well as in the Chinese and international research literature. Only recently has the problem started to attract scholarly attention (cf. Chen 2004; Cook 2007; Holdaway 2008; Ling *et al.* 2014; Xiang 2005; Zhang 2007; Zheng 2006; see also Chapter 2 of this book). From a sustainable livelihoods perspective,[1] Heather Zhang (2007) argues that despite the prominent role of migration as a strategy that rural households use to manage livelihood challenges, there has been insufficient attention paid to the link between migration, health, risk and poverty in livelihoods research. Zhang (2007: 196) asks whether the cash-earning jobs of rural migrants "in Chinese towns and cities would, in the longer term, necessarily lead to better lives for themselves and their families". And, thus, wonders how these migrants would be supported if their health deteriorated due to harsh labour conditions (ibid.).

Taking up Heather Zhang's (2007) suggestion to broaden the concept of livelihood resources by including health and well-being as an important component of sustainable livelihoods, this chapter frames health as an important asset for migrants in search of non-agricultural employment and higher cash incomes, and examines the dynamics of health risks, health consciousness and health strategies of migrant workers. Health risk is defined here as physical, behavioural, psychological, social or environmental factors that increase the vulnerability of rural migrants to adverse health outcomes in the city. This definition includes objective as well as subjective dimensions of perceiving, defining and calculating health risks. The chapter argues that the health strategies adopted by individual rural migrants are unable to sustain livelihoods unless government policies are changed to recognise and respond to the situation of migrants.

The chapter is partly based on the analysis of 50 fieldwork interviews with rural migrants in the urban villages of Guangzhou City conducted between November 2007 and February 2008 as part of the German-Chinese research project "Informal migrant communities and health strategies in urban villages of the Pearl River Delta, China".[2] Guangzhou, the capital of Guangdong Province in southern China, has been a popular migration destination since China's economic reforms started at the beginning of the 1980s. As one of the first important target areas to attract foreign direct investment in China, Guangdong has experienced the impact of global market forces and has been increasingly integrated into the global capitalist system. According to China's sixth census (conducted in 2010), Guangzhou had a total of 12.7 million regular residents (*changzhu renkou*), of whom 4.76 million did not hold local *hukou* (*wailai renkou*), accounting for 37.48 per cent (*Nanfang Daily* 2011). Like labour migrants in other Chinese cities, most of the rural migrants in Guangzhou are working in manufacturing, construction and the service sector (National Bureau of Statistics of China 2008, hereafter NBSC). They are also concentrated in informal employment, doing odd jobs, or as street peddlers and small shopkeepers (Cai *et al.* 2009; Zhou *et al.* 2007). It is reported that some migrants have managed to save money and establish their own businesses in the city after a period of working for others (Bork *et al.* 2010: 76).

With the rapid increase in the number of rural migrants, the need arose for affordable housing at the urban destination. In Guangzhou, this has been provided in what are known as "urban villages" or "villages-in-the-city" (*chengzhongcun*) (Wu *et al.* 2014). It is estimated that approximately half of the migrant population in the city is living in Guangzhou's 139 urban villages (Bork *et al.* 2010: 73; Li 2003). According to the requirements of local authorities, which are frequently ignored, however, local landlords and tenants from outside the city must sign rental agreements and the latter must register with the local police. The native rural population in the "villages" (i.e. the original villagers) whose farmland has been appropriated during the process of city expansion, have managed to maintain their residential housing space, and thus the right to their own housing, as well as constructing extra housing on the village's collectively-owned territory – a resource that is not available to other urban residents or the migrants. This special resource is the foundation for erecting extra buildings that the original villagers have used to rent out for income as a compensation for their lost agricultural livelihoods associated with farmland. Over the years the local population in these urban villages discovered the profitable business of renting to migrants and started to build more floors onto their existing houses. Hardly any space remains between the buildings, so people now need to walk down narrow, dark alleyways. Despite their incorporation into the city, urban villages in Guangzhou still retain their original village names as well as the village gate (Figure 4.1) – the symbol of their collective identity, shared ancestral worship, and collective rights and interests distinct from both the

Figure 4.1 An urban village in Guangzhou.
Source: Photo by Heather Zhang, November 2008.

urban government and residents alike and the rural migrant "outsiders" who now live in the urban villages.

Until very recently, these urban villages were not subject to the municipal administration, so local permanent residents could modify or renovate the buildings for rental purposes with few official restrictions. However, with the massive urban renewal projects that have been pushed by mega-events such as the 2010 Asian Games in Guangzhou, the rural status of the urban villages is being discontinued and the villages – at least those in the central business districts (CBDs) – are being demolished and reconstructed in the urban planning processes according to the municipal regulations.

This chapter documents the work and living conditions, and examines health risks and health strategies of rural-to-urban migrants in Guangzhou's urban villages. In particular, it focuses on the coping strategies of migrants regarding health and healthcare as they attempt to secure and sustain livelihoods. It first identifies and summarises the main health risks for rural migrants before demonstrating that these health risks are aggravated by a lack of health insurance and access to healthcare services, due in turn to the migrants' lack of financial resources as well as lack of knowledge about healthcare and information about health services. This is followed by an examination of the health risk consciousness and the health strategies that rural migrants have used to sustain their livelihoods in Guangzhou. The final section examines the coping strategies of migrants regarding health and healthcare, and provides some policy suggestions for making migration a more effective and sustainable livelihood strategy for the mobile population.

Main health risks and issues for rural migrants

Based on surveys of international and Chinese documentary literature, and data collected during our own fieldwork, we summarise the main health risks for rural migrants as follows: work-related death, work injuries and chronic illness; infectious diseases (including HIV/AIDS and STDs); environmental hazards (including poor diets and poor living conditions); reproductive health problems; non-vaccination of migrant children; and psychological problems and mental disorders.

Work-related death, injuries and chronic illnesses

Industries with high rates of fatalities are mining, construction and manufacturing, and the percentage of rural migrants employed in these sectors is high. Mining is the most dangerous industry in China, accounting for more than half of the fatalities that occurred each year between 2000 and 2005 (Zheng and Huang-Li 2007: 392). Rural migrants account for the majority of workplace deaths in mining, construction and in industries using harmful chemicals (Wu 2007: 15). According to estimates from the 1990s, 1–2 per cent of all male migrant workers had suffered accidents at work (Xiang 2005: 162).[3] Compared to other Chinese provinces, Guangdong with its concentration of export industries has a very high rate of occupational accidents. In the first half of 2003, there were 483,829 accidents of all kinds in China, with a death toll of 61,519. Of this total, 41,965 accidents including 6,129 deaths occurred in Guangdong Province (International Labour Organisation 2005: 55, hereafter ILO). Long working hours and high work intensity increase the risk of occupational accidents. The hazardous nature of the so-called 3-D jobs (dirty, dangerous and demanding) has already left a large group of people disabled. The problem will continue without the effective formulation and implementation of occupational health measures and adequate healthcare (Xiang 2005: 162–163).

Work-related diseases are another serious consequence of the vulnerable situation of labour migrants. These diseases sometimes only become evident after workers leave their jobs, making it even more difficult for victims to establish the work-related source of their conditions. According to China's Ministry of Health (hereafter MOH, cited in ILO 2005: 54), "occupational diseases are one of the major problems that affect the health of workers and cause them to lose their ability". Some 180,802 new cases of occupational diseases of all kinds in China were reported between 1990 and 2001, with an average of 15,000 new cases reported every year. Of particular significance is the problem of pneumoconiosis caused by dust generated at production sites, with a reported 433,000 sufferers nationwide, and some experts putting this figure at 600,000 (Zheng and Huang-Li 2007: 392). According to statistics from the MOH, pneumoconiosis sufferers made up 70 per cent of all occupational diseases in 2005, with 170,000 patients having already died. Accidents involving toxic substances have been reported in Hebei and other provinces. Among migrant workers in the clothing and leather processing industries, there have been clusters of benzene poisoning (Xiang 2005: 163). Given the low rate of health checks for workers and a problematic occupational disease reporting system, the real situation might be more serious than is evident from the statistics, as shown in the following remarks of an interviewee:

> The most frequent work-related illnesses are acute and chronic leukaemia caused by toxic benzene. The second most frequent disease is silicosis, and then there are hearing disorders caused by noise.
>
> (Interview with a representative of a legal-aid NGO providing services for migrant workers in Guangzhou)

Other chronic diseases are related to poor ventilation, dust and toxins in the workplace. Referring to the large number of female migrants who work in manufacturing facilities, Ngai Pun (2005: 169–170) points to toxic chemicals in the electronics industry that cause chronic diseases with symptoms such as headache, sore throat, flu and coughs, stomach problems, eyestrain, dizziness and aggravated menstrual pain. Outmoded equipment and a shortage of safety systems, including adequate fire protection, may be described as "risks due to organised irresponsibility" (Wu 2007: 18).

Infectious diseases

Migrants contract infectious diseases more than local permanent populations do. This is mainly due to poor living conditions, lack of knowledge about healthcare, and unhealthy practices. During the SARS crisis in 2003, a considerably higher number of cases were found among migrants at construction sites who were living in crowded accommodation with poor hygiene and ventilation. Migrants also have a higher risk of contracting infections because they often work in public spaces where there is a greater concentration of infectious agents. According to a survey carried out in Guangzhou from 1997 to 1999, the incidence of infectious diseases, such as tetanus in infants, encephalitis, HIV/AIDS, malaria and measles, was higher among migrants than among the local population. More cases of measles were found among migrants' children in Guangdong because of their exclusion from the free public immunisation schemes (Chen 2004: 86; Zheng 2006). According to a survey conducted in Guangdong Province between 1997 and 2001, the incidence of measles among the urban migrant population increased from 34.3 per cent to 53 per cent of total cases in the province. Another survey undertaken in Shenzhen in the first half of the 1990s showed that 76 per cent of all newly reported cases of tuberculosis were among migrants (Zheng and Huang-Li 2007: 362–363).

Migrants also contract STDs (including HIV/AIDS) at disproportionately high rates when compared with local populations. Factors contributing to this are identified as:

- *Demographic characteristics*: Migrants are predominantly young sexually active individuals and many male migrants have to endure lengthy separations from their sexual partners in their rural origins. They, therefore, may seek alternative channels to meet their sexual needs, leading to risky behaviour. Young adults are more adventurous sexually than people of other ages, but migrants are particularly vulnerable because of a lack of knowledge or means to appropriately protect themselves from such sexual and reproductive health hazards.
- *Working environments*: Some migrants engage in sex work due to poverty or lack of skills required by the urban labour market. They are thus particularly exposed to greater health risks specifically related to such occupations.
- *Economic situation*: Migrants are exposed to greater health risks because of the low income and poverty that they have suffered in the city. They are therefore deprived of the economic means of accessing appropriate healthcare, which has been increasingly commercialised and charging high user fees.
- *Awareness and education*: Migrants often lack information and knowledge about HIV/AIDS and STD in order to protect themselves against HIV infection. Some migrants also use drugs and share needles when injecting drugs, unaware of the threat posed by these behaviours to their sexual and reproductive health (Yang 2004: 216–222; Zheng and Huang-Li 2007: 362).

The risk of infection from HIV/AIDS and other STDs is different for individual groups of migrants, depending on their specific working and living conditions, and therefore the general claim that migrants are at higher risk is debatable. It is, however, feared that migrants are more likely to be infected due to their vulnerability and social disadvantage, and, in turn, their mobility means they tend to carry the virus with them to their sexual partners and families in the countryside where the medical facilities are poorly equipped. Commercial sex work, drug use and shared needles as routes of HIV/AIDS infection are more common among self-employed migrants and those not living in shared dormitories where sexual freedom tends to be restricted. With respect to male migrants as clients of sex workers, one could speculate that they purchase sex more often than rural residents but less frequently than urban dwellers (Xiang 2005: 165), presumably because of their unmet sexual needs and lack of awareness of the high risks involved.

Environmental health risks

Environmental health is defined here as all human health-related aspects of both the natural and built environments. With more and more migrants bringing their families with them and staying in urban areas for longer periods of time, environmental health risks are increasingly becoming an issue. Air pollution, lack of access to clean drinking water, food poisoning, and waste disposal problems are all serious challenges for migrants as well as for local populations working and living in the city. Additionally, migrants living in Guangzhou's urban villages are particularly exposed to environmental health risks, such as deprivation of sunshine due to the high density of the built environment, inadequate sanitation facilities and poor living conditions, such as prolonged periods of living in basements.

The water in the Pearl River is of poor quality and contains micro-toxic substances, such as pesticides and industrial waste discharged into the river. Normally, migrants in Guangzhou have access to piped water, but it is not drinking water quality. On the streets of the urban villages there are automatic vending machines where people may bring their own bottles and fill them with drinking water. But it seems that these new machines are not used much. One reason may be that people still have to carry the water from the machines to their apartments. One migrant living in a large urban village in Guangzhou's Tianhe District tries to deal with the situation thus:

> We [now] have a drinking water device, a filter unit that you can use to filter water directly. We bought it ourselves. We used to have these large water containers, but we stopped buying them because we're on the fourth floor here and no one helps [carry them up]; so we thought we'd be better off buying a filter unit.
>
> (Interview with a migrant resident in an urban village)

Migrants can be exposed to different levels of air pollution. Many male migrants working in the transport or delivery sectors ride their bicycles or tricycles all day long through streets jammed with traffic, or are exposed to other work-related pollution. Food safety is another important issue of environmental health. As a result of pesticide residues in vegetables, there were 28 incidents of mass food poisoning between 1997 and 2001 in Guangzhou, causing 415 people to be poisoned (Lu and Liu 2006: 9). Contaminated soil is not the only factor to influence the safety and quality of products; food poisoning itself occurs more frequently among the migrant population. Despite their strenuous working conditions and the resulting greater need for nutrition, migrants' food is often not very good, especially the food on construction sites. From 2001 to 2005, some cases of food poisoning occurred every year among migrants at construction sites, leading to approximately 40–100 victims in each case (Zheng and Huang-Li 2007: 365). During fieldwork, we saw posters on walls in urban villages warning migrant residents against fake food products and explaining how to distinguish these from real food products, underscoring the problem of unsafe food and the risks it poses to migrants' health.

Reproductive health risks for female migrants

For pregnant female migrants, there is a lack of systematic healthcare compared with the urban population. As sample surveys (in Hangzhou, Wuchang and Yiwu) show, the proportion of prenatal check-ups is much lower for pregnant migrant women than for local women. This situation results in a higher maternal mortality rate among migrants and a higher infant mortality rate among migrant children compared to the local population (Zheng and Huang-Li 2007). According to a survey undertaken by the Guangzhou Municipal Bureau of Population and Family Planning (Guangdong Research Team 2006), nearly two-thirds of the pregnant migrant women in Guangzhou returned to their hometowns to give birth. In the opinion of an urban village doctor in Guangzhou, this decision is due not only to the high costs of delivery in urban hospitals, but also to considerations of care and trust at the rural origin:

> Most pregnant migrants go home to have their babies. First of all it's too expensive [to give birth] here, and also they trust their doctors at home more; they also have family there to take care of them … The feeling of having family around, whereas without being with your family you are emotionally isolated.
>
> (Interview with an urban village gynaecologist)

Lack of information about their rights and not being in possession of a temporary household registration seem to be the two major obstacles for pregnant migrant women to receive government services in urban areas. They are also probably unaware that authorised hospitals are not permitted to impose baby delivery charges higher than 1,600 yuan (Anon. 2006). Most of the pregnant migrant women in Guangzhou who did not go back to their rural origin gave birth at small private clinics (Zheng and Huang-Li 2007). Migrant women who have an unwanted pregnancy and thus need an abortion also tend to seek the service from private clinics despite the fact that the price of the procedure at a private clinic is nearly the same as at state-run medical institutions estimated at 1,000–2,000 yuan per abortion but the former involves much higher risk, according to an urban village doctor in Guangzhou. Premarital sex among young migrants is more likely to be unprotected due to lack of information or hesitation to use services. Migrant women are therefore more vulnerable to reproductive ill-health, more likely to have an abortion at a younger age, or at an advanced stage of the pregnancy.

Migrant women also have a high prevalence of reproductive tract infections (RTIs) (Zheng et al. 2013). A doctor in an urban village estimated during the interview that around 10 per cent of the female migrants are suffering from gynaecological diseases, such as cervical or pelvic infections, or ovary abnormality. Since most migrants are of childbearing age, reproductive and maternal health and healthcare services are of particular importance to them. Maternal health is provided mainly by government services and should cover everyone, but our research shows that migrant women are still systematically excluded from urban health screening and reproductive healthcare programmes.

Health risks facing migrant children

The health situation of migrant children in Guangdong Province is closely connected to the specific migration situation of their parents. Infant tetanus occurs more often in migrant children, because migrant women frequently cannot afford hospital deliveries (Chen 2004). Until very recently, migrant children were not covered by the urban public health system, and as a result could not receive the routine vaccinations as urban children did.[4] According to a survey conducted in Beijing, Shanghai, Guangzhou and Hangzhou, only 45 per cent of migrant children were provided with local public health services compared to 95–98 per cent for local urban children (Zheng and Huang-Li 2007: 363). Similarly, the health situation of migrant children in general is comparatively poor. In 2004, the infant mortality rate per 1,000 live births and the under-five mortality rate per 1,000 for the mobile population were 13.8 and 24.8, respectively, compared with the rates of 10.1 and 12.9, respectively, for the local urban population (Zheng and Huang-Li 2007: 363). The higher incidence of migrant child mortality is also due to a lack of basic emergency obstetric and neonatal care (Department of Labour and Social Security of Guangdong Province 2006). Migrant children get less nutrition containing milk products, meat, fish, eggs and fruit than local urban children, resulting in a higher incidence of malnutrition-caused problems, such as rickets, anaemia, and stunted growth. Thus far, patchy health service coverage for preventable childhood diseases in the city has represented another risk for migrant children.

Stress and mental disorders

Migration stress has to be seen as a potential risk factor increasing the likelihood of adverse health outcomes. A survey of acclimatisation problems for migrants in Guangzhou clearly shows a link between feelings of loneliness and the overall sense of health (Chen 2004). Migration stress may result from facing survival pressures such as employment and financial problems, losses, cultural differences and unfulfilled expectations after settling in the city. Language barriers, poor living conditions and discrimination may be particularly stressful. Loss of social networks may also lead to depressive symptoms (Wong et al. 2008). On top of all this, migrants have to deal with a discriminatory and rigid urban bureaucracy, causing further frustration and distress, as illustrated below:

> There is a very high level of stress in my life, especially when I spend money. The children have to learn that four grandparents expect to be taken care of, and my wife is not so strong physically. I call my parents twice a week to hear how they are doing, that eases my mind too. But there's also another kind of stress: government officials create problems regarding household registrations, hygiene inspections for my business registration, etc.; every two or three days they come by and you start losing the motivation to do business.
>
> (Interview with a migrant shop keeper)

Despite the vulnerability and risk of migrants to mental and psychological ill-being, with only a few exceptions (cf. Wong et al. 2008), the issue has not featured much in either the research literature or related policies. Our fieldwork interviews, however, showed that counselling services are particularly needed for migrants who face difficulties in the city.

Access to health insurance and healthcare

The recent reform of the healthcare system has been carried out separately for the urban and rural sectors, making access difficult for rural-urban migrants (see Chapter 2 of this book). Because health insurance in the city – just like other components of social security – is based on employment and local *hukou* status, and because of the existence of a large informal sector, where the more expensive formal employment contracts are frequently replaced with informal employment relations without welfare benefits, and where most migrants find their jobs, only a very small proportion of migrant workers have been covered by health insurance and retirement plans. Since 2004, all firms have been required by government regulations to put in place work-related injury insurance to cover their workers, including migrants. However, when accidents occur, migrants have to prove that they have a formal employment relationship with the firm in order to claim compensation, but according to some research, only around 22 per cent of migrant workers have written work contracts (Cheng and Darimont 2005: 87–88). Urban employers have tried every means to avoid giving compensation to migrant workers who are injured at work while relevant city government departments turn a blind eye on such practices, as one interviewee pointed out:

> There are these instances [of buying insurance only for some workers]. Occupational insurance means paying insurance premiums. However, firms buy accident insurance for some of the workers, but not for others. If an accident occurs, the firm sends the victim to the hospital under the name of an insured person, and then cheats by asking the insurance company to pay. After the firm receives the money, it doesn't give it to the worker, because first it has to pay for the hospital, and then it wants to make a bit out of it itself. You frequently find such cheating in Guangdong. Once we went to the Department of Labour and Social Security to sort the problem out, but the Department doesn't care either.
> (Interview with a representative of a legal-aid NGO providing services for migrant workers in Guangzhou)

Once injured at work, financial concerns often make the migrants unable to continue the follow-up treatment needed after emergency care at hospitals. The external injury department at the People's Hospital of Guangdong Province has treated 200 migrants a year on average, of whom more than one third were unable to pay the bill. Some hospitals have subsequently refused to admit migrants as patients. This has caused migrants to adopt a wait-and-see attitude upon the initial signs of illness instead of seeking treatment – which can lead to much more serious conditions developing (Xiang 2005). Faced with a very tight budget and financial pressure to earn enough not only for themselves but also to support their families in rural areas and pay for their children's education, migrants have hardly any resources left to provide for retirement or health insurance.

Since the late 1990s, Guangzhou and other cities in the Pearl River Delta, such as Shenzhen, Zhuhai and Dongguan, have experimented with health insurance for migrant workers; however, only a small proportion of the migrant workers have participated in these insurance programmes (Guangdong Research Team 2006). One reason is that the health insurance scheme is strictly employment-based, whereas most migrants enter the job market informally. Another reason is that the money for the health insurance fund is partly through the migrant's individual contribution combined with the employer's contribution, meaning that the low wages of migrant workers often prohibit them from joining such schemes. A third reason is that nearly half of the migrants are self-employed and, therefore, are not covered by the programme. However, the biggest problem is the conflict between migrants' mobility and the localised operational pattern of healthcare funds. The geographically fragmented operational pattern of the healthcare system discourages migrants from joining (Xiang 2005). If migrants change their jobs across county or provincial administrative boundaries, their medical accounts have to be cancelled at their health safety management bureaus and then reregistered in the bureaus of the new county or province, a process frequently involving huge technical, operational and bureaucratic obstacles. If migrant workers return to the countryside (which happens often), their health insurance has to be cancelled altogether. The tension between the high level of migrant worker mobility and the low level of their social security (including healthcare) account's portability is the main reason why migrants often cancel their health insurance (Xiang 2005).

The ways in which migrants are excluded from the formal healthcare system are ultimately reflections of China's urban-rural dualistic structure. In the countryside, China used to have a rural cooperative medical system supported by rural collectives, which met the basic health needs of their members. But the system collapsed in the 1980s when the commune system was replaced by the individual household responsibility system. This development was accompanied by a substantial decline in support from the government for public health and a sharp increase in the cost of medical care, meaning that peasants now have to shoulder around 90 per cent of healthcare costs themselves. The State Council initiated a new cooperative medical scheme (NCMS) in the countryside in 2002, which has been implemented by the MOH and financed by the central government, local governments and individual households. The scheme is voluntary with each party contributing 10 yuan per person per year. The NCMS is characterised by an emphasis on covering serious illness (Feng 2007). Officially considered part of the rural population based on their rural *hukou* status, migrants are supposed to claim medical benefits at the rural locations, but, given the low level of coverage of the rural healthcare system, migrants cannot expect much (if anything) from it.

The urban healthcare system faces different problems. After 1949, China established a low-cost healthcare system for government staff and the employees of SOEs that covered both these groups via their places of work. However, this urban public healthcare system saw serious erosion following market reforms and the state's retreat from its support for public health. Healthcare services became expensive commodities, which only a minority could afford. In 1998, a nation-wide reform of the urban health insurance system was carried out and a basic health insurance system was introduced. It is administered by the Ministry of Human Resources and Social Security[5] and includes widespread access to primary healthcare, joint premium contributions by employers and employees, and the integration of individual medical savings accounts and social pooling accounts (Feng 2007). All employees of urban enterprises are required to join this programme, while the funding is managed externally and not confined to the enterprises. Thus, employees can accumulate money in their accounts and change jobs without changing accounts. However, this programme does not cover migrants (Xiang 2005).

The healthcare system reforms in China, aimed at reducing government subsidies and giving greater financial autonomy to healthcare providers, have led to market-oriented financing strategies that have driven up costs, reduced the provision of preventive services, and created huge barriers for the poor to access healthcare services (see Chapter 2 of the book). Hospitals now have to obtain the revenue required for their operating expenses, leading to increased user-fee charges. A dual-track pricing system allows the government to set prices only for personnel wages, basic examinations and surgery, while drugs and high-tech treatments are priced according to market principles. Thus, hospitals and clinics can make more profit from selling drugs (Feng 2007). As stated above, migrants have to meet nearly all the costs for health check-ups and treatments them-selves, and most of them cannot afford these expenses. Given that healthcare is becoming increasingly unaffordable in cities, including areas where large migrant populations reside (such as the urban villages), many small informal health stations and medical practices have arisen as providers for migrant healthcare. These facilities range from district-level government health centres to purely private and commercially-oriented offices, as well as non-profit, third-sector options. In the process, a wide variety of different types of public-private partner-ships have arisen. However, not all of these newly established facilities are legal and possess the necessary licence, as indicated in the following observations:

> They [private clinics] have some doctors who practise without licences. Or they have only forged licence. There are many [private clinics] that oper-ate under fake licence ... I have seen people that specialise in forging certificates ... Migrant patients normally don't ask to see the licence. It is embarrassing for them. If they ask [about a licence], they would have to doubt whether the doctor should be conducting a medical examination, they also would have to doubt whether the doctor will prescribe the right medicine ... Besides, from the certificates you cannot see that they are fake

unless you check the licence on the Internet. Each licence has a number, as a protection against forgery. But normally no one will check it.

(Interview with a doctor in a family planning bureau)

In recent years, Guangdong Province has increasingly included rural migrant workers into its health insurance schemes and community health programmes. In May 2006, for example, the Labour and Social Security Bureau of Guangdong issued a Circular on the Expanded Participation of Rural Migrants in Health Insurance (Cai *et al.* 2009: 346). Governmental health institutions at the local and community levels are nowadays expected to offer specific health services to migrants – especially prenatal exams for pregnant women and vaccinations for migrant children. Health institutions in Guangzhou at the district level are cooperating in this area with large hospitals by offering services that are also open to migrants. However, unlike urban residents who are covered by health insurance, rural migrants have to pay out of their own pocket, as shown in the following:

Twice a year the street committees offer reproductive health checks for women free of charge. Local women as well as female migrants may participate. The district health centre offers vaccinations for children, the street committees inform the people, but they have to pay by themselves ... Migrants may participate in this system too. Medical examinations have to be paid for by the patients themselves. For hospital stays, local people will receive a refund of 50 per cent, migrants have to pay by themselves.

(Interview with the secretary of an urban village health centre)

Given the marginalisation, discrimination and exclusion of migrants who are victims of work-related injuries and diseases, civil society organisations have emerged that advocate the legal rights of migrants. Some of these organisations have been founded by individuals who came to the cities themselves as labour migrants. As noted by one interviewee, staff at migrant service centres would like to incorporate some health services into their agenda, but encounter financial and other difficulties:

Originally we organised a lot of medical training and health education lectures, including the prevention of work-related diseases, health knowledge in everyday life, health protection knowledge, etc., we also offered consulting hours. For the lectures we had to rent a rather large room, we also had to pay the lecturers ... The workers welcome this because if people visit a hospital for minor ailment they have to spend a lot of money. But here we could provide them with some free health services and health education. The life of migrants around here is hard, so if we can help them a bit, they would feel much better. But we don't have the resources for this [these activities], so we had to stop.

(Interview with a representative of a legal-aid NGO providing services for migrant workers in Guangzhou)

Many NGOs face funding constraints, and sometimes become the target of official suspicion and restriction. Trust, support and stronger public and third sector partnership are required in order to meet the needs of the migrant population.

Health risk consciousness and health strategies of rural migrants

As discussed above, rural migrants are a social group facing high risks in terms of health and healthcare. However, many of them are not aware of such risks, as illustrated by the following remarks, which demonstrate migrants' own perceptions of their health status, "Health-wise I'm doing well, I've hardly been sick the last few years – at most, a small cold" (interview with a house-wife in an urban village); "Now while I'm young, I don't have any illnesses" (interview with an employee in a service centre). Subjectively, rural migrants tend to emphasise the physical strength of their bodies. This clearly para-doxical finding might be explained by the following factors. First, the rela-tively young age of migrants may be one reason for an optimistic health outlook. Second, one may also speculate that the health risks for migrants living in Guangzhou's urban villages are not as high as those for migrant factory or construction workers, because urban village dwellers tend to reside with their families and are self-employed, whereas those working in factories or construction live mainly in crowded dormitories or construction sites with limited private space and without the emotional support from close family. Third, living and hygienic conditions are probably similar to or even slightly better in the urban village than those in the rural origins, particularly in poorer regions.

Moreover, despite growing media attention to high rates of work-related injuries, chronic diseases and other types of health vulnerabilities experi-enced by migrant workers, the interviewees in our fieldwork seemed not to be aware of these risks as something that could happen to them. The image of a strong body goes hand in hand with gender images and is mainly associated with the young male body. When vulnerability or illness comes up, it does so mainly in the context of aging, e.g. "All in all, I still feel in good physical health, I used to be a soldier. I'm generally rarely sick, only my stomach has a few age-related troubles" (interview with a small shop owner); or the female body, e.g. "I'm still doing very well physically, but my wife is a little weak, although she's reluctant to pay for a health check at the hospital. I've never been sick, only occasionally have a cold" (interview with a small shop keeper). More research is needed on the gender implications of the images of health and body.

Migrants' self-representation of physical strength and good health is reflected to a certain degree in the strategies employed and measures undertaken (or not undertaken) in the event they become ill. Health strategies employed by rural migrants have to be seen against the backdrop of the limited financial resources available to them. Analysis of our interview data identifies five interrelated health strategies used by rural migrants:

1   Constructing a self-image of being strong and healthy.
2   When becoming ill, adopting a "wait and see" attitude, hoping the illness will go away.
3   Going to pharmacies and buying medications based on one's own knowledge when the illness becomes more serious; however, because this medical knowledge is limited, the situation may worsen, or minor illnesses may turn into serious conditions.
4   Seeking affordable health services at substandard semi-legal or illegal institutions in urban villages.
5   Returning to the countryside in the event of serious illness.

The most common attitude among migrants when facing illness is to "wait and see", as shown in the following observations:

> Sure, there are people who are ill but do not go to see a doctor ... Some have financial difficulties, and therefore cannot afford to see a doctor. Others think they can solve the problem by themselves and therefore do not need a doctor.
>
> (Interview with a doctor in an urban village in Guangzhou)

Furthermore, migrants' locality-based social networks and the associated trust mean that they are reluctant to use the services of private clinics unless these are managed by people from their home regions: "If I have a bad cold, I go to a clinic run by people from my hometown (*laoxiang zhensuo*) and get a shot, because such facilities are cheaper [I wouldn't be overcharged by *laoxiang*]" (Interview with a small shop owner).

Health strategies employed by rural migrants have to be viewed in light of the various personal but mostly institutional constraints that migrants have to face in the city. These include a shortage of financial resources; constraints imposed by the *hukou* institution, such as obstacles that migrants encounter when trying to access the urban labour market, especially skilled labour and the formal employment sector; lack of access to information about local healthcare available to them, including also family planning services; lack of health and accident insurance; lack of social and family networks; lack of knowledge about hygiene, infectious diseases, HIV/AIDS, other STDs, and so forth. Low awareness of the health risks among migrants often exacerbates such risks. The inadequate legal and social protection of migrants' rights, together with the low awareness among migrant workers themselves of their own rights and of the channels to seek justice in the event of work-related injury or illness, has led to the individualisation of migrants' health problems, with migrants themselves frequently being held responsible for the risks and the materialisation of such risks, namely the damages and harm done to their health and livelihoods.

Conclusion

Rural migrants constitute a large but relatively powerless group in Chinese society, without political representation or a lobby to influence policy. Their self-representation as possessing a strong and healthy body, which stands in harsh contrast to their numerous health risks discussed above, may be viewed as a type of psychological armour, against not only the hazardous aspects of their working and living conditions, but also an urban environment that is frequently discriminatory and exclusionary, denying their equal rights. This self-defensive image itself, however, may paradoxically contribute to their vulnerability.

The main health risks for rural migrants can be summarised as high levels of work-related death, injury and chronic illness, unhealthy and unsafe living conditions, and a high risk of disease infection (including HIV/AIDS and other STDs). In addition, migrant women and children face reproductive health problems including a higher incidence of maternal and child mortality. This situation is exacerbated by an institutional framework that excludes migrants from China's urban healthcare system, and by a lack of insurance systems tailored to the needs of the mobile population. Better tailored healthcare and insurance systems would need to provide the migrants with more options to stay in urban areas or return to the countryside and make a living there if they wish to do so. It is thus suggested that health insurance schemes should be made "portable". This could contribute to better protection for migrants against the risk of impoverishment in cases of illness and accidents while working in the cities. Such insurance schemes would also provide pregnant women with better healthcare and more choices regarding where to give birth. The design of health and insurance schemes should contribute to making migration a more effective and secure strategy of sustaining livelihoods in rural or urban settings.

This chapter argues that the coping strategies that migrants employ to stay healthy and obtain healthcare so as to secure and sustain livelihoods are limited. Migration as a rural household livelihood strategy to fight poverty and earn a decent cash income seems to be dependent on the migrant individual's "super-natural ability" to stay healthy under harsh labour conditions without affordable healthcare provision and appropriate health insurance coverage in Chinese cities. If migrant workers suffer from a serious health problem, lose their ability to work and lack the necessary social safety net, their rural families will have to bear the financial and healthcare burdens for the migrant returnees. Under such circumstances, migration may well become the source of additional risks and impoverishment for many rural households.

Ultimately, the highly complex and dynamic issues related to migrants' health risks and vulnerability cannot be solved by their individual health strategies or behaviour change alone. National and local policies with the proper institutional support are needed in order to contribute more effectively to sustaining livelihoods for migrants and their families. For a few years now, Chinese government policies have been shifting towards recognising and responding to the situation of migrants. Local experiments with various forms of social insurance for migrants, including health insurance, pension and so forth are under way (see Chapters 2 and 3 in this book), but there is still a long way to go before we reach a situation where the health of migrant workers can be described as a valuable asset in sustainable livelihood strategies, or where migrants' rights to health are no longer sacrificed for the so-called "comparative advantages" in the global market.

Notes

1 For a review of the debate on sustainable livelihood perspectives, see Scoones (2009).
2 Directed by Bettina Gransow and Frauke Kraas, funded by the German Research Foundation (DFG).
3 For a more detailed analysis of Chinese migrant workers and occupational injuries, see Gransow *et al.* (2014).
4 The five basic vaccinations in China include BBC (vaccine for TB), measles, PDT (pertussis, diphtheria, and tetanus), polio, and hepatitis B.
5 Formerly called the Ministry of Labour and Social Security.

References

Anon. (2006), Childbirth problems for migrant workers in Guangzhou. Available at: http://english.gov.cn/2006-06/14/content_309317.htm (accessed 17 February 2008).
Bork, Tabea, Frauke Kraas and Yuan Yuan (2010), Migrants' health, health facilities and services in villages-in-the-city in Guangzhou. In Bettina Gransow and Daming Zhou (eds), *Migrants and Health in Urban China*. Berlin: Berliner China-Hefte Vol. 38, pp. 72–93.
Cai, He, Linping Liu and Xiangdong Wan (2009), *Chengshihua jinchengzhong de nongmingong: Laizi zhujiang sanjiaozhou de yanjiu* [Migrant workers in the urbanisation process: A study from the Pearl River Delta area]. Beijing: Social Sciences Academic Press.
Chen, Hua (2004), *Guangdong wailai renqun de shiyingxing* [Adaptability of floating people in Guangdong Province]. Hong Kong: International Yanhuang Culture Press.
Cheng, Yanyuan and Barbara Darimont (2005), Occupational accident insurance reform and legislation in China. *International Social Security Review* 58(1): 85–97.
Cook, Sarah (2007), Putting health back in China's development. *China Perspectives* 71: 100–108.
Department of Labour and Social Security of Guangdong Province (2006–2007), *Guangdong sheng laodong he shehui baozhang ting 2006–2007*, Unpublished report on the situation of migrants in Guangdong.
Feng, Zhiqiang (2007), Marginalization and health provision in transitional China. In Heather Xiaoquan Zhang, Bin Wu and Richard Sanders (eds), *Marginalisation in China: Perspectives on Transition and Globalisation*. Aldershot: Ashgate, pp. 97–116.
Gransow, Bettina, Guanghuai Zheng, Apo Leong and Li Ling (2014), Chinese migrant workers and occupational injuries: A case study of the manufacturing industry in the Pearl River Delta. United Nations Research Institute for Social Development (UNRISD) Working Paper 2014-1 (January): 1–39.
Guangdong Research Team [*Guangdongsheng diaoyanzu*] (2006), *Guangdongsheng jiaqiang nongmingong guanli he fuwu zhuyao zuofa* [Main methods of strengthening peasant workers' administration and services in Guangdong Province]. In *Guowuyuan yanjiushi*

ketizu [State Council Research Team] (ed.), *Zhongguo nongmingong diaoyan baogao* [Research report on Chinese peasant workers]. Beijing: Zhongguo yanshi, pp. 432–446.

Holdaway, Jennifer (2008), Migration and health in China: An introduction to problems, policy and research. *The Yale-China Health Journal* 5: 7–23.

ILO (International Labour Organisation) (2005), *National Profile Report on Occupational Safety and Health in China*. Beijing: Chinese Labor and Social Security Press.

Li, Junfu (2003), *Guangzhou chengzhongcun tudi liyong yanjiu* [Research on land use in Guangzhou's urban villages]. Ph.D. thesis, Sun Yat-sen University.

Ling, Li, Manju Rani, Yuanyuan Sang, Guiye Lv and Sarah L. Barber (2014), Two decades of research on migrant health in China: A systematic review – lessons for future inquiry. Working Paper 2014-8. United Nations Research Institute for Social Development (UNRISD), (May): 1–65.

Lu, Dadao and Hui Liu (2006), Urbanization and environmental issues in China. In Wuyi Wang, Thomas Krafft and Frauke Kraas (eds), *Global Change, Urbanization and Health*. Beijing: China Meteorological Press, pp. 3–10.

Nanfang Daily (2011), *Mei sange guangzhou ren zhong you yige wailai renyuan: zuixin tongji shuju xianshu* [One-third of Guangzhou residents are non-local *hukou* holders as shown in the latest statistics]. Available at: http://epaper.nfdaily.cn/html/2011-05/17/content_6961085.htm (accessed 18 March 2014).

National Bureau of Statistics of China (NBSC) (2008), *2008 nianmo quanguo nongmingong zongliang wei 22542 wan ren* [225,420,000 rural migrants at the end of 2008]. Available at: www.stats.gov.cn/tjfx/fxbg/t20090325_402547406.htm (accessed 31 March 2009).

Pun, Ngai (2005), *Made in China: Women Factory Workers in a Global Workplace*. Durham, NC: Duke University Press.

Scoones, Ian (2009), Livelihood perspectives and rural development. *The Journal of Peasant Studies* 36(1): 171–196.

Wong, Daniel, Keung Fu and He Xue Song (2008), The resilience of migrant workers in Shanghai: The roles of migration stress and meaning of migration. *International Journal of Social Psychiatry*, 54(2): 131–143.

Wu, Fulong, Fangzhu Zhang and Chris Webster (eds) (2014), *Rural Migrants in Urban China: Enclaves and Transient Urbanism*. London: Routledge.

Wu, Linbin (2007), *Nongmingong zhiye jiankang yizhi xiaojie huayu jizhi* [Discourses that dispel migrant workers' consciousness of work-related ill health]. M.A. thesis, Sun Yat-sen University.

Xiang, Biao (2005), An institutional approach towards migration and health in China. In Santosh Jatrana, Mika Toyota and Brenda S.A. Yeoh (eds), *Migration and Health in Asia*. London: Routledge, pp. 161–176.

Yang, Xiushi (2004), Temporary migration and the spread of STDs/HIV in China: Is there a link? *International Migration Review* 38(1): 212–235.

Zhang, Heather Xiaoquan (2007), Conceptualising the links: Migration, health and sustainable livelihoods in China. In Heather Xiaoquan Zhang, Bin Wu, and Richard Sanders (eds), *Marginalisation in China: Perspectives on Transition and Globalisation*. Aldershot: Ashgate, pp. 195–214.

Zheng, Gongcheng and Ruolian Huang-Li (eds) (2007), *Zhongguo nongmingong wenti yu shehui baohu* [The rural-urban migrant workers issue and migrants' social protection in China], two vols. Beijing: People's Press.

Zheng, Zhenzhen (2006), Health vulnerability among temporary migrants in urban China. In Wuyi Wang, Thomas Krafft and Frauke Kraas (eds), *Global Change, Urbanization and Health*. Beijing: China Meteorological Press, pp. 197–207.

Zheng, Zhenzhen, Ciyong Lu and Liming Lu (2013), Reproductive health and access to services among rural-to-urban migrants in China. United Nations Research Institute for Social Development (UNRISD) Working Paper 2013-4 (December): 1–27.

Zhou, Daming, Jianxin Zhou and Zhijun Liu (2007), *'Ziyou' de dushi bianyuanren – zhongguo dongnan yanhai sangong yanjiu* [The 'free' marginalised people in cities: A study of odd-job workers in Chinese southeast coastal areas]. Guangzhou: Sun Yat-sen University Press.

5   Legal activism or class action?

The political economy of the "no boss" and "no labour relationship" in China's construction industry

Ngai Pun and Yi Xu

Introduction

A global China is made spatially possible by the huge construction workforce, which is composed of more than 40 million migrant workers hailing from all parts of China's countryside. Recent years have seen increasing numbers of individual and collective actions among construction workers pursuing delayed wages or demanding compensation for injury or death. These actions include legal litigation, such as suing subcontractors or companies, as well as collective actions, such as property damage, physical assault, and even suicidal behaviour. Should these be understood as class actions, especially when framed by a discourse of human and legal rights? What is the relationship between legal action (supposedly a realm of civil society) and collective resistance (supposedly an area of class conflict driven by production relations)? In the area of labour consciousness, how can workers make sense of their actions, both legal and/or collective, and negotiate with a hegemonic discourse? Do they transform legal action into class action at a particular juncture and thereby transgress the construed hegemonic language of legal rights? Addressing these questions requires an understanding of the political economy of the construction industry that shapes the politics of labour resistance among migrant construction workers. The first part of this chapter discusses changes in the political economy of the construction industry and the rise of the labour subcontracting system that has resulted in a "double absence" – the absence of a boss and management, and the absence of a capital–labour relationship in the reform period. The second part focuses on how this "double absence" generates a variety of legal and collective actions among construction workers, and how the workers take and understand their actions.

The rapid development of the construction industry and the accompanying structural changes in China have led to the rebirth of a highly exploitative labour subcontracting system that was abandoned during the socialist period (Lei 2005; Shen 2007). This labour system embodies two processes: (1) the rapid commodification of labour through non-industrial social relations organised by a quasi-labour market in rural villages; and (2) the subsumption of labour in the production process of the construction sector in urban areas. These two processes have shaped a specific labour subcontracting system in reform-era China, result-ing in a perpetual process of wage arrears and the struggle of construction work-ers to pursue delayed wages in various ways, sometimes involving violent collective action (Pun and Lu 2010). China's construction industry has experi-enced astonishing growth in the world market in recent years.[1] By 2007, the Chinese construction industry was consuming half of the world's concrete and a third of its steel for building its global cities, and was employing more than 40 million workers, most of them migrant workers from all parts of the country. About 30 per cent of all migrant workers are employed in the construction industry (*China Daily* 2007). In order to transform Beijing, Shanghai, and Guangzhou into China's core global cities and speed up the process of urbanisa-tion, China has invested about US$376 billion in construction each year since the Tenth Five Year Plan (2001–2005), making construction the country's fourth largest industry. By the turn of the twenty-first century, the construction industry had become a strategic industry accounting for approximately 6.6 per cent of China's GDP. By the end of 2007, the industry's total income had risen by 25.9 per cent to 5.10 trillion yuan, and total output value reached 2.27 trillion yuan in the first half of 2008 (National Bureau of Statistics of China 2008, hereafter NBSC).

This study draws on research conducted in seven cities – Beijing, Shenyang, Chengdu, Guiyang, Wuhan, Changsha and Guangzhou – in 2008 and 2009. More than 1,500 supervisors and workers were interviewed on 12 construction sites in these seven cities. In January 2009, the study followed workers back home to a rural village in Tang County, Hebei Province, where more than 1,500 working adults out of a population of 6,000 were construction workers. The village study allowed for a deeper understanding of the social origins of the labour subcontracting system and how it served as the bedrock for collective action among the migrant construction workers.

It became clear to the research team that in contrast to the enormous gross profits and output value of the construction industry, construction workers remain a poorly protected Chinese working class.[2] We were also struck by the violent individual or collective action taken by workers. The working lives of construction workers involved acts of individual and collective conflict, attempts to damage buildings, physical assault, and even suicidal behaviour. At the construction site we observed a variety of violent actions that were no doubt engendered by changes in the history and political economy of the industry.

The labour subcontracting system

The socialist structure of the Chinese construction sector was radically trans-formed during the reform period. The reforms, accompanied by a discourse of modernisation, paradoxically brought an end to the "socialist" practices of the construction industry. The year 1980 marked the beginning of the end of the planned economy in industry, and the resumption of the bidding and contract system in the construction industry (Lei 2005: 391–392). A World Bank project,

Lubuge Hydropower in Yunnan Province, radically changed socialist practices in the construction sector through the use of international competitive bidding in 1980. This represented the beginning of changes in the nature of capitalisation of the industry. As early as 1978, Deng Xiaoping pointed out that the construction industry could be profitable. The reform objectives set for the construction industry included restructuring the industry's administrative system, opening construction markets, granting autonomy to state-owned enterprises (SOEs), establishing a competitive bidding system and improving project managerial skills (Mayo and Liu 1995).

As the pioneer industry undertaking a series of reform programmes, the construction sector was the first to introduce "capitalistic" market mechanisms into its operations. In 1984, the State Council promulgated a regulation stating, "State-owned construction and installation enterprises shall gradually reduce the number of permanent workers. In the future they shall not, in principle, recruit any permanent workers except skilled operatives necessary to keep the enterprise technically operational."[3] Another significant 1984 regulation, the "Separation of Management from Field Operations", stated that general contractors or contracting companies should not directly employ their blue-collar workforce.[4] Rather, they should employ labour subcontractors who were to be responsible for recruiting the workforce. Needless to say, the regulations initiated an abrupt change in the capitalisation as well as the management of the construction industry and the composition of its workforce, leading to problems in the labour subcontracting system that became evident in the later stage of the reform. Driven by state initiatives, construction enterprises were further marketised, and field operations were alienated from direct management via the labour subcontracting system.

By the late 1990s, the restructuring of the capital–labour relationship in the construction industry was almost complete.[5] While this series of dramatic changes arguably increased efficiency and productivity in the operation of construction projects, the direct result was the emergence of a multi-tiered labour subcontracting system. Today, irrespective of the location of construction projects and the form of capitalisation, be it through an SOE or privately-owned company, the labour contracting system is the most significant form of labour in the industry. Organised through a subcontractor who recruits a team of migrant workers from rural areas to work on construction sites, more than 40 million workers are now part of this labour subcontracting system (All China Federation of Trade Unions, hereafter ACFTU 2004).

Looking deeply into the labour process of the industry, we see that a double delinking of capital and industry, and of management and production has created a power imbalance in the production chain that favours top-tier contractors. In the production chain, the top-tier contractors control construction projects through their relationship with property developers and the local state, while at the same time outsourcing their work to lower-tier subcontractors. In this hierarchical structure, the top-tier contractors, without contributing substantial capital to the construction operation, seek to profit from the transfer of investment risk and labour recruitment to their subcontractors. "They don't

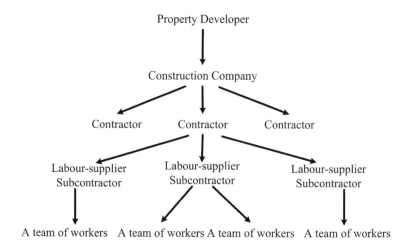

Figure 5.1 The subcontracting system.

bother to get their hands dirty. They transfer all the risks to us. They make us face the workers at times of wage arrears when the money doesn't arrive from above," said Lao Fang, a third-tier subcontractor. This was the most frequent complaint against top-tier contractors that we heard from labour-supply subcontractors at the construction sites.

Let us take a typical construction project in Beijing or Guangzhou as an example (Figure 5.1). The subcontracting system usually began with a giant property developer responsible for land reclamation and the architectural design of the project. This property developer can be an SOE or privately-owned enterprise. The actual construction was then shifted down the production chain through a bidding process to a construction company, which was often an SOE that only took charge of project management and equipment arrangements for its contractors. The first tier of the subcontracting process in the construction industry was monopolised by SOEs because of their strong foothold in the industry. SOEs usually had a number of contractors (mostly private companies) from all over the country. These contractors were called big contractors (*dabao*), responsible for providing raw materials and labour for the project. Sometimes these contractors would set up a labour service company to help recruit rural labourers, but in reality they usually relied on labour-supply subcontractors (*xiaobao* or *qingbao*) to recruit labour, manage daily work assignments, and pay out wages upon completion of the project. In return, these subcontractors further depended on their labour-use facilitators (*daigong*), usually their relatives or co-villagers, to recruit workers from their own or surrounding villages. In this way, construction workers were organised into a number of small subcontracting teams that worked on the construction site for construction projects. The number of workers in each subcontracting team ranges from a dozen to a hundred.

The construction projects that we studied in the Beijing migrant community brought very low profit margins for subcontractors, who often lacked sufficient funds to tide them over until their final payment. The task was to build 108 villas of 300–500 square metres. Lao Fang, an experienced subcontractor, provided us with detailed information: to build a block of villas with an estimated sale price of about 10 million yuan, the bidding price was only 760,000 yuan (including the costs of raw materials, labour and administration) for the first-tier contractors. These first-tier contractors then outsourced the construction work to second-tier contractors, who further subcontracted the work to labour-supply subcontractors. The standard unit price set for labour costs was 80,000 yuan, which meant that third-tier and fourth-tier labour-supply subcontractors had only this lump sum from which to pay the workers they recruited and to make a profit. Lao Fang explained, "We almost lost money in building the villas.[6] Sometimes we run up debts but still have to keep ourselves in the production chain, otherwise we'll be left out." Coming from places such as Hebei, Anhui, Sichuan and Shandong, most contractors and subcontractors had little bargaining power with the construction companies, which were mainly from big cities such as Beijing and Guangzhou and were well connected with political power, e.g. the municipal government, and wealth, e.g. big and influential private developers. Contractors and labour subcontractors often faced serious arrears even in the modest payments owed to them at the early stages of construction, and they were in a weak position to stand up for themselves against locally influential developers and construction companies. All these factors combined to make wage arrears an intractable and unresolved problem (Pun and Lu 2004).

The subsumption of labour in the production process

China's rapid urban and industrial development and the further expansion of the construction industry in the 1990s were accompanied by a tremendous demand for cheap labour. The labour subcontracting system subsequently stood out as the single greatest means of labour expropriation, laying the foundation for the subsumption of labour in the production process in its specific form. According to Marx, there are two forms of the subsumption of labour under capital, i.e. the formal subsumption of labour and the real subsumption of labour.[7] Today's labour expropriation in the construction industry can be considered a form of formal subsumption of labour, under which the labour power of construction workers is subsumed by the manipulation of capital through the labour subcontracting system. In addition to the valorisation of surplus value for capital, it also creates the following effects: further separation of the means of production from construction workers; prolonged reliance on subcontractors to recruit labour; the absence of a direct capital–labour relationship; small-scale production organised through small subcontracting teams; and, last but not least, the perpetual process of wage arrears. In China, the subsumption of labour in its specific form was not only a product of industry restructuring, serving the process of capital accumulation, but was also a joint creation of state and capital – because it was the state that took the lead in changing ownership and management–labour relations in the industry by instructing the construction industry to rely on subcontracting (without proper regulation to protect labour), and by privatising SOEs or turning them into profit-seeking entities (frequently at the expense of the interests of labour).

In the late 1990s, the development of the labour market operating via the labour subcontracting system left the rural workforce with no state or social protection. Workers had no health coverage, and no casualty insurance or disability payments. By the end of the 1990s, subcontractors were recruiting migrant workers as temporary labourers who were not even provided with a legal contract as required by the 1995 Labour Law.[8] None of the construction workers we interviewed received regular monthly payments, and not one had signed a labour contract. Although the Labour Contract Law enacted in January 2008 has made signing of a labour contract compulsory, neither the contractors nor the subcontractors observed the new law, and only a few workers whom we spoke to were aware of the new legal obligations binding contractors. Workers typically responded to our questions by saying, "What's a labour contract? No, we don't have it. I've never heard of it."

All of the workers we interviewed in Beijing, Shenyang, Chengdu, Guiyang, Wuhan, Changsha, and Guangzhou from December 2007 to January 2009 had been promised a daily pay rate ranging from 50 yuan to 120 yuan, depending on the type of job and the skills required.[9] Notwithstanding the promised pay rate, we observed that workers ran a significant risk of ultimately being paid at a substantially lower rate, as well as a significant risk of never being paid at all, and without contracts they had very limited recourse to the court. This failure of the state to provide legal and social protection to migrant workers has reduced legal reforms to little more than lip service.

The growing incidence of non-payment of wages is a case in point. Since developers do not pay contractors and subcontractors until after the project is completed, the workers are penalised by delayed payments – and, as we will illustrate in this chapter, this puts them at great risk. Instead of weekly or monthly wages until the completion of the project or the end of the year, construction workers are usually paid an irregular "living allowance" (*shenghuo fei*) arranged by their labour-supply subcontractors, which is barely enough to cover food and other daily expenses. The allowance ranges from one hundred to a few hundred yuan per month (about 10 to 20 per cent of their promised monthly income), depending on the quality of the subcontractor. Many subcontractors had to use their own money to provide a living allowance for their workers. Some workers received no living allowance at all because their subcontractor claimed to have no money. The subsumption of labour value in the production process was made possible when wages were replaced by living allowances and when subcontractors justified this practice by claiming a lack of funds for labour costs from their contractors.

On the first day of 2008, Beijing was numbingly cold, and most of the construction sites were already idle. In a shack on the outskirts of the metropolis,

Lao Chen, a 50-year-old worker from Hubei, was waiting anxiously to receive his wages from the subcontractor. As we gathered round him in the cold, Lao Chen opened his record of the past year's work, showing meticulously how he had worked 286 consecutive days with neither a day off nor a penny to show for it. In his dorm at a construction site, he explained:

> We're not even workers. Workers sell their labour to the boss and in return they receive wages … But as construction workers, we're different! I've been working 286 days for the boss and I still can't get my pay. I'm waiting for my work money (*gongqian*)[10] just as I'm always waiting for my luck.

Who is my boss?

The rapidly changing social relations in rural areas further fuel problems and conflicts derived from a labour subcontracting system that was supposed to operate through kin and ethnic networks. The research team were in a village in Tang County, Hebei Province, in the first week of January 2009. As in most Hebei villages, a major share of family income relied on earnings from working outside the village (*dagong*), especially in the construction industry. It was not a particularly poor village, with an average annual family income of around 15,000 to 20,000 yuan. We visited more than 30 families that had one or more members working on construction sites in Beijing. Having a long tradition in the construction industry, most families had a father and son, that is, at least two generations, working in the sector. These families were keen to show us their "papers of debt" that they had collected over the years, each telling a story of unpaid toil. One case of unpaid wages that we observed in the village was more than five years old: a 45-year-old man, Hai, who had worked continuously in the construction industry for 10 years, showed us a piece of worn paper that stated "XXX owes Hai 3,000 yuan only." The debtor had signed it, making the paper evidence of a debt owed to the worker. In this village, most labour supply subcontractors recruited from their own or surrounding villages. Every time we encountered cases of outstanding debt, we enquired into the debt and the reasons for non-payment. "Do you mean the subcontractor intentionally kept your money, or he couldn't pay you because the money didn't come through?" we asked. "Who knows? We didn't know who the boss was. We haven't even seen the boss," the worker usually would say.

The boss the workers referred to was not the labour-supply subcontractor, but the second or third-layer contractor who outsourced the work to the labour-supply subcontractor. The subcontractor was the only target for seeking wage payment because it was he who had recruited the workers, even though he was not the boss in a legal sense.[11] At the beginning of the Chinese New Year, the subcontractor would use his network in the village to recruit a group of workers, the exact number depending on the size of the construction project, and he would promise the workers a daily pay rate. All of the workers knew that their wages would not be paid until the completion of the construction project or the end of the year, a practice that had already become routine in the village. As long as their wages were received by the time they returned home to help with the harvest, or by the end of the Chinese New Year, workers consented to this payment delay, though not altogether willingly. In this sense, the exchange value of labour as a commodity is not reliant on legally required standards or accepted norms in society at large. This commodification process was special in that non-industrial social relationships were manipulated to serve the purpose of labour expropriation while at the same time helping to disguise the wage–labour relationship with capital. The "real" boss has become something of a myth in China's construction industry.

Construction workers' trust that they would be paid regularly was based on kin and co-villager networks. In the construction industry, workers were led to believe that their subcontractor, as their relative or co-villager, would not run away with the money. According to a saying popular among the workers, especially the older generation, "A monk may run away but a temple stays." This means that the subcontractor still had a family in the village, and it was difficult for the whole family to run away. This faith was destroyed, however, when wage arrears and debt became routine in the late 1990s. The rapid commodification of labour in the rural community through labour-supply subcontractors has eroded trust.[12]

A number of workers emphasised their constant search for a new small subcontractor that would be better than the previous one. The reason for this practice was clear: no one was trusted enough in the village any more. But in times when jobs were badly needed, middle-aged workers in particular had little choice of subcontractors. Even if the subcontractor had a poor record of wage payment, there was still hope that he would be able to pay at the end of the Lunar Year. We observed tense social relations in Hebei's rural villages, with serious worries and anxieties among workers that wages would not be paid and that subcontractors, either relatives or co-villagers, would run off. Trust had been destroyed, and normal human relationships were somewhat distorted. As middlemen with personal networks who fed the construction industry with cheap labour, subcontractors were the main agents in the process of commodification of labour. Rural non-industrial social relationships were manipulated to serve the purposes of labour subsumption, which in turn intensified hidden social conflicts on the construction site and in the village.

Collective action

The political economy of the construction industry has shaped a specific labour use system – labour subcontracting – that generates a specific capital–labour relationship in which the legal labour identity and labour relationship are highly subsumed. It creates a double absence in the legal sense: an "absent" boss and an "absent" labour relationship. This double absence has led to a perpetual process of wage arrears and the struggle of construction workers to pursue delayed wages in various ways, usually involving collective action. It is interesting to note that even though the issue of this "double absence" has surfaced as a legal problem, few labour disputes have actually reached the courts through formal legal procedures. Instead, most labour disputes, following a series of labour actions, have been settled through informal legal channels (see also Chapter 2 in this collection), and particularly through direct negotiations that often involve violent struggles with the construction company.

Collective actions by construction workers have centred largely on wage arrears and injury compensation. Under an unreasonable labour subcontracting system, construction workers have gradually learnt that their labour rights can hardly be protected. Unlike the studies by Lee (2007) and Gallagher (2005), which emphasise legalism regarding the labour rights of Chinese migrant workers, our study found that few construction workers attempted to take action through litigation or even labour arbitration. Most workers launched direct individual or collective actions against construction companies or put pressure on local governments. The reason for this, paradoxically, is also the "double absence" of the boss and the capital–labour relationship in a legal sense. The workers usually did not take action until the bottom line of their consent – receiving wages at the end of the Lunar Year – was broken. Once action was taken, it was often of a violent nature, involving fighting, physical injury, suicidal behaviour, or attempts to damage buildings.

On a freezing winter's evening in January 2008, we met Lan and her co-workers in the workers' dorm of a construction site in Beijing. Work had ended a few days earlier, but workers' wages had not arrived, leaving workers waiting anxiously to return to their hometowns. Lan and her co-workers, all from a village in Hebei, were arguing with their subcontractor, who was trying to convince the workers to wait patiently for their payments. The argument was so loud that it attracted workers from other dorms to gather around. "You have to give us justice (*gongdao*); working for no money is simply against the law of heaven!" one worker protested. "We trusted you and we relied on you to chase up our money – our money tainted with blood and sweat! Keeping our wage is against the law (*weifa*)!" another worker followed. During the argument with the subcontractor, workers often used the terms *gongdao* (the principle of justice) and *weifa* (against the law).

The language the workers learned to claim their rights originated in the central government's discourse of legal labour rights. In order to alleviate the industrial tensions engendered since the 1990s, the Chinese government has issued a series of labour regulations and laws, not only to protect labour rights but also to resolve social conflicts between capital and labour. "Rule by law" has become not only a slogan of contemporary Chinese society but also a means of political legitimacy for the Chinese government (Lee 2007). It also represents a process of de-politicisation (de-ideologisation) of the state in its attempts to regain political hegemony through a legal rationale. Hence an imagined "irrational" ideological society in the socialist period is replaced by a "rational" legal society in the reform era, with "rule by law" used to defend an evolving constellation of property rights and class relations. Faith in the law is a political device to safeguard a changing political regime in the process of privatisation and neoliberalisation that has led to a rapid transfer of wealth and a reconfiguration of social class and status. Legalism has never been intended to support greater civic participation, and even less to protect labour rights. The workers had to learn this "truth" through their own actions.

The concepts of justice and law have nevertheless embodied different meanings when employed by workers. Using the term *gongdao* is a call for morality derived from a basic belief in human fairness embedded in the order of heaven and the cosmos. In the eyes of construction workers, *gongdao* is more basic and fundamental once it is challenged. *Gongdao*, with its faith rooted at the community level, is therefore a habitus concept,[13] while the concept of law, with its provisions by the state, is a formal legal concept. We found that workers made stronger claims under *gongdao* than under *weifa*, and that they were angrier when *gongdao* was transgressed. Law is a new faith in Chinese society created by the Chinese state. As a new ideology, it occupies a key position in providing an understanding of the normative behaviours of social agents, be they farmers, workers, or bosses. However, if "building a legalised society" is a "modernising" attempt in the eyes of the Chinese elite, it is less so to migrant workers, who understand their social lives through the principles of justice, humanity and morality. To demand an explanation – "*Tao yige shuofa*" – an expression often employed when construction workers go to the office of the construction company demanding their delayed payments, is to fight for justice based on moral grounds rather than a legal rationale.

Workers are usually very anxious to receive their wages before they reunite with their families for the Chinese New Year. As a mother of three children, Lan was less patient than the men in waiting for her delayed payment. She had been away from home for half a year working on the construction site, and her only reason for leaving her children was to earn money for her family. Working hard for nothing was simply unacceptable. Taking action to demand their money was morally legitimate, whether legal or illegal. She further complained:

> A group of Henan workers took action to fight for their wages yesterday. Why do we still have to wait? Wait for what? The Henan workers threatened to damage the villas they built and surrounded the office of the contractor on the construction site and didn't allow the office staff to leave. The staff then called the police and two police cars came. The manager of the company finally showed up and promised to pay the workers three days later … But how about us? We haven't managed to "*nao*" (literally means to make noise and create a disturbance)! How can we get our wages?

Arguments and fighting were a frequent phenomenon on the construction site. Workers called for *nao* instead of legal means to resolve their labour disputes. The tense relationship between subcontractors and workers often triggered violent acts arising from verbal disagreements. On several occasions we observed severe fighting, usually collective, between workers and their subcontractor, or between the subcontractor and his workers against their contractor, or some-times between different subcontract teams over work conflicts on the construc-tion site. One case we observed was in December 2008, when a subcontractor called 20 of his workers to surround the office of his contractor to demand a delayed payment. This ended up in collective fighting when the contractor called in his own hired hands. Workers on both sides were injured.

Lan's group had been told by their subcontractor that they would receive their wages on 26 December. Some of her co-workers had already bought train tickets, hoping to return home immediately after receiving their three months' payment. On 29 December, the subcontractor came and said the company still had not paid him the money he needed to pay the workers. Since the New Year's holiday was imminent, the workers would have to wait until 3 January. When 3 January arrived, the workers still had not seen their money. Anxiety and anger mounted. One of Lan's co-workers, Tian, jumped into the conversation:

We have to *nao*. We have to show our muscle. When we were working, they [the quality controllers sent by the contractor] came to monitor and fuss over our job. Every day we were watched. But now that our work is finished, we've been dumped. We are nobody. We have to *nao* to demand our wages!

Both in the city and in the village, creating a disturbance (*nao*) was the word most frequently used when workers talked of demanding delayed wages. *Nao* means action involving challenges to "face", breaking up a relationship, and disturbing social harmony by petitioning the manager's office, the labour bureau, the Ministry of Construction and, if needed, by blocking national highways to gain media attention. Most workers labouring in the construction industry for a few years found no way to resolve their wage arrears other than *nao*, and *nao* therefore became a last resort, a weapon of the weak, and an act of rightful resist-ance (O'Brien and Li 2006).

The bargaining power of workers became minimal once their work was completed and they were eager to return home. Staying on the construction site without work was like a punishment, and they still had to pay for their meals and other daily expenses. Waiting in the city, therefore, meant a big loss in a number of senses from the migrant worker's perspective: they could not return home to unite with long-separated families causing emotional distress, or in time to help with the harvest, which can lead to reduced household income at the rural end, and they were unable to earn money while paying for daily living costs in the city. Lan's co-workers insisted on taking action to back up their wage demands. The workers feared simply waiting: "What do we do if 6 January comes and the boss still has no money to pay us? We can't wait any more." The workers discussed the issue fiercely until they finally reached a consensus to visit the offices of Ministry of Construction and ask officials for help the next day. While some workers prepared a petition letter, others collected information about their contractor and evidence of their labour relationship with this contractor, and still others tried to find the address of the Ministry. Three workers, including

Tian, were chosen as representatives to meet with officials. It is common practice for the disadvantaged in need of help to request a meeting with upper-level government officials. Even so, this was recourse to government support beyond a sense of legal rationality. In the eyes of the construction workers, the responsibility of officials to "resolve the difficulties" of ordinary people (*shujie minkun*) was the grounds for official legitimacy.

The workers travelled three hours by bus to reach the Ministry building, only to be told that they were at the wrong place; because they lacked a labour contract, they had to go to the Labour Bureau for help. It took another hour to reach the Labour Bureau, where staff directed them to the District Labour Bureau: in accordance with the bureaucratic protocol, the workers had to begin requesting assistance from the lowest level at their work location. Late that afternoon, the workers finally reached the district office, which was crowded with workers from other construction sites, all caught in the same impasse of wage arrears. Tian observed:

> Some workers were squatting quietly in the corridor waiting to see the officials. Some, however, were very agitated, and shouted that if they still couldn't receive their wages, they would climb to the top of the building and jump off.

Workers from other groups applauded this suggestion and screamed loudly that only a suicide attempt would make the boss listen to them and repay them on the spot. "No boss has a conscience," or, "All bosses are black-hearted (*heixin*)" were the most frequent utterances. Self-destructive action or violent protest was often threatened when construction workers saw no way out. During the same month in 2009, at another construction site we visited, a worker climbed onto a bulldozer in a threat to commit suicide if his pay continued to be withheld. The construction company called the police, who arrived and ordered the worker to climb down while also asking the company to pay his delayed wages.

Other workers were known to pick up axes or sledgehammers and damage the villas they had built. In June 2008, a group of construction workers surrounded and wrecked a sales office as it prepared to welcome customers one morning. The workers yelled, "The company cares about customers, but not us!" This drew the attention of the property developer, who put pressure on the construction company to resolve the wage arrears. Blocking a major highway in order to attract the attention of top officials in the central government was also a frequently resorted method of resistance. Only by disrupting urban life were the city's builders – these transient migrant workers – able to secure their wages.

Tian and his co-workers were nevertheless still at the point of seeking redress by appealing to the authorities. He and his co-workers waited for an hour and a half to get in the door of the legal aid department of the District Labour Bureau. The first question put to them was whether they had a labour contract. They were told that if they did not, the Labour Department could not help them, as they did not have a legal employer, and hence did not have a legal labour relationship. Only if their labour relationship could be legally proven could workers request help from the Labour Bureau. The staff at both the Construction Ministry and the District Labour Bureau knew that most workers in this industry were not given labour contracts. Tian asked, "If a labour contract is that important, why doesn't the government enforce it seriously? Why do none of us have contracts?" He felt very angry after being shuttled from one department to another. A hegemonic discourse on legalism was self-defeating, if not self-deceiving, in the eyes of the agitated workers. The workers finally learned that they were not protected by the law but excluded by it. As wage-labour, they were not recognised as "workers" simply due to the lack of a legally required written labour contract.

The failure of the construction companies to abide by labour laws and workers' disappointment at the local government drove them to the brink of violent action. When three of the workers returned to their construction site late that evening, they were unable to calm down and repeatedly proclaimed to their co-workers that if their money did not arrive, they had no choice but to fight: "It's not a normal industry! We workers have worked for no wage! … If they don't give us our money, I'll lay down my life to fight them! How dare they refuse us our money?" But that evening Tian had not yet reached a point of pushing for actual violence. Instead, he began mobilising other workers to make a protest banner reading, "Return my money tainted with my blood and sweat!"[14] Such demonstrations were often one step away from physical conflict.

These acts of labour conflict were not isolated cases we observed at construction sites in Beijing and other cities. Rather, various efforts against wage arrears, often culminating in violent acts, became particularly severe at the end of the year. As a result, most of the workers we interviewed had, at some point, participated in collective action of some kind.

Conclusion

The struggle at the construction site – simply to fight for delayed or embezzled wages – can be understood as a "bottom-line" struggle, as it exposes the nature of the subcontracting system and the failure of the politico-legal system to protect the basic labour rights of migrant workers in China. Construction workers are well aware of the exploitative nature of the labour subcontracting system, because it often results in wage arrears and lack of compensation for bodily injury (see also Chapter 2 of this book). During their struggles, the situation of "no boss" and hence "no labour relationship" is not a legal issue to them but rather a class issue disguised by a legal discourse. While the workers seldom use the word "class", they replace it with the language of justice and law. In short, the principle of injustice (*bu gongdao*) refers to unfair treatment by the more powerful in the construction industry and beyond, who violate the minimum moral standards of society at large. In this scenario, a discourse of "rightful resistance" seems to overshadow the discourse of "class action", in that workers make sense of their suffering in terms of an embedded morality rather than of class exploitation.

On deeper examination, however, we find that accusations of injustice lie at the very core of the capital–labour relationship, i.e., the production relations of the construction industry, which has been affected by a rapid shift in the nature and structure of the industry during the reform period. The political economy of "no boss" and "no labour relationship", a delinking of capital and industry and of management and labour, is also directly linked with the specific form of subsumption and exploitation of labour in the subcontracting system. All labour struggles stem from this changing political economy of the construction industry. It is not a "normal" industry for either subcontractors or workers, since there is no boss, and no employer who is directly responsible for their employment, pay and livelihood security. The capital–labour relationship has been entirely disguised: the workers literally do not know the identity of the developer or the construction company who is ultimately responsible for the non-payment of wages owed to them. This misrecognition has been made possible through a labour subcontracting system that sustains the valorisation of capital without always recompensing subsumed labour: an invisible hand, the market, operating several steps removed from the workforce, enables the dealing out of a rigged losing hand to a transient army of migrant labourers.

The specific struggles and practices involved in this rapidly changing construction industry induce angry, largely violent actions, and sometimes a mixture of legal and non-legal collective action by migrant construction workers. Actions taken by workers usually surface as a fight for legal labour rights, as the violation of their basic rights is legally sanctioned. This does not mean, however, that the minds of construction workers have been indoctrinated by the hegemonic discourse of "a legalised society" or legalism. Rather, faith in legalism acts as a double-edged sword since once workers discover that the law enforcement institutions are frequently allies of, and thus side with capital against their interests, their faith collapses. Furthermore, workers learn that their basic labour rights are often ignored rather than protected by law (which is also demonstrated in Chapter 2 of this book). In short, this chapter shows that the labour subcontracting system is a core problem of China's post-socialist construction industry, generating a series of collective actions usually carried out in non-legal realms. When trust and faith in the law are severely eroded by the legal system itself and its enforcement mechanisms, the phenomenon of widespread delayed or default payment of wages becomes unacceptable and the workers' consent breaks, the class conflicts and struggles over livelihood and rights are turned into militant labour action.

Acknowledgements

We are grateful to Huilin Lu, Dajun Li, Zicun Liang, Huipeng Zhang, Lijuan Zhou, and Qingsu Li, who provided unfailing research support. We are also grateful for financial support from two research grants, "Working Class Community: Space and Labour Resistance in China" and "The Making of

Transborder-Community in the Pearl River Delta", the Department of Applied Social Sciences, Hong Kong Polytechnic University. An earlier version of this chapter was published as "Legal Activism or Class Action?: The Political Economy of the 'No Boss' and 'No Labour Relationship' in China's Construction Industry", *China Perspectives* 2 (2011): 9–17.

Notes

1 In China, the construction industry is defined as the sector that creates buildings and other structures. See Shenghan Sun and George Ofori (2001).
2 "Poorly protected working class" refers to work conditions such as intensity, hours, and payment methods, but not necessarily the pay rates of construction workers compared with workers in the manufacturing or service sectors.
3 This was the Tentative Provisions for Construction Industry and Capital Investment Administration System Reform (Ministry of Construction 2000: 7–8).
4 See the Ministry of Construction (2000: 8).
5 In August 1995, the State Planning Commission, the Ministry of Electric Power Industry, and the Ministry of Transportation jointly issued "The Circular on Granting Concessions to Foreign Financed Capital Projects." The Construction Law was put into effect on 1 March 1998, covering a wide range of issues such as qualifications for entry into the construction industry, procurement and delivery of work, construction supervision, construction safety, construction quality, legal liability, market regulations, and procedures in construction projects.
6 The structure of villas is more complicated than that of a high-rise building, requiring subcontractors to contribute more labour days to the completion of the work.
7 According to Marx's Economic Manuscripts of 1861–1863, the form that produces absolute surplus value is called the formal subsumption of labour under capital. It is distinguished only formally from other modes of production in which the actual producers provide a surplus value, i.e., work more than the necessary labour time, but for others rather than for themselves. The real subsumption of labour under capital is developed in all forms that produce relative, as opposed to absolute, surplus value. With the real subsumption of labour under capital, Marx argued, a complete revolution takes place in the mode of production itself, in the productivity of labour, and in the relation – within production – between the capitalist and the worker, as well as in the social relationship between them.
8 The 1995 Labour Law was supposed to lay a foundation for workers' legal and contractual rights, and create a framework for resolving labour disputes. In the 2000s, the Beijing leadership began to channel labour disputes into arbitration committees and the court system through bureaucratic and legal procedures (see also Chapter 2 in this book). The Labour Contract Law, which came into effect on 1 January 2008, is considered the most significant change in Chinese labour law in the reform period. See www.gov.cn/ziliao/flfg/2007-06/29/content_669394.htm.
9 Women workers were paid 5–10 yuan less per day than their male counterparts on the same job. Pay rates reached a peak in 2007 and 2008 due to the shortage of labour that became evident in the early to mid-2000s. In 2006, the daily pay rates for cement pourers and carpenters were 30 yuan and 50 yuan respectively, and they soared to 50 yuan and 100 yuan in 2008.
10 In the construction industry, migrant workers use the term *gongqian* (work money) to describe their wages. But in the manufacturing and service sectors, workers usually use *gongzi* (work payment), a more formal concept referring to wages. *Gongzi* means wage, and it bears a formal capital–labour relationship, but the term *gongqian* does not have the same connotation.

11 Strictly speaking, according to the Company Law and the Construction Law, labour-supply subcontractors do not have corporate status and hence do not have a legal status to employ workers.
12 This finding contradicts Yuan Shen's study on migrant construction workers. Shen (2007) argues that kinship and co-villager relationships among the workers were able to construct a relation-hegemony in which the workers' interests were disguised.
13 "Habitus" refers to a set of socially learned dispositions, skills, and ways of acting that are often taken for granted, and that are acquired through the activities and experiences of everyday life.
14 The next morning, Tian and his co-workers launched a demonstration. After surrounding the management office for three hours, the workers were able to collect their delayed wages.

References

All-China Federation of Trade Unions (ACFTU) (2004), A survey on the situation of construction peasant-workers. Available at: http://finance.sina.com.cn/g/20041111/17381148918.shtml (accessed 1 November 2010).

China Daily (2007), Construction workers alienated. *Zhongguo ribao*, 9 July 2007.

Gallagher, Mary Elizabeth (2005), *Contagious Capitalism: Globalisation and the Politics of Labour in China*. Princeton, NJ: Princeton University Press.

Lee, Ching Kwan (2007), *Against the Law: Labour Protests in China's Rustbelt and Sunbelt*. Berkeley, CA: University of California Press.

Lei, Guang (2005), The market as social convention: Rural migrants and the making of China's home renovation market. *Critical Asian Studies* 37(3): 391–411.

Mayo, Richard E. and Gong Liu (1995), Reform agenda of Chinese industry. *Journal of Construction Engineering and Management* 121(1): 80–85.

Ministry of Construction (2000), *Xin zhongguo jianzhuye wushinian* [Fifty years of new China's construction industry]. Beijing: Zhongguo sanxia chubanshe.

National Bureau of Statistics of China (NBSC) (2008), *Zhongguo jianzhuye tongji nianjian* [China construction statistical yearbook]. Beijing: Zhongguo tongji chubanshe.

O'Brien, Kevin and Lianjiang Li (2006), *Rightful Resistance in Rural China*. Cambridge: Cambridge University Press.

Pun, Ngai and Huilin Lu (2010), A culture of violence: The labour subcontracting system and collective actions by construction workers in post-socialist China. *The China Journal* 64: 143–158.

Shen, Yuan (2007), *Shichang, jieji yu shehui* [Market, class and society]. Beijing: Social Sciences Academic Press.

Sun, Shenghan and George Ofori (2001), Construction industry in China's regional economy, 1990–1998. *Construction Management and Economics* 19: 189–205.

Part II

Sustainable livelihoods

6 Biotech politics in an emerging economy

Is China a developmental risk society?

Jennifer H. Zhao, Peter Ho, Dayuan Xue and Jac. A. A. Swart

Introduction

It is forecast that in the near future the area devoted to genetically modified (GM) crops in developing countries will exceed that in industrialised countries. However, agro-biotech applications have been criticised because of the perceived risks to the environment and to human health (along with the corresponding socio-economic consequences), particularly in the Global South.[1] Over the past decade or so, China has become one of the largest producers of GM crops in the world, in part as a result of international and domestic biotech corporations' attempts to conquer the Chinese seed market (Ho *et al.* 2009). This has led to the fear among some observers that the pressures surrounding food security and increased international competition, coupled with a relatively less developed civil society in China, might lead to a disregard for risks associated with genetically modified organisms (GMOs).

In this chapter, we examine whether China might evolve into a "developmental risk society". The "risk society" thesis predicts that the forces of civil society (through "sub-politics") combined with newly emerging institutions could eventually trigger a "reflexive modernisation" able to rein in new technological and industrial risks (Beck 1992a, 1992b; Beck *et al.* 1994). This process would lead to potentially adequate responses to the hazards wrought by the new risks in the "risk society". In a developmental risk society, in contrast, the state is still struggling to solve major "developmental dilemmas" on its selected path to industrialisation and modernity (Ho 2009), while civil society forces are relatively constrained or underdeveloped. Coupled with relatively limited state capacity and effective regulatory institutions, states in developing countries tend to overlook or even disregard risks in favour of overall development. Having said this, we shall argue that in dealing with the risks of biotechnology, China does not entirely fit the profile of a developmental risk society. In fact, Chinese biotech politics feature more complex dynamics with, on the one hand, a fledging civil society working against a strong push for GM technology by commercial and industrial interests, and, on the other, a certain level of regulatory checks and balances, and strong central state institutions that, despite their inner contradictions, are committed to controlling the biotech sector and its risks.

There are several arguments why biotechnology developments in China merit close scholarly attention. In the 1990s, the publicist Lester Brown shocked the Chinese government with his prediction that the People's Republic of China (PRC) would face critical food shortages in the near future (Brown 1995).[2] For decades, food security has been a source of major concern for the Chinese government, partly due to the fact that one-fifth of the world's population live in China, while the area of per capita farmland is limited. Based on current demographic trends, it has been estimated that the demand for food production would rise by at least 60 per cent in order to feed the growing Chinese population (Zhang 2000).[3] Given GM crops' advantages of producing higher yields and having stronger resistance to diseases, many experts maintain that such crops may help China to attain this goal. At the same time, more cautious observers fear that China's relatively underdeveloped regulatory and legal institutions, and a lack of political transparency, combined with the absence of a strong civil society, might result in a too hasty adoption of new and uncertain technologies with potential social, environmental and health risks.

Further, some fear that it would be unlikely that public concerns over GMOs would increase to such a level that would prompt the government to take effective action. While a study on Taiwanese and Japanese consumer views found a relatively high level of resistance to GM foods as compared to their peers in the USA (Chern and Rickertsen 2002; Macer and Ng 2000), GMOs are a non-issue among consumers in China (Ho et al. 2006).[4] Another important reason why the Chinese biotechnology developments should be followed closely is China's rapidly expanding area where GM crops are cultivated. Various crops have been approved for or already gone into commercial production, e.g., GM tomatoes, papayas, disease-resistant green peppers, short-straw morning glories (petunia), tobacco, and two types of cotton modified with genes from the *Bacillis thuringiensis*, called "Bt cotton" (Qing and Wade 2000: 2; Wang 1999: 8; Zhao 2002: 30). For years China was the world's largest cultivator of pest-resistant Bt cotton, and was not overtaken until 2006 by India. Furthermore, the way in which China deals with the control of GMOs has global implications, as China's leadership on such emerging issues will be critical for Asian regional institutions and organisations, e.g., the Association of South East Asian Nations (ASEAN), and Asia Pacific Economic Cooperation (APEC), in which China has actively participated.

Dangerous developments? Core questions and concepts

Ulrich Beck (1992a), in the risk society thesis, envisioned a bleak future for human development. He regarded current environmental problems such as global warming, nuclear waste, and the loss of biodiversity as serious challenges, which late modern societies might not be able to meet. Old risks of the nineteenth century, such as industrial accidents and hazards, were often considered to be discrete, statistically describable and thus "predictable", and "subject to supra-individual and political rules of recognition, compensation and avoidance"

(Beck 1992b: 99). In contrast, modernisation has unleashed a new generation of incalculable hazards that have been dubbed a "new species of trouble" (Erikson 1994). These hazards are undetectable by direct human sensory perception, can cause irreversible harm, and can transcend generations and the boundaries of nation-states. Paradigmatic examples are the increase in radiation exposure as a result of nuclear bomb testing in the 1950s and the resultant health hazards; the depletion of the ozone layer due to chemical substances; the widespread use of dichlorodiphenyltrichloroethane (DDT) as a pesticide causing serious distur-bances to ecological food chains; and the development of GM crops and their adverse effects on biodiversity and ecological change. According to Beck, politi-cal and socio-economic institutions of contemporary society are unable to deal with this new category of risks:

> This means that the calculation of risk as it has been established so far by science and legal institutions collapses ... Science's rationality claim to be able to investigate objectively the hazardousness of risk permanently refutes itself. It is based on a house of cards of speculative assumptions, and moves exclusively within a framework of probability statements, whose prognosis of safety cannot even be refuted by actual accidents.
>
> (Beck 1992a: 22, 29)

In effect, late modern society would create a sense of false security based on the institutionalisation of techno-bureaucratic – but ineffective – norms and regulations, which form an intractable logic of self-destruction, i.e. the risk society, which will lead to problems with the political legitimacy of the state.[5]

Whereas Beck was writing based on Western (in particular, German) develop-ment experiences,[6] the question of state legitimacy in the face of environmental risks and their management might be even more pertinent in developing coun-tries. Beck and others charted a possible way out of the pitfalls of the "Western" risk society by positing the concept of "reflexive modernisation" – a development trajectory by which state and civil society in post-industrial countries might turn the self-destructive tide through the dissolution of traditional institutions, the launch of "sub-politics", the rise of transnational forces (such as a global civil society), and the incorporation of principles of sustainability and precaution (Beck *et al.* 1994). Against this backdrop, one might wonder how well equipped nations in the Global South would be in dealing with issues of biosafety and risks of GMOs. In fact, in developing countries where "sub-political activities" might be, to varying extents, restrained, and where state capacity is weaker, yet, serious developmental dilemmas and socio-economic problems still await solutions (Ho 2009), there might be a significantly greater danger that the state disregards the risks of new technologies. Kydd *et al.* (2000: 1137) remark that these issues are sometimes "dramatised" as a "genetic Bhopal". These authors also state: "Regulatory arrangements may be weaker in LDC [less developed countries], more difficult to manage (more farmers and distributors) or more easily subverted, leading to lower standards for food safety and environmental protection" (ibid.: 1137).

China is – similar to other East Asian states – considered by some scholars to be a developmental state, which, rather than taking a *laissez-faire* free market approach, has strategically and actively managed the domestic market and promoted growth by effectively channelling national resources to its perceived priority areas. This means, however, that non-state actors have a much smaller scope to influence or reshape the priority agendas set by the government. For example, Diamond and Myers categorise China as an "authoritarian state, which rules out formal political opposition of any kind" (2000: 368).[7] With its large population but serious resource constraints, as well as a lack of systemic checks to state power, the central government can show a tendency to look for short-term ready (and sometimes drastic) solutions to imminent development problems ranging from energy supply to food security without first carefully balancing their potential longer-term benefits and risks.

Therefore, the question is whether China fits the description of what we term a "developmental risk society". This would imply a society where government and science are incapable of dealing with technological risks in the absence of an effective system of checks and balances, as well as in the face of large-scale "dilemmas of development".[8] When confronted with major development problems – such as food security versus population pressure; economic growth versus environmental degradation; and rural poverty versus agricultural modernisation – the government of a developmental risk society would be prone to sacrifice principles of sustainability and precaution for rapid development and economic growth. In a wider development context, transnational and domestic companies would – in pursuit of profit and their own interests – seek to avert, generate or spread risk, benefiting themselves at the expense of other social groups, increasing the latter's exposure and vulnerabilities to risks, disregarding the relevant government regulations, and the environmental and social impact. A case in point is the 2008 Chinese milk scandal in which the chemical melamine had been added to milk (including infant formula) so that it appeared protein-rich, leaving six infants dead, 860 babies hospitalised, and over 300,000 others affected. This food safety incident involved four leading Chinese diary companies, namely the Sanlu Group, Mengniu, Yili and Yashili.[9] Another food safety incident involving a multinational company occurred in 2003 when the Swiss company Nestlé's Nesquik milk powder was tested positive for GM material without proper labelling. The multinational was immediately accused by Chinese consumers of using "double standards" as the same product was labelled in the European market, but not in China, despite the Chinese government's regulations on GM labelling introduced a year before (Ho *et al.* 2006: 9).

However, despite these incidents, we will argue that China and its biotech sector do not entirely fit the features of a developmental risk society. Although China lacks a vibrant civil society and democratic polity, biotech politics reflect intricate dynamics of various countervailing forces in the society that balance the different – and often conflicting – interests of diverse social and political actors. The Chinese state plays a vital role in this. First, strong central government authority enables China to deflect and check, to some extent, the power of multinational and domestic corporations, thus enabling a stronger regulatory regime towards them. Second, the Chinese government's approach to biosafety is often in two minds, suggesting a certain degree of awareness, hesitation and precaution about the widespread use of agro-biotechnology, and the associated uncertainties and potential risks. For instance the government has vigorously promoted biotech development, while, at the same time, attempting to regulate more effectively the international and national flows of GMOs into the food chain and the environment, sometimes under pressure from domestic consumer groups, public opinion, and national and international non-governmental organisations (NGOs). This socio-political constellation allows China to confront the "new risks", albeit in a less consistent and coordinated manner. In this sense, China might be considered a quasi- or semi-developmental risk society.

In order to substantiate our argument, in the next three sections we review the role, risk perceptions, and vested interests of three groups of political and social actors involved in the politics of GMOs in China: the central state, the transnational biotech companies, and the NGOs and independent experts. The final section provides concluding observations and a prognosis for future biosafety governance in China.

The state

Wavering between public and private interests

At present, China is the sixth largest grower of GM crops in the world with cultivated areas reaching 4.2 million hectares, which is only less than the USA (70.1 million hectares), Brazil (40.3), Argentina (24.4), India (11.0) and Canada (10.8) (ISAAA 2013: 1). In addition, the national research budget for plant biotechnology has hugely expanded over the past two decades.[10] With one-fifth of the world's population living off less than half of the world's average per capita arable land, the Chinese state is certainly facing a number of pressures related to safeguarding the nation's food security, agricultural modernisation, and keeping up with increased international competition. For the reasons above, some international media have portrayed China's biotech sector as balancing on the brink of an ecological biotech disaster with the potential for an imminent environmental crisis related to, for instance, uncontrolled gene flow and biodiversity loss (Kirkby 2002: 1).

However, the situation is more complex than the critics would like us to believe. For instance, as a signatory to the United Nations Convention on Biological Diversity, China has played an active role in negotiating and drafting the Cartagena Biosafety Protocol (CBP).[11] In addition, China was also among 18 other countries that joined an international pilot project for the development of a National Biosafety Framework. The project, established by the

United Nations Environment Programme (UNEP) and funded by the Global Environment Facility, was meant to build and improve capacity on biosafety management in developing countries. This project has supported and stimulated China to establish a comprehensive regulatory framework that covers most relevant areas, including risk assessment, labelling, production, use, storage, import and export, and the release of GMOs into the environment. However, China has not yet included specific regulations for the implementation of the CBP's "Precautionary Principle" and the "Advance Informed Agreement", but a drafting group has been engaged in harmonising national laws and regulations with the CBP.[12]

When it comes to the choice of which GMOs should be allowed entry to the domestic market, Chinese central authorities have been wavering between considerations on the side of precaution versus the pressure of commercialisation.[13] Although some prominent Chinese scientists were pushing for the commercialisation of a wide variety of GMOs,[14] the government delayed the granting of permits for most of these to enter into the food chain for more than a decade.[15] By the turn of twenty-first century, Bt cotton (a non-food crop) accounted for the majority of commercially cultivated GM crops in the country (China Science and Technology Newsletter, hereafter CSTN 2002: 2). The turning point occurred in 2008, when the State Council announced the approval of a plan to use genetically modified crops as a major strategy to attain agricultural sustainability (Peters 2008). Since then, various vegetables and fruits have gone into legal commercial production, such as transgenic papaya, green pepper, tomato, and potato.

The case that perhaps best illustrates the Chinese central government's contradictory stance on the biotech issue is the development of Bt rice. As early as 2004 it was announced that China was about to approve GM rice for commercial production.[16] However, due to an incident involving the illegal cultivation and sale of Bt rice in Hubei Province (which was brought to light by Greenpeace in 2005), the biosafety approval of the crop was abruptly halted.[17] In early 2010, the Chinese Ministry of Agriculture (MOA) approved safety certificates for two types of paddy rice, which sparked heated debates during the subsequent session of the National People's Congress. The Deputy Director of the CCP Central Committee's Rural Work Leading Group, Chen Xiwen, commented on the Ministry's approval: "Before reaching the shelves, the products need to be certified by government agencies from the health and quality inspection sectors... Any of these agencies might stop the GM rice from entering the market" (cited in Shan and Wu 2010).

Today, more than a decade after its initial announcement, there are still no clear signs that the Chinese government is going to approve the market release of Bt rice any time soon (Shan and Zhu 2010). The Bt rice approval process is just one illustration[18] of the central government's difficult task of juggling the controversial issue of GM crops with regard to their benefits and risks.[19]

China's biotech governance

A critical and potentially destabilising factor in China's biotech governance is the fragmentation of authority, which results partly from the novelty of the issue and partly from the various readjustments to the central and local state bureaucracy that have taken place since the late 1990s. The novelty of biosafety and GMOs as political issues implies that newly created state institutions or newly accorded responsibilities need to be defended against older, established agencies with vested interests. On top of this, China has, during the recent decades, engaged in a major restructuring of the state's bureaucracy, which has affected two important institutions concerned with biosafety: the State Science and Technology Commission (SSTC) and the National Environmental Protection Agency (NEPA). During the restructuring in 1998, the SSTC was downgraded to the ministerial level and renamed the Ministry of Science and Technology (MOST) while NEPA was administratively elevated half a rank below the ministerial level and renamed the State Environmental Protection Agency (SEPA). Reflecting the increasing importance of environmental issues on the government's agenda, in 2008, SEPA was once again promoted to the current Ministry of Environmental Protection (MEP).

The state institution that was allegedly in charge of the nationwide control of biosafety is the MOST. In the early 1990s, a National GMO Biosafety Committee was established under MOST to be responsible for the supervision, administration and approval of activities related to biotechnology. For years, the most important national rules on biotechnology were the "1993 Safety Administration Regulations on Genetic Engineering" issued by the former SSTC (the predecessor of MOST).[20] In addition to MOST, there are four other state institutions with overlapping duties in the law-making, control and supervision of biosafety and GMOs:

1   MEP, and in particular its subordinate Department of Nature and Ecology Conservation;
2   MOA, and notably its Office for Security Management of Agricultural Genetically Modified Bioproducts and the Experts Committee on Agricultural Genetic Engineering Safety;
3   the Ministry of Health (MOH), and particularly its Centre of GMO Food Safety Evaluation and the State Human Genetic Resources Administration, jointly set up with MOST;
4   the State Administration for Entry-Exit Inspection and Quarantine.

Of these four institutions, MEP most likely plays a coordinating role in national biosafety control. Traditionally MEP was concerned with (agro) industrial pollution issues, but since the signing of the CBP in 2000, it has also been in charge of the conservation of biodiversity. Under the protocol, MEP is also the executory agency for the drafting of the National Biosafety

Framework, and the agency maintains that it will continue to build a national system for the inspection and technological support of biosafety in accordance with this framework. At the same time, the older (and more powerful) MOA is charged with biosafety control and the assessment of agricultural GM products and crops.[21] Although the MOH has left most biosafety concerns to the MOA, this Ministry is also active in the testing, approval, labelling and industrial standards setting for new foods. In fact, the MOH is in the midst of drafting new GMO Food Safety Regulations, and therefore its role overlaps with MOA in some areas.

At present, it is unclear how the different responsibilities of the various ministries and state departments relate to each other with regard to biosafety. Canfa Wang, a member of the NPC drafting group for new comprehensive legislation on biosafety, stated:

> There is no ministry that has systematically stipulated comprehensive rules on biosafety and its administration from the national perspective. As a result, there is no coordinated and uniform administration ... which has already influenced China's management of biosafety, and the coordination of biosafety administration with the international community.
>
> (Interview by Peter Ho, Beijing, 23 November 2003)

After an initial period during which it appeared that the Chinese state – typical of a developmental risk society – would trade biosafety concerns for a rapid development of the biotech sector, a set of substantially more stringent rules came into place. In 2002, China approved new regulations on the production and use of GM products. Under these rules, Chinese-foreign joint ventures and foreign-owned companies should seek government approval to research or test GMOs, while traders of GM seeds, seedlings or animals need official permits. Furthermore, the rules also stipulate that 17 different species of agricultural GM products divided into five classes in the MOA's Identification Catalogue must be labelled before being put on sale on the domestic market. This is different from, for example, the European Union, Japan or Switzerland, where labelling is compulsory above a certain percentage threshold of transgenic material.[22] Also, for GM products that are already available in stores, labelling is required (CSTN 2002: 3). No major regulations have been promulgated since 2002, though a new Biosafety Law (*shengwu anquan fa*) is in the making.

Promulgating laws and regulations are one thing, but their effective and efficient implementation is quite another. A clear illustration of the problems with the enforcement of biosafety regulations can be seen in the issue of labelling. Various studies have found that the majority of GM products on sale in the Chinese market have limited labelling (e.g. small print, difficult to read), or no labelling at all (Ho et al. 2006; Shan 2010). To strengthen biosafety enforcement, the coordination and integration of policies between MOST, MEP, MOA, MOH and the State Administration for Entry-Exit Inspection and Quarantine will prove essential. However, whether Chinese society might or might not develop into a developmental risk society not only hinges on how the central state balances conflicting interests of environmental protection, food security, and biotech development, but also depends on the input from, influence of and interaction with a range of corporative, social and civic actors, including, e.g., NGOs and independent experts, and companies, particularly transnational corporations.

Biotech companies

US-based Monsanto is by far the most important transnational player in GM crops – both internationally and in the Chinese market.[23] The two main products that Monsanto attempts to market in China include GM soybean known as Roundup Ready® soybeans, and Bt cotton sold under the name BollGard® cotton. Roundup Ready soybeans contain an enzyme capable of neutralising glyphosphate, an active ingredient in herbicide. This gives it a comparative advantage over non-resistant weeds. BollGard cotton has been modified with genes from *Bacillis thuringiensis*, and therefore produces biotoxins that kill its main pest – the bollworm. Monsanto claims its GM crops are environmentally friendly, cost- and labour-efficient, and help guarantee food security. In their words:

> Why are farmers adopting biotech crops at a rate that some compare to the rate at which tractors replaced horses during the early 20th century? The reasons are simple: With no change in safety or quality of the harvested products, these crops are easier and cheaper to grow than their counterparts without herbicide or insect resistance. In addition, the environmental bonuses represent, arguably, the greatest benefits to resource conservation and environmental quality of any technology introduced since the beginning of agriculture.
>
> (James R. Cook, quoted in Monsanto 2002: 1)

Monsanto's rationale for entering the Chinese market is obvious – China is one of the world's largest producers of both cotton and soybeans.[24] The research and development of Bt cotton are one of the world's largest undertakings in the commercial production of GM cotton to date. In the early 1980s, the Institute of Biotechnology of the Chinese Academy of Agricultural Sciences (CAAS) and Monsanto independently engaged in research on bollworm-resistant cotton. This resulted in two types of Bt cotton: Monsanto's BollGard cotton and the Chinese variant of Bt cotton developed by the Institute of Biotechnology of CAAS. Chinese authorities allowed commercial use of the two Bt cotton types in 1997, after the domestic cotton harvest was badly affected by pests while field experiments with Bt cotton proved successful (He 2000: 1).

China's major cotton-producing regions (which are prone to the bollworm pest damage) are located along the fluvial plains of the Yellow and Yangtze rivers, stretching from the state farms of Xinjiang in the northwest to the coastal provinces of Shandong and Zhejiang in the east and southeast. Since Monsanto obtained a licence for commercial sale of BollGard cottonseeds, it made considerable investment in promoting the product in China. Initially this effort led to the rapid increase of its market share in the country: from 1996 to 2000 the total cotton-growing area using Monsanto's Bt cotton rose from zero to 65.9 per cent. In addition, by collaborating with local seed companies, Monsanto took the lion's share of the market in Hebei Province. Monsanto and the Chinese Delta and Pine Land Company established a joint venture with the Hebei Provincial Seed Company to sell its Bt cottonseeds (He 2000: 2). Although Monsanto's application to Hubei Province was rejected, it did receive approval to sell its Bt cottonseeds in Shandong Province (Smith 2000). In the past few years, however, Monsanto's initial domination of the Chinese cottonseed market has significantly declined as domestically developed Bt cottonseeds, and hybrid seed varieties have started entering the market and taking growing market shares (Ho et al. 2009).

The operations of transnational biotech companies in China are confined within the boundaries set by the central state. Unlike most industrialised nations where biotech research is privately financed, the Chinese government funds almost all plant biotech research.[25] In their attempt to govern the biotech arena, the Chinese authorities have not shown any fear at the prospect of a trade war with one of their largest trading partners – the USA. The decision of the MOA to proclaim new biosafety rules in 2002[26] caused concern in the USA, which produces 70 per cent of the world's GMOs, including GM soybeans. Confusion over the upcoming rules brought new orders of US soybeans to a virtual halt – 70 per cent of which are bio-engineered – as Chinese buyers worried cargoes might not be approved. Half a year before the regulations' official proclamation, the USA and China reached a formal agreement over GM products, and soybean sales resumed.[27] Today China is the largest global export market for GM soybeans,[28] and exports from the USA amounted to over 19 million metric tonnes (or 63 per cent of total exports) during the period from 2009–2010 (US Export Statistics 2010).

At the time of the USA–China trade war over GM soybeans, John Killmer, Monsanto's Greater China president, was frustrated by the Chinese government's stance on biotech development, which he considered contradictory:

> China has imposed the most restrictive regulations on the production, research and importation of GMO crops in the world. The ban is specifically designed to shut foreign companies out of the world's largest government-funded biotechnology-development programmes. They have one foot on the accelerator, which is funding biotech research and development, and they have the other foot on the regulatory brake.
>
> (cited in Kyne 2002: 1)

As we have already seen above, the central government's motives for stepping up control over biosafety are not driven by environmental concerns alone. Weirong Wang, a researcher at Fudan Xinyang Biotech, commented on the new rules: "Most GM-related products in China are currently made from imported material ... The regulation is thus likely to form trade barriers to foreign competition" (Wang, cited in Jia 2003: 836). In fact, one of the underlying reasons for the Chinese leadership to allow the presence of transnational biotech companies might be to facilitate field trial experiences and gain expertise through technology transfer – being, at times, even suspected of involving pirating (Ho *et al.* 2009: 356). Yet, whatever the central state's motives, it is clear that the authorities would not allow the monopolisation of the market by either transnational or domestic corporations, and have taken every measure to govern and, where necessary, curb corporate power.

Chinese civil society and academia

The complexity of biotech politics in shaping China's stance on risk management is also visible in the public debate. At present, Chinese NGOs are relatively weak and incapable of providing sufficient countervailing power against the proponents of biotechnology (state or business actors). At the same time, however, as Chinese politics has gradually opened up to pressure groups and public participation, the environmental arena has sprung up as one of the most active sectors in civil society. That being said, green NGOs still face many political and institutional constraints, and their impact on society and polity has been limited (Ho 2001; Ho and Edmonds 2008; Wu 2002). In a survey of 10,495 households conducted by MEP between 1998 and 1999, only 4 per cent of the respondents believed that environmental protection should be enhanced through increasing the role played by green NGOs, while almost 57 per cent opted for other measures such as strengthening environmental education, environmental laws and regulations, and increasing investments in environmental protection (SEPA 1999: 22, 29).[29] Another survey found that less than 3 per cent of 1,000 respondents had heard of GM food through environmental NGOs.[30] Most significantly, there are few domestic NGOs that have made biotechnology their key activity in China.[31]

Many commentators worry that the lack of civic actors in the area in large developing countries like China and India would lead to low awareness and the neglect of the environmental and socio-economic risks associated with biotechnology. The *New York Times* reported on the situation in China:

> Enthusiasm for the new science abounds. There is no public debate to stir up the opposition that has brought the development of genetically modified crops to a near standstill in India ... Though with no independent news coverage ... consumers are unaware that they are eating modified food, in any case.
>
> (Smith 2000: 1)

Although there is a kernel of truth in such reports, we cannot assume that biotech risks in China "are underestimated, compared out of existence or made anonymous causally and legally" as Beck predicted would happen in the risk society (Beck 1992b: 105). In fact, unknown to most foreign – and probably also domestic – observers, the Chinese authorities have actually tried to provoke a societal debate on biosafety by inviting scientists or others in positions of authority on the subject to write articles in leading newspapers. The first scientist who was invited for a critical contribution on the safety of GM crops in China was Keqiang Mang, professor at the Institute of Microbiology of the Chinese Academy of Sciences (CAS) (pers. comm. with Peter Ho, 3 November 2002). The high priority that had been accorded to this issue was illustrated by its publication as early as 1996 in China's main official newspaper: the *People's Daily*. Professor Mang warned that "once agricultural transgenic plants and microorganisms are released and spread into the environment, they might be difficult to control" and hoped that the "involvement of other concerned experts in the discussion would bring these questions to the attention of governmental policy-makers and the administrative departments in charge of research funds" (Mang 1996). However, the government's attempt to start a national debate on biosafety did not succeed at the time.

Such a debate, to a certain extent, was stimulated later by Greenpeace, an influential transnational environmental NGO. In 2002, Greenpeace (probably with the tacit support of the Chinese government) helped publish a report on the Chinese experiences in the Bt cotton cultivation. The report, written by Dayuan Xue, the then deputy chief of the Biosafety Management Office of SEPA, focused on the environmental impact of Bt cotton (Xue 2002). The study was based on a scientific review of Chinese research conducted by four academic institutes: the National Institute of Plant Protection and the Cotton Research Institute in Anyang, Henan Province (both associated with the CAAS); the Department of Plant Protection of China Agricultural University; and the Department of Plant Protection of Nanjing Agricultural University.

In his report, Xue drew several important conclusions. First, "although in the Chinese studies there are no significant impacts on predatory pests associated with Bt cotton, there are associated adverse impacts on the parasitic pest of cotton, i.e. bollworm". Second, "Bt cotton is ineffective in controlling many secondary pests, especially sucking pests … such as cotton aphids, cotton spider mites, and thrips". Third, "cotton bollworm can develop resistance to Bt cotton". Actually, laboratory tests indicated that "susceptibility of bollworm to Bt cotton fell to 30 per cent after 17 generations" while the resistance index "increased 1,000 times when the selection continued to the 40th generation". Fourth, "farmers must use pesticide 2–3 times more than the normal amount to control bollworm, particularly from mid-July to the end of August" because "the resistance of Bt cotton to bollworm decreases over time, and control is incomplete in the third and fourth generations". In other words, the cultivation of Bt cotton results in an increased, rather than decreased pesticide use as claimed by Monsanto (Xue 2002: 3; Zhao et al. 2011). As there are no effective measures to resolve the resistance problem, Xue argues that Bt cotton had been released into the environment prematurely.

Immediately after publication, the report came under heavy attack. According to Monsanto's scientific director Eric Sachs, the Greenpeace report was "misleading and flawed". He added that: "There is no evidence of resistance to Bt crops ... and while this purports to be a review of the relevant information, it doesn't present all information available, even that which contradicts it" (Sachs, quoted in Reuters 2002). The report was also fiercely criticised by two prominent scientists at the CAAS, Shirong Jia and Yufa Peng, who wrote: "The context of many research data is garbled in accordance with the author's own interest and will." They added that "the greatest environmental impact of Bt cotton was its benefit to the environment that was a significant reduction (70–80 per cent) of the chemical pesticide use" while "risks to beneficial insects and the environment are negligible" (United Nations Industrial Development Organisation Biosafety Information Network and Advisory Service, 2002: 1–2, hereafter UNIDO-BINAS). However, the question of whether Xue's argument regarding the longer-term benefit and cost of Bt cotton in the Greenpeace report was valid or not is of secondary importance to the fact that a Chinese debate on the risks of GMOs – albeit confined to scholarly and commercial circles – has been initiated through the action of an international NGO.

Conclusion: the future dynamics of biotech politics

Over the past decade, China has embarked on nothing less than a biotech "Great Leap Forward". With an area of approximately 4.2 million hectares devoted to GM crops, China became the sixth largest cultivator in the world in 2013. Some China observers fear that China's relatively weak civil society and independent media, combined with a conventional top-down governance style, might lead to the hasty adoption of GM technologies with scant regard for environmental risks and their socio-economic impact.

Partly drawing on social theories of risk and the risk society, this chapter examines the question of whether the particular constellation of the Chinese polity and society does indeed constitute a developmental risk society, construed as a society in which government and science are incapable of dealing with the new technological risks in the absence of an effective system of checks and balances, and in the face of the mounting challenges and dilemmas of development. Through a deep analysis of the main social actors involved in China's biotech politics – the state, domestic and transnational biotech corporations, and NGOs and academics – we conclude that the answer to this question is much more complex and dynamic. The type of governance that the Chinese state has adopted in the sector is characterised by a relatively strict regulation and management of biotech risk and concern over biosafety. Different from many other developing nations, China has been proactive in drafting and promulgating rules for the national, as well as international control of GMOs. China signed the CBP, and proclaimed a comprehensive and stringent set of regulations on the risk assessment, labelling, research and environmental release of GMOs. In addition, even though certain GM foods, such as potato, papaya, tomato and green pepper, have been allowed for commercial production, the only GM crop that has been commercially cultivated on a large scale is a non-food crop: Bt cotton. Some would argue that this points to the government's caution in allowing GMOs to enter the food chain.

On the other hand, even if the main implementation of agricultural biotechnology to date has been primarily limited to non-food crops, this does not exclude the possibility that food products might soon gain official approval for commercial release. Substantial investments have been made in the research and development of transgenic varieties of major staple crops, such as wheat, potato and, most notably, rice. Sooner or later the domestic and transnational biotech companies would want to see the returns on these investments. Furthermore, the regulations on labelling and risk assessment have generally been ineffectively implemented. As a consequence, large quantities of non-traceable and unregulated GM material may have entered China's food and meat processing industries, suggesting an ambiguous stance taken by the Chinese state on biosafety issues. For one thing, the underlying motives that determine the type of biotech governance adopted by the central leadership are clearly not only related to environmental concerns alone. In the biotech arena, the Chinese state is facing various developmental pressures, such as securing food for its huge and ever-growing population, agricultural modernisation without harming small-scale subsistence farmers as the current mainstay of rural society, and keeping up with international competition. Internationally, the USA is the largest producer and exporter of GMOs. To shield its own emerging biotech sector against international competition, the Chinese government's responses have been marked by intensive investment in research and protection of the domestic market, as any state would do to protect national interests.

Adding to the complexity of Chinese biotech politics are the relatively weak countervailing forces represented by civil society actors. However, the alarmist reports by Western media of a complete neglect of the risks of the new technologies fail to identify the many positive developments with respect to biosafety and cautious measures against risks in China. As early as 1996, years before the public debates took off in selected member states of the EU, the Chinese government made an attempt to initiate a public discussion over GMOs. A prominent researcher of the CAS was invited to write and publish articles about biotech risks in the People's Daily. However, a wider public debate failed to follow at the time. The debate that did take off in 2002 caused the controversy over Monsanto's Bt cotton. The publication of a Greenpeace report written by a leading Chinese scientist criticised the promotion and premature commercial production of the crop by Monsanto though the associated potential deficiencies and risks were not made public. Nevertheless this stimulated a heated debate in commercial and academic circles in China.

The chapter identifies three prominent features relating to the biotech politics in China. First, the central state has been, in recent decades and to a great extent, committed to stimulating societal debates over GMOs with reference to their risks as well as benefits, and will remain influential in balancing the diverse and often conflicting interests over the development and adoption of biotechnology. Second, even though the discussion over environmental effects is important in its own right, in the Chinese debate, many other dimensions of the issue have been left unsaid, in particular, the socio-economic impact of GMOs on the rural populace. Third, although the role played by domestic NGOs in the biotech arena is relatively small, public discussions over the risks of GMOs have been stimulated through the active participation of international NGOs. In spite of the apparent indifference of the Chinese public to issues of biosafety, as shown in the several surveys discussed in this chapter, this is clearly a new field to be explored by domestic NGOs in the near future as the public awareness of the risks increases. The 2002 survey of 1,000 urban residents mentioned earlier in this chapter came up with a few remarkable findings, such as the fact that 87 per cent of the respondents found that food producers and supermarkets were obliged to provide consumers with the information on which foods contain transgenic material, and 83 per cent of respondents deemed a labelling system necessary for this purpose (Green Community Research Centre 2002: 2).

We argue that though China today may not be deemed a developmental risk society, there are potentially dangerous counter-currents both presently and in the longer run, such as the fragmentation of state authority over regulating and managing GMO-related risks and securing biosafety, the inertia of domestic civic groups in considering biotechnology an issue for public awareness and debate, the pressures and lobbying by powerful domestic and international biotech companies due to various motivations and vested interests, and the lack of involvement and absence of voice of small landholding Chinese farmers in the debate. In this sense, we might see China as a semi-developmental risk society. What is certain, however, is that how China will deal with biosafety and its related risks will have a crucial impact on the future dynamics of biotech politics both within the country and globally.

Acknowledgements

This chapter is based on a substantially revised and updated version of a paper that was originally published in the *International Journal of Environment and Sustainable Development* 4(4) (2005): 370–394.

Notes

1 For an extensive review of the literature on this topic, see Azadi and Ho (2010).
2 It should be noted that Brown has been heavily criticised by scholars for neglecting the role of agricultural intensification, and making no specifications for the quality of land resources in his analysis. In addition, some surveys of the arable land area have shown that there has been significant under-reporting in the land statistics (up to 25 per cent) (Wu and Kirke 1994).

3 Furthermore, the rapid urbanisation and structural changes in the agricultural sector have led to a considerable loss of arable land.

4 See also Green Community Research Centre 2002.

5 For more discussion of Beck's risk society thesis, see Barry (1999) and Cohen (2000).

6 As Brent Marshall wrote: "The explanatory power of the risk society is strongest when applied to 'welfare states' where the material needs of most of its citizens are met via wealth redistribution through taxation and social security" (1999: 267).

7 Yet, on the other hand, ample studies have examined and described the various arenas in which modest political reforms are taking place in China, e.g. the village elections since the mid-1980s; the growing power of the national and provincial People's Congresses; and the nation's first experiment with democratic elections at the township level since 1949. See, for example, Li (2002).

8 This is different from Beck's conception of the Western risk society where the redistribution of wealth, around which social cleavages and class distinction centre, is considered to be replaced by an equal exposure to the new risks regardless of the traditional social differentiations. In fact, though social divisions and cleavage related to unequal distribution of wealth still feature prominently in developing nations (as well as in post-industrial societies), this does not preclude the emergence of the new risks.

9 This was not the first time that a milk-related scandal had occurred in China. In a separate incident in 2004, watered-down milk had resulted in 13 infant deaths from malnutrition, mainly in Anhui Province (Buckley 2008).

10 Over the period from 1986 to 1999 the budget increased 14 times from US$8 million to US$112 million. China already accounts for more than half of the developing world's expenditures on developing plant biotechnology. In 2001, Chinese officials announced plans to raise the research budget by 400 per cent before 2005, which implied that China would account for nearly one-third of the world's public spending on plant biotechnology (Huang et al. 2002: 675).

11 The CBP developed from the Convention on Biological Diversity of the United Nations Conference on Environment and Development held in 1992 in Rio de Janeiro. In 2000, China signed (but has still not ratified) the CBP, joining another 71 signatories (Stilwell and Van Dyke 1999).

12 The "Precautionary Principle" states that in the absence of scientific evidence or certainty on risks, decision-makers should be free to refrain from granting approval for the use and production of GMOs and products made with GM materials. The requirement of the "Advance Informed Agreement" for export is to prevent developing countries from becoming dumping grounds for GMOs. The nation receiving GMOs or products made with GM materials must be notified by the exporting party in written communication, while export can only proceed when approval from the receiving country has been given (Meyer 2000).

13 China has also firmly opposed any experiments in the area of human cloning. This was expressed by the national delegate to the UN ad hoc Meeting for the International Convention against Reproductive Cloning of Human Beings (Chen 2002: 1).

14 The varieties developed and pushed for commercialisation were many, including rice, wheat, Chinese cabbage, cauliflower, carp, pig and sheep (Wang 1999: 7).

15 Until 2000, permission had only been granted for two varieties of GM tomatoes and green pepper, but these crops did not go into commercial production at that time because of concerns over domestic food safety regulations on the part of investors (Qing and Wade 2000: 2).

16 See the report by Newsweek (Science and Technology 2004).

17 It is estimated that between 950 and 1,200 tonnes of Bt rice had illegally entered the food chain in 2004. In April 2005, Greenpeace China found that unapproved Bt rice was being sold and grown illegally in Hubei Province (Greenpeace 2005).

18 Another case concerns GM tobacco. GM tobacco was commercially grown in China between 1993 and 1998. According to the ISAAA, the area growing GM tobacco

was more than one million hectares (accounting for 60 per cent of the total tobacco-growing area in 1996 and 1997. However, in 1998, the cultivation of GM tobacco was suddenly halted in anticipation of stricter regulations on biosafety proclaimed by the MOA in 2002 (ISAAA 1997; Greenpeace 2002).

19 Not only environmental, but also trade concerns with regard to the impact that GM rice might have on Chinese exports have been driving the government to make this balancing act.

20 The regulations also stipulate that "the SSTC is responsible for the nationwide genetic engineering safety work" (SSTC 1993).

21 By the end of 2001, the MOA had received over 700 applications for security-oriented assessment of agricultural GM products from 52 domestic and 4 foreign biotech companies (CSTN 2002: 2).

22 For the EU, this is 0.9 per cent, Australia, 1 per cent, Brazil, 4 per cent, Japan, 5 per cent and Switzerland, 5 per cent (Jia 2003: 835).

23 Worldwide, three large transnational corporations – Monsanto, Syngenta and Aventis CropScience (acquired by Bayer), have monopolised the market (accounting for almost all the GM crops that are commercially grown. Of these three, Monsanto products alone accounted for 91 per cent of the total cultivated area for GMOs (Greenpeace 2002: 1).

24 In 1998, when Monsanto started commercial operations in China, the country ranked first in cotton output with an annual production of over 4.5 million tonnes, and ranked fourth in soybean output with more than 15 million tonnes (He 2000: 1).

25 In 1998, 50 per cent of the total expenditure of 461 billion yuan on R&D in natural sciences and technology came from the government (National Bureau of Statistics of China, hereafter NBSC 1999: 678). It was estimated that in the periods before 1995 and between 1995 and 1999, private investments in biotechnology only accounted for 5 per cent and 10 per cent respectively (Huang *et al.* 2002: 675). Today, the situation is not much different, though private investments have gradually grown.

26 These are: (1) the "Methods on Security Evaluation and Management of Genetically Modified Agriculture Bioproducts"; (2) the "Methods on Security Management of Imported Genetically Modified Agriculture Bioproducts"; and (3) the "Methods on Identification Management of Genetically Modified Agriculture Bioproducts" (CSTN 2002: 3).

27 On 11 March 2002, China extended its trade agreement with the USA on GM soybeans until April 2004. At the time, the issue even caught the attention of US president George W. Bush, who discussed the problem with Chinese leaders during a meeting in October 2001 in Shanghai (American Soybean Association 2001).

28 A large proportion of the soybeans are used for oil extraction. Soybean seed contains about 19 per cent oil. To extract soybean oil from seed, the soybeans are cracked, adjusted for moisture content, rolled into flakes and solvent-extracted with commercial hexane.

29 The survey was conducted between July 1998 and July 1999 in all provinces of China. The response rate was 87.7 per cent. Of the remaining 43 per cent, 13.6 per cent opted for better law enforcement; 10.6 per cent for public participation in environmental protection; 9.7 per cent for monitoring and control of enterprises in the area of pollution; and 5.4 per cent for innovation in environmental technologies. When asked to rank who had the greatest responsibility for environmental protection, NGOs came last with the central and local governments in first and second places, companies in the third, and the individual in the fourth (SEPA 1999).

30 Some 37.2 per cent had heard about GM food through the media, 12.8 per cent through friends, 12.3 per cent through books and articles, 2.8 per cent through school, 2 per cent through the government and 1.5 per cent through companies (Green Community Research Centre 2002).

31 To date, only Greenpeace has actively taken up the issue of GM crops in China. However, it has faced constraints on its activities. For instance, in 1995 their office was closed down because of an incident in August of that year when public security personnel arrested six foreign Greenpeace demonstrators, detained them for one day, and expelled them from China for unfurling an antinuclear banner in Tiananmen Square. The office was not reopened until spring 2002.

References

American Soybean Association (2001), ASA confident U.S. soy shipments to China will now resume, October 23. Available from: www.soygrowers.com/newsroom/releases/2001%20releases/r102301.htm (accessed 3 March 2011).

Azadi, Hossein and Peter Ho (2010), Genetically modified and organic crops in developing countries: A review of options for food security. *Biotechnology Advances* 128: 160–186.

Barry, John (1999), *Environment and Social Theory*. London: Routledge.

Beck, Ulrich (1992a), *Risk Society: Towards a New Modernity*. London: Sage Publications.

Beck, Ulrich (1992b), From industrial society to the risk society: Questions of survival, social structure and ecological enlightenment. *Theory, Culture and Society* 9(1): 97–123.

Beck, Ulrich, Anthony Giddens and Scott Lash (1994), *Reflexive Modernization: Politics, Tradition and Aesthetics in the Modern Social Order*. Stanford, CA: Stanford University Press.

Brown, Lester R. (1995), *Who Will Feed China?: Wake-Up Call for a Small Planet*. New York: Norton.

Buckley, Chris (2008), Second infant death in China milk scandal, Reuters, 16 September. Available at: www.asiaone.com/Health/News/Story/A1Story20080916-88026.html (accessed 3 March 2011).

Chen, Xu (2002), Statement by the Representative of the People's Republic of China Mr. Chen Xu at the Ad Hoc Committee on the Convention Against the Reproductive Cloning of Human Beings. Available at: www.china-un.org/eng/xw/t27710.htm (accessed 29 July 2014).

Chern, Wen S. and Kyrre Rickertsen (2002), Consumer acceptance of GMO: Survey results from Japan, Norway, Taiwan and the United States. Working Paper of the Department of Agricultural, Environmental and Development Economics, AEDE-WP-0026-02. Ohio: Ohio State University.

Cho, Young Nam (2002), From "rubber stamps" to "iron stamps": The emergence of Chinese local People's Congresses as supervisory powerhouses. *The China Quarterly* 171: 724–740.

Cohen, Maurie J. (ed.) (2000), *Risk in the Modern Age: Social Theory, Science and Environmental Decision-Making*. London: Macmillan.

CSTN (2002), *The Ministry of Science and Technology, People's Republic of China* no. 287, 28 February.

Diamond, Larry and Ramon H. Myers (2000), Elections and democracy in China. *The China Quarterly* 162: 365–386.

Erikson, Kai (1994), *A New Species of Trouble: Explorations in Disaster, Trauma and Community*. New York: W.W. Norton and Company.

Green Community Research Center (2002), *Guangzhou shimin zhuanjiyin anquan yishi diaochao fenxi baogao* [Research report on awareness of transgenic safety by Guangzhou citizens]. Guangzhou: Zhongshan University and Greenpeace.

Greenpeace (2002), GE crops – increasingly isolated as awareness and rejection grow. *International Genetic Engineering Campaign: Background Information 03/02*.

Berlin: Greenpeace. Available at: www.greenpeace.org/international/en/publications/reports/ge-crops-increasingly-isolat/ (accessed 12 January 2011).

Greenpeace (2005), Illegal GE rice contaminates food chain in China. *Greenpeace Press Release*, 13 April. Available at: www.greenpeace.org/international/en/press/releases/illegal-ge-rice-contaminates-f-2/ (accessed 12 January 2011).

He, Sheng (2000), GMO research stirs hot debate. *China Daily*, 25 September. Available from: www.biotech-info.net/hot_debate.html (accessed 9 January 2011).

Ho, Peter (2001), Greening without conflict? Environmentalism, NGOs and civil society in China. *Development and Change* 32(5): 893–921.

Ho, Peter (ed.) (2009), *Developmental Dilemmas*, 2nd edn. New York: Routledge.

Ho, Peter and Richard L. Edmonds (eds) (2008), *China's Embedded Activism: Limitations and Constraints of a Social Movement*. New York: Routledge.

Ho, Peter, Eduard B. Vermeer and Jennifer H. Zhao (2006), Biotech and food safety in China: Consumers' acceptance or resistance? *Development and Change* 37(1): 227–253.

Ho, Peter, Jennifer H. Zhao and Dayuan Xue (2009), Rethinking agro-biotech innovations in emerging economies: The case of Bt cotton in China. *Journal of Peasant Studies* 36(3): 345–364.

Huang, Jikun, Scott Rozelle, Carl Pray and Qinfang Wang (2002), Plant biotechnology in China. *Science* 295: 674–677.

ISAAA (1997), Global status of transgenic crops in 1997. *ISAAA Briefs* 5. Available at: www.isaaa.org/resources/publications/briefs/default.asp (accessed 11 January 2011).

ISAAA (2006), Global status of commercialized biotech/GM crops: 2006. *ISAAA Briefs* 35. Available at: www.isaaa.org/resources/publications/briefs/default.asp (accessed 14 February 2011).

ISAAA (2013), Global status of commercialized biotech/GM crops: 2013. *Executive Summary ISAAA Brief* 46. Available at: www.isaaa.org/resources/publications/briefs/46/executivesummary/default.asp (accessed 10 December 2014).

Jia, Hepeng (2003), GM labeling in China beset by problems. *Nature Biotechnology* 21(8): 835–836.

Kirkby, Alex (2002), GM crops find friends in China. *BBC News: Science and Technology*, 24 January. Available at: http://news.bbc.co.uk/1/hi/sci/tech/1778132.stm (accessed 2 July 2002).

Kydd, Jonathan, Janet Haddock, John Mansfield, Charles Ainsworth and Allan Buckwell (2000), Genetically modified organisms: Major issues and policy responses for developing countries. *Journal of International Development* 12: 1133–1145.

Kyne, Phelim (2002), China's ban on biotech investors may violate WTO obligations. *Dow Jones News Wires*. Available from: www.djnewswires.com (accessed 13 May 2002).

Li, Lianjiang (2002), The politics of introducing direct township elections in China. *The China Quarterly* 171: 704–723.

Macer, Darryl and Mary Ann Chen Ng (2000), Changing attitudes to biotechnology in Japan. *Nature Biotechnology* 18(9): 945–947.

Mang, Keqiang (1996), The safety issue of transgenic plants, Parts I and II. *People's Daily*, 13 June, p. 12; 20 June, p. 11.

Marshall, Brent K. (1999), Globalisation, environmental degradation and Ulrich Beck's risk society. *Environmental Values* 8: 253–275.

Meyer, Hartmut (2000), The Cartagena protocol on biosafety. *Biotechnology and Development Monitor* 43: 2–7.

Monsanto (2002), Spokane, spokesman review: Biotechnology has been great for farmers, environment. Available at: www.monsantopakistan.com/news (accessed 19 March 2002).

NBSC (1999), *China Statistical Yearbook 1999*. Beijing: China Statistical Press.

Peters, Meghan (2008), Green light for plan to boost GM crops. *China Daily*, 11 July. Available at: www.chinadaily.com.cn/language_tips/cdaudio/2008-07/11/content_6838501.htm (accessed 6 July 2009).

Qing, Xiang and John Wade (2000), China: Trade policy monitoring – current status of Chinese GMO development and regulation 2000. *USDA, Foreign Agricultural Service*. Beijing: Global Agriculture Information Network.

Reuters (2002), China GMO cotton bad for environment – Greenpeace. Available at: www.planetark.org/dailynewsstory.cfm/newsid/16251/story.htm (accessed 4 June 2002).

Science and Technology (2004), Coming soon to China: brave new rice. *Newsweek*, December 20, pp. 37–38.

SEPA (1999), *Quanguo gongzhong huanjing yishi diaocha baogao* [Research report on public environmental awareness in China]. Beijing: Zhongguo huanjing kexue chubanshe.

Shan, Juan (2010), Shelves stacked with GM foods. *China Daily*, 12 February. Available at: www.chinadaily.com.cn/china/2010-02/12/content_9465789.htm (accessed 27 February 2010).

Shan, Juan and Jiao Wu (2010), GM grain still long distance away. *China Daily*, 11 March. Available at: www.chinadaily.com.cn/china/2010npc/2010-03/11/content_9570242.htm (accessed 12 March 2010).

Shan, Juan and Jin Zhu (2010), China turns to GM rice for food supply. *China Daily*, 4 February 2010. Available at: www.chinadaily.com.cn/china/2010-02/04/content_9424300_2.htm (accessed 12 March 2010).

Smith, Craig S. (2000), China rushes to adopt genetically modified crops. *New York Times*, 7 October, p. 5.

SSTC (1993), Safety administration regulation on genetic engineering. *Order of the State Science and Technology, Commission of the People's Republic of China* 17, December 24. Available at: http://faolex.fao.org/docs/texts/chn19138.doc (accessed 3 March 2011).

Stilwell, Matthew and Brennan Van Dyke (1999), *An Activist's Handbook on Genetically Modified Organisms and the WTO*. Washington, DC: Center for International Environmental Law.

UNIDO-BINAS (2002), Chinese scientists criticize Greenpeace Bt report. Available at: www.binas.unido.org/binas/news/2002-07_2.html (accessed 2 July 2002).

US Export Statistics (2010), United States Census Bureau. Available at: www.census.gov/foreign-trade/ (paid subscription).

Wang, G.Y. (1999), *Zhongguo nongye shengwu jishu yanjiu jiqi anquanxing pingjia* [Research on agro-biotechnology and an evaluation of its biosafety]. In D.Y. Xue and I. Virgin (eds), *Shengwu anquan guanli yu shijian* [Regulation and practice of biosafety]. Beijing: China Environmental Science Press, pp. 6–8.

Wu, Fengshi (2002), New partners or old brothers? GONGOs in transnational environmental advocacy in China. *China Environment Series* 5: 45–58. Available at: www.wilsoncenter.org/topics/pubs/ACF3C9.pdf (accessed 12 January 2011).

Wu, Ziping and Alan W. Kirke (1994), An assessment of some key Chinese agricultural statistics, *China Information* 9(1): 42–76.

Xue, Dayuan (2002), *A Summary of Research on the Impact of Bt Cotton in China*. The Hague: Greenpeace.

Zhang, Qifa (2000), China: Agricultural biotechnology opportunities to meet the challenges of food production. In G. J. Persley and M. M. Lantin (eds), *Agricultural Biotechnology and the Poor*. Washington, DC: World Bank CGIAR, pp. 45–50.

Zhao, Jennifer H. (2002), Eating GMOs with chopsticks? Risks of biotechnology in China. *International Institute for Asian Studies Newsletter*, 29 (November): 30.

Zhao, Jennifer H., Peter Ho and Hossein Azadi (2011), Benefits of Bt cotton counterbalanced by secondary pests? Perceptions of ecological change in China. *Environmental Monitoring and Assessment*, 173(4): 985–94.

7 Small cotton farmers, livelihood diversification and policy interventions in Southern Xinjiang

Max Spoor, Xiaoping Shi and Chunling Pu

Introduction

This chapter investigates the recent changes in livelihood strategies of small cotton farmers in the Xinjiang Uyghur Autonomous Region (XUAR) in north-western China. As pointed out in Chapter 6 of this book, Xinjiang is a large producer of cotton, which has been grown as a near mono-culture for a long time, especially in the southwestern parts of the region. Of the Chinese provinces[1] Xinjiang is the largest cotton producer, followed by Shandong and Hebei. The crop is produced by Uyghur minority farmers on tiny farms and by large-scale Han-Chinese populated state or "regiment" farms (*bingtuan*), which are part of the Xinjiang Production and Construction Corps (XPCC).

Increasing resource constraints (in particular land and water) in Xinjiang are leading to difficulties that are forcing small farmers to look for strategies to diversify their livelihoods. National government policies changed in the 2000s, from issuing direct "instructions" on what to grow and to whom to sell the output, to more indirect policy instruments that stimulate changes in crop mix. However, farming households are now more affected by market price fluctuations, especially for cotton, and in a context where non-farm employment opportunities are sparse (e.g. fewer members of the Uyghur minority have migrated out of the region partly due to language barriers), the government is aware of the need for diversification.

Policies at the regional level have been developed and implemented that focus directly on promoting diversification of farm produce through subsidies on the expansion of grain production (for food security reasons) and the planting of fruit and nut trees (Spoor and Shi 2009). The latter is known in southwestern Xinjiang as the 6311 campaign, which was initiated in 2006–2007. The name 6311 stands for the planned planting acreage of fruit and nut trees, i.e. 600,000 mu[2] of apricots, 300,000 mu of almonds, and 100,000 mu of other fruits and nuts such as jujube and walnut (Spoor *et al.* 2010). This complements other widespread programmes such as the Fruit and Forest Tree Plantation Programme (Sun 2009).

The chapter is divided into six sections. Following the introduction, the second section analyses the diversification from the predominant cotton crop towards more fruit and nut production in Xinjiang, emphasising the role of "push" and "pull" factors that are well documented in the economic literature. We show that the introduction of fruit and nut trees is more policy-driven than market-induced, as it is strongly promoted by the regional government, which acknowledges that cotton production alone does not provide sufficient income for small-scale Uyghur farmers. Policy interventions include technical assistance, subsidised seeds, credit facilities, and so forth. In the third section we introduce the research area of Awati County, Aksu Prefecture, and discuss the existing rural income inequality in Xinjiang, connecting it to a high rate of income dependency on crop agriculture (mainly cotton and to a lesser degree grain), unequal land distribution and limited opportunities for non-farm activities. The fourth section further analyses the income dependency on crop agriculture looking at the effect of land availability and farm size on income. In the fifth section we analyse the recent attempt to diversify livelihoods through massive intercropping of cotton with fruit and nut trees, in particular, apricot, jujube, almond and walnut, and the promotion of vegetable production in greenhouses. We point out that while this has the potential to improve the income of small farmers, it is still unclear where the markets are for the newly introduced produce. Finally, we conclude by focusing on the impact of this livelihood diversification strategy on small-scale Uyghur farmers in Xinjiang.

We argue that the success of the regional government-initiated crop diversification project will depend on the development of rural markets (labour, finance, input and output) in this remote region of China, and will further be influenced by what impact these shifts will have on the already scarce land and water resources, which may paradoxically limit the potential benefits of the new strategy. Finally, the "fallacy of composition" problem could appear, as a massive shift towards more fruit and nut production is being stimulated without a good understanding of the markets for the produce.

Cotton monoculture and livelihood diversification in XUAR

Our research focuses particularly on the "cotton dependency" of small-scale Uyghur farmers in the southwestern part of Xinjiang. While cotton has been produced for decades, income derived from cotton production in small farms is low, resulting in high incidence of poverty (Becquelin 2000, 2004; Chai *et al.* 2004; Heilig *et al.* 2005). Before factor market liberalisation took place in China during the late 1990s and early 2000s, these small farmers had no choice but to produce cotton, since within the planned economy sector production targets were sent down to provinces, prefectures, townships and villages, and local farmers were expected to follow these instructions. With the liberalisation of markets, a rapidly changing economic and institutional environment has emerged. While provincial production targets are still set and announced, much more freedom is allowed for farming households to decide what to produce, giving them incentives to find alternative ways to secure and sustain their livelihoods, rather than relying on cotton production alone.

Various factors influence the diversification behaviour of farming households, especially in developing countries. There is ample economic literature that tries to identify and explain these factors. Two categories, identified as "push" and "pull" factors, are often emphasised (Awudu and CroleRees 2001; Démurger *et al.* 2010; Ellis 1998; Shi 2007, Shi *et al.* 2007; Wouterse and Taylor 2008). Push factors are mostly related to livelihood vulnerability and low incomes from crop production. These are quite relevant for Uyghur farming households in Xinjiang. To reduce income risks and fluctuations, farming households often engage in a more diversified portfolio of farm and non-farm activities (Carter 1997). For example, uncertainty caused by price volatility in cotton markets and changes in water availability and distribution in Xinjiang may prompt farming households to diversify into fruit and nut tree production, and sheep farming. Research shows that poor farming households tend to have higher absolute risk aversion (Rosenzweig and Binswanger 1993), and therefore try to diversify productive activities and income sources.

Pull factors often emerge from new livelihood opportunities created through market development (Davis and Pearce 2001) and policy initiatives. Non-farm employment generated by rural industries is a possible pull factor in diversifying farm labour (Shi 2007). However, Xinjiang is geographically remote and has a relatively low population density, therefore rural industries are much less developed than in other parts of China. Most industry in the region is concentrated in a number of cities, and intra-regional labour migration is relatively limited. Large-scale Uyghur rural out-migration to China's more industrialised eastern areas seems to be hindered by the language barrier. However, new urban markets for fruits and vegetables can stimulate investment in crop diversification and lead to an increase in production, especially in areas surrounding these urban markets.

In Chinese policy circles there is an awareness of these factors, and policy interventions (e.g. poverty reduction measures, rural social security programmes, and investment in the countryside) have been initiated to diminish the push and stimulate the pull factors. For example, in the programme to encourage planting fruit and nut trees, different levels of local government have assisted farming households to develop and access local agricultural product markets, and even made attempts to extend these markets beyond Xinjiang in order to create new income-generating sources for farming households. This massive campaign aimed at encouraging the planting of fruit and nut trees in Xinjiang may contribute to the further development of factor and commodity markets, and assist in the diversification and increase of farm incomes. Credit constraints can prevent farming households from undertaking a wider range of livelihood activities and reducing income risks. The 6311 fruit and nut tree planting programme, which will be discussed in detail below, initiated and strongly supported by local governments, also provides direct credit support for farming households (CCPC-XUAR 2007).

Here we intend to provide a detailed examination of how local governments can assure the success of certain types of fruit and nuts in local and intra-regional markets, how the direct intervention in the cultivation of fruit and nut trees can reduce risks in production and investment, and what impact the project may have on land and water resources. We will show that if local governments in Xinjiang fail to take full account of the local market demand factor and the related prices of the tree products, and formulate an appropriate strategy to tackle the associated challenges, the Uyghur farming households affected by the policy could be worse off – not only because they might not gain much from crop diversification, but also due to the fact that their income from the traditional crop (i.e. cotton) could decline because of the decrease in cotton-growing acreage as a result of inter-cropping with fruit or nut trees. The unintended outcomes of the policy are a central concern in this context.

The need for livelihood diversification: poverty and agriculture

Regional income differences in Xinjiang

Xinjiang has a relatively high poverty incidence, particularly in its far southwestern prefectures, such as Aksu, Kashgar and Khotan (Spoor and Shi 2009). Rural income is low in Xinjiang compared with other parts of China. According to the recent official data, annual rural net income per capita in Xinjiang was estimated at 3,883 yuan in 2009, and in 2006 the per capita income for the autonomous region was ranked 25th out of China's 31 provinces and autonomous regions. Intra-regional income inequality is also substantial (Table 7.1). According to data obtained from household surveys carried out in 2006 in eight of the 11 prefectures of Xinjiang, the average income for the region as a whole was 2,737 yuan, with the lowest being 1,417 yuan and 1,873 yuan in Khotan and Kashgar, respectively, and the highest being 5,004 yuan in Changji (some 3.5 times higher than that of Khotan). Aksu Prefecture, which we examine in greater detail in this chapter with a case study from its Awati County, had an above average rural per capita income of 3,360 yuan (Table 7.1).

Table 7.1 Rural income differentiation and share of agricultural income in XUAR, 2006

Prefecture	Rural net income (yuan/ person)	Agricultural share of gross income (%)	Rural population	Rural population share (%)	Income share (%)
Changji Counties	5,003.7	71.2	734,807	7.3	13.4
Directly Under Ili	3,164.7	57.0	1,410,660	14.1	16.3
Tacheng	4,003.3	72.4	489,123	4.9	7.2
Altay	3,302.6	43.3	274,149	2.7	3.3
Bayangol Mongol	4,459.3	72.3	420,831	4.2	6.9
Aksu	3,360.0	81.4	1,326,607	13.3	16.3
Kashgar	1,872.9	65.6	2,576,260	25.8	17.6
Khotan	1,417.3	44.0	1,500,051	15.0	7.8
Average/Total	2,737.4	68.0	10,002,681	100.0	100.0

Source: Household Survey Data published in aggregate by the Statistical Bureau of XUAR (2007).

Income inequality could be partially explained by the following factors from the disciplinary perspective of classic economics. First, there are spatial differences in infrastructure (such as roads and communication facilities) in part related to the government's development strategies and priorities, leading to differential access to markets, transportation costs, and so forth. Second, proximity to fast growing industrial or natural resource extraction centres affects the spin-off effects on rural areas, such as migration and the supply of primary commodities. These serve as pull factors in diversifying agricultural and farm-based production, in that they facilitate the development of a non-farm rural economy, such as processing companies and services. Third, differences could further be explained by the availability of water resources, which are generally scarce in Xinjiang, and by the influence of seasonal fluctuations in the water supply and the positioning of the small farms in relation to the main irrigation canal of the river basin. Finally, the original land allocation could be crucial, as, unlike many other areas in China where land has been periodically reallocated to reflect the demographic dynamics of rural families and communities (Unger 2002; Ho 2009), there has been no regular redistribution of land in Xinjiang (Spoor and Shi 2009).

As shown in Table 7.1, Xinjiang is still largely rural. Official statistics show that the Uyghur population is the largest ethnic group in Xinjiang today despite the in-migration of Han Chinese since the 1950s (Statistics Bureau of XUAR 2010). This trans-migration was first initiated to exploit the vast virgin land in rural areas and establish state *bingtuan* farms. However, many Han Chinese now live in cities while in rural areas, particularly in the southwest, the majority of the population are still of Uyghur origin. For example, in Aksu Prefecture, the Uyghur account for about 73 per cent of the total population in 2006, and in Awati County, where our survey was conducted, they account for around 78 per cent of the population (Statistics Bureau of XUAR 2007). While state *bingtuans* have contributed to infrastructural improvement, they, at the same time, have competed for scarce resources, particularly water, with small-scale farmers in the region. In 2009, Xinjiang's Uyghur population was about 10 million, accounting for 46.4 per cent of the total population of about 21.6 million. The Han population, the second largest ethnic group, was 8.4 million, representing 38.9 per cent, while the third largest group, the Kazakhs, had a population of some 1.5 million accounting for 7 per cent of the total population (Statistics Bureau of XUAR 2010). These figures show how the trans-migration process has affected the region's ethnic composition and the livelihoods of the ethnic groups.

The research area and data collection

As demonstrated in Table 7.1, with regard to per capita income, Kashgar and Khotan in the southwest are the poorest prefectures in Xinjiang. Kashgar is also one of the main cotton-producing prefectures (second after Aksu) (Statistics Bureau of XUAR 2010), which suggests a link between income poverty and single-crop dependency. Contrary to the assumption that a cash crop would bring more monetary rewards for farming households, in Xinjiang cotton does not generate sufficient income to allow small-scale Uyghur farmers to escape poverty. The contribution of cotton to income depends on the availability of natural resources, primarily land and water, the distance to markets, conditions of rural infrastructure and the institutional environment, such as tax and procurement policies and crop diversification. In order to investigate this further, we analyse in some detail Aksu Prefecture, which has an average rural per capita income in Xinjiang and a typical cotton-based local economy. In Aksu Prefecture we chose Awati County (close to the Taklamakan Desert) as the study area to undertake the village and household surveys. Given its physical and socio-economic conditions, Awati County is considered typical of Aksu Prefecture.

Awati County produces around one quarter of the cotton in Aksu Prefecture. Its physical conditions are reasonably favourable for cotton growing. The total land area of Awati County is 13,233 square kilometres (Statistics Bureau of XUAR 2010). It is located on the alluvial plain at the convergence of the Aksu, Yarkant, Kashgar and Hotan rivers, which are the main tributaries of the large Tarim River. Awati, which means "prosperity" in Uyghur, was an important trading post along the ancient Silk Road, a trans-continental trade network linking China to the Mediterranean. The county, with a total population of 218,600 in 2008, has five rural and three urban townships, and three large state-owned *bingtuan* farms. It has a continental temperate arid climate, with light and scarce precipitation, significant levels of evaporation, a hot summer and a relatively long frost-free period – the climate, therefore, is favourable for growing cotton as well as grains such as wheat.

The data are drawn from a village and household survey undertaken in nine villages in Awati County in December 2008. The survey was conducted as part of a collaborative research project undertaken by the College of Economics and Management of Xinjiang Agricultural University and the International Institute of Social Studies, The Netherlands. Survey questionnaires were jointly designed, and the interviews were carried out by a team of graduate students of Uyghur origin. According to official statistics, the rural population of Aksu Prefecture in 2009 represented 41.7 per cent of the prefecture's total population (Statistics Bureau of XUAR 2010). For Awati County, this was 46.0 per cent. However, taking into account the fact that the land of some farmers falls within the administratively defined "city" boundaries, in reality, the "agricultural population" would be much larger than these statistics suggest. It was estimated that the actual proportion of the rural population more broadly defined was 78.0 per cent and 77.3 per cent in Aksu Prefecture and Awati County, respectively (ibid.).

The household and village survey was conducted just after cotton was harvested. The villages were chosen in three different townships, namely (using both their Uyghur and Chinese names), Bex erik baziri (Baishi airiki) to the north of the Awati County seat; Horiqol baziri (Wuluquele) to the southeast; and Yengi erik yezizi (Ying airiki) to the west. In total, nine villages – three per township – were selected according to criteria such as land size and quality, water availability, poor versus non-poor ratio of the population, and distance to urban centres. A random sample of 361 households was selected across the nine villages. The sample was taken from detailed household lists provided by the village committees. All the interviews were conducted by the research team in December 2008 during a period of nine days.

Agricultural and cotton dependency

In Xinjiang, the dependence of rural income on agricultural production is substantial (Table 7.1). In Aksu Prefecture the dependency rate is as high as 81.4 per cent. Aksu was often described by village officials as an area with "many people, little land" (Field notes, March and December 2008). Initial land division without later readjustments, few non-farm employment opportunities (including migration) and limited livelihood diversification have partially resulted in income inequality, and the average income shows substantial variation across Xinjiang. In prefectures with the largest rural population, including Kashgar and Khotan (whose populations account for 25.8 and 15.0 per cent of the total rural population in Xinjiang respectively), the share of total rural income in Xinjiang was disproportionately only 17.6 and 7.8 per cent, respectively. For Aksu Prefecture the figures were slightly better: 13.3 per cent of Xinjiang's total rural population earned 16.3 per cent of total rural income (Table 7.1).

Table 7.2 provides data for two strategic crops, cotton and grain (mainly wheat) in Awati County between 2001 and 2009. The sown area of cotton expanded substantially during this period, leading to a significant rise in output while average yields remained relatively constant. The sown area of grain reduced substantially in 2007 and 2008, which reflected the increase in the sown area of cotton, a trend which also occurred in Aksu as a whole (interviews with officials from the Aksu Reform and Development Commission, 19 March 2008). However, the rising prices for wheat and other grains during 2008–2009, combined with a policy to increase food security through grain subsidies (which is examined in detail in Chapter 10 of this collection), helped to redress the imbalance, leading to substantially increased grain production in 2009 (Table 7.2).

Table 7.2 Grain and cotton production in Awati County, 2001–2009

Year	Grain sown area (hectare)	Grain output (tonne)	Grain yield (tonne/ hectare)	Cotton sown area (hectare)	Cotton output (tonne)	Cotton yield (tonne/ hectare)
2001	13,110	79,961	6.10	30,000	42,000	1.40
2004	12,850	82,166	6.39	28,000	45,972	1.64
2006	11,290	74,938	6.64	35,670	53,575	1.50
2007	4,627	31,247	6.75	43,333	63,213	1.46
2008	6,980	48,095	6.89	61,590	73,030	1.19
2009	24,040	159,539	6.64	66,590	87,363	1.31

Source: Statistical Bureau of XUAR (2002, 2005, 2007, 2008, 2009, 2010).

Our fieldwork interviews showed that officials of the Development Commission of Aksu were worried in 2008 that the sown area of grain was decreasing so fast that it was threatening food self-sufficiency in the region. The regional government had already applied to higher levels of government for more subsidies to promote grain, particularly wheat production, as the sown area of cotton in 2008 was even higher than planned. The latter is an interesting phenomenon in itself, as it might suggest that farmers could not always decide what to grow. Although the practice of the centrally planned production quotas had been largely abolished, there was still a system of cotton and grain targets at the prefecture (or provincial) level, which were then implemented downwards to county, township and administrative village levels. Finally, within natural villages, these targets (mostly measured as sown acreage) were distributed, with some autonomy for farmers to decide on the crop mix and "what and where to grow". It was often stressed that farmers were not asked, but instead "guided" to grow this or that kind of crop (Field notes, March and December 2008).

The household survey in Awati County shows that small-scale Uyghur farmers' dependency on cotton was very high as indicated in the crop's share of farmers' income. As Table 7.3 shows, agriculture's income share for a typical Awati farmer was 79.0 per cent and 80.6 per cent in 2006 and 2007, respectively, and the share of income deriving from cotton production was 65.6 per cent and 73.1 per cent respectively, corresponding to the expansion of the cotton sown area during these years.

Figure 7.1 shows the cotton price change from 1999 to 2010. While the price increased over the years, this is shown in current rather than relative terms compared with input prices. With factor market liberalisation, the prices of inputs have substantially increased and therefore real cotton prices may have been either stagnant or even reduced over time. What is clearly shown in Figure 7.1 is that there has been considerable price fluctuation over the years and this has created uncertainties and insecurity for rural household income and livelihoods. Since these small farmers have relied heavily on cotton production, their income has varied over the years due to sometimes dramatic fluctuations in

Table 7.3 Income structure of an average Awati Uyghur farmer (%)

	2006	2007
Crop agriculture	79.0	80.6
Cotton	65.6	73.1
Grain	8.3	3.4
Fruit	4.7	4.1
Forestry	2.8	2.5
Animal husbandry	12.8	12.2
Non-farm industry	5.4	4.7
Total	100.0	100.0

Source: Awati County Agricultural Bureau (data provided during our field visit in 2008).

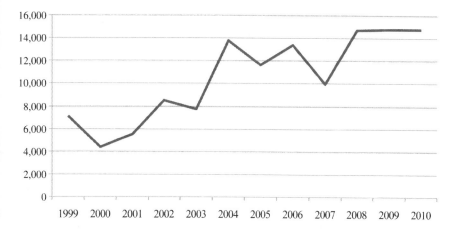

Figure 7.1 Change in cotton prices, 1999–2010 (yuan per tonne).
Source: Based on data from NBSC (1999–2010), *China Agricultural Statistical Yearbook*.

cotton prices. Before market liberalisation there was no choice other than to deliver the planned quotas of cotton. While there is more freedom and choice nowadays, small Uyghur farmers have had to face the significant price volatility of the cotton market and related risks.

In the household survey we also investigated the importance of animal husbandry for rural livelihood and its diversification. While representing a small proportion of gross rural output, animal husbandry has the potential to be of strategic significance for small farming households, particularly with regard to a household's food security (meat and milk) and its resilience, i.e. the ability to absorb external shocks, such as sudden high expenses caused by the calamitous illness of a family member, harvest failure, and so forth. Our survey findings indicated that many small farmers had a flock of sheep, which was often considered a form of safety net or savings, to finance unexpected expenditure due to medical care, festivities, etc. One farmer told us that he sold his sheep in order to buy urea for his cotton crop due to the scarcity of rural credit for these farmers (Field notes, March 2008).

Income dependency on land

Rural income inequality at the local level (using data of average income differences between localities) seems to be linked to the relatively fixed original land allocation, and further determined by the high dependency of agricultural income on land. In Xinjiang, most farmers received their small plots of land in the early 1980s. The contracted land was, in the decades that followed, supplemented by reclaimed land. While in other parts of China there was regular re-allocation of farmland (Ho 2009; Ho and Spoor 2006), this was not the case in Xinjiang.

Our initial expectation was, therefore, that the per capita land size would decrease over the years, but the official data show that this was not the case. However, for Aksu, there is considerable intra-prefecture inequality in terms of average per capita landholding, which slightly increased over the years (Table 7.4). For example in Aksu Prefecture, where original per capita landholding during land distribution when agriculture was decollectivised was relatively high, in 2001 the average per capita cultivated land size was 4.3 mu at the county level, with a standard deviation of 1.4. In 2006, the average per capita land size was 4.3 mu, with a standard deviation of 1.2. In Awati County, average rural cultivated land per capita stood at 5.1 mu in 2001 and 5.3 mu in 2006 (not differentiating between contracted and development land), which was higher than the prefecture's average. This could be explained by the emerging rural out-migration and some newly reclaimed land. However, the latter is somewhat surprising as during our fieldwork regional officials stressed that, out of environmental concerns, since 2001 reclamation of land has been discouraged through policies restricting water allocation and use for newly reclaimed land, which is not surprising given that there has been an overall reduction of the water supply in Awati County (Field notes, March 2008).

Table 7.5 shows differentiations in per capita landholding at the village level in Awati. Data provided by the village heads during the survey on per capita contracted land was somewhat lower than the average figures obtained in the household survey.[3] However, in nearly all the villages these differences are within reasonable margins, with Raidang Village being the only exception. This might be caused by the inclusion of a considerable number of Han Chinese farmers in the survey sample, who held larger than average contracted land.

Table 7.5 only includes land for which the farmer has a contract certificate, but excludes land which has been sublet by others. Most contracted land is between 2 and 3 mu per capita on average, but when development (or reclaimed) land is included, the landholding size is larger. The land size difference between

Table 7.4 Rural cultivated land in Aksu, 2001–2006 (mu/capita)

County	2001	2004	2006
Aksu City	4.78	4.58	5.25
Wensu (Onsu)	6.34	5.89	6.08
Kuqa	3.10	2.64	3.15
Xayar	4.98	4.48	4.83
Xinhe (Toksu)	4.51	4.26	4.47
Baicheng (Bay)	5.08	4.17	4.09
Wushi (Uxturpan)	2.86	2.32	2.19
Awati	5.06	4.83	5.29
Kalpin	1.81	3.00	3.37
Aksu Prefecture	4.28	4.02	4.30
Standard deviation	1.41	1.15	1.23

Sources: Statistical Bureau of XUAR (2002, 2005, 2007, authors' calculations).

Table 7.5 Average landholding at the village level, Awati County, 2008

Township	Village	Contracted land/ household (mu)	STDEV	Contract-ed land/ capita (mu)	STDEV	Village data/ capita (mu)	N
Bex erik	Ustunki imampaxa	15.48	7.12	3.41	1.70	2.88	49
Bex erik	Towenki dong huxlak	8.98	4.03	2.07	0.84	2.37	30
Bex erik	Ustunki hojiwaska	15.68	4.42	3.15	0.79	3.03	23
Horiqol	Kizil dong	17.39	10.35	3.56	2.10	2.18	15
Horiqol	Raidang	32.09	21.49	7.16	5.35	1.97	22
Horiqol	Kum erik	14.96	9.28	3.34	2.03	2.90	45
Yengi erik	Su yaydi	15.48	8.38	3.52	2.03	2.82	63
Yengi erik	Ustunki togra osteng	7.27	3.89	1.58	0.81	1.41	74
Yengi erik	Latkilik	11.63	7.66	2.88	1.56	2.70	36
Average/ Total		12.39		3.10		2.47	357

Source: Xinjiang Agricultural University (XJAU) and International Institute of Social Studies (ISS) Household and Village Survey (December 2008).

a household's own contracted land allocated by the collective/village and its land on others' subletting is fairly small, since most land contractual transactions have taken place within the village. Of the 361 households surveyed, 357 provided data on contracted land, with an average of 3.10 mu per capita. This increased slightly to 3.28 mu per capita when the "sublet" land is included. Given the specific conditions of Xinjiang, reclaimed wasteland or development land is an important component of local farmers' landholding. In total, 79 of the 361 households in the survey sample (Table 7.6) said that they had additional "development land", which was often larger than their contracted land. In addition to the contracted and development land, nearly half of the surveyed households (N = 157, plot size = 0.88 mu) reported having a small privately owned plot. The per capita data are calculated on the basis of the reported numbers of household members in the survey.

While in most villages the large majority of farmers were of Uyghur origin, in Su Yaydi kenti (Su Yayidi) Village in Yengi erik yezisi Township, a total of 25 Han Chinese farmers (39.7 per cent) and one Hui Muslim farmer (1.6 per cent) were included (out of 63 households) in the surveyed sample. In addition, in Raidang Village a total of nine Han Chinese farmers (41.0 per cent) and nine Hui Muslim farmers (41.0 per cent) were represented in the sample of 22 households. Further, one other village – Latkilik kenti or Lateleke in Yengi erik Township – is inhabited mainly by Han Chinese farmers. The inclusion of these

Table 7.6 Contracted land, development land and household private plots, Awati County, 2008

	Farm size per household (mu)	Farm size per capita (mu)	No. of house-holds surveyed
Contracted land	12.39 (10.31)	3.10 (2.37)	357
Total managed contracted land (including rented-in/excluding rented-out land)	13.24 (12.74)	3.28 (2.76)	357
Total managed developed land (including rented-in/excluding rented-out land)	19.74 (50.29)	4.06 (10.49)	79
Household private plot	0.88 (1.18)	0.20 (0.27)	157

Source: XAU and ISS Household and Village Survey (December 2008).

Note: Figures in brackets are standard deviation.

villages, which are inhabited by either mixed ethnic groups or largely Han Chinese farmers, aims to generate comparative data. Table 7.5 shows that Su Yaydi Village has an average per capita landholding of 3.52 mu. Raidang Village has a much larger average per capita landholding of 7.16 mu. The survey data suggest that the average per capita landholding of Han Chinese farmers in Su Yayidi Village (4.2 mu) is slightly higher than that of Uyghur farmers in most other villages. The nine Hui Muslim farmers' average landholding (in Raidang Village) is 5.9 mu per capita while the average per capita landholding of Han Chinese farmers (2.88 mu) in Latkilik Village is similar to, or even smaller than that of the Uyghur farmers in most other villages. These data (Table 7.5) also suggest greater than expected heterogeneity and differentiation within ethnic groups. For development land, differences in landholding are fairly small, being 4.12 mu (Uyghur), 4.84 mu (Han), and 4.28 mu (Hui) per capita. For the privately-owned household plots, Han Chinese farmers have a larger average landholding than that of Uyghur farmers (Household survey, December 2008). Further research would be required to examine the underlying factors for such landholding differences.

Awati County is relatively well endowed in terms of water supply (though this is a recent development due to the construction of a large irrigation canal nearby). However, under the policy of water conservation in the Tarim Basin and supported by environmental considerations, the water supply for Awati has been reduced by 10 per cent during the past decade. This means that while there has not been a ban on wasteland reclamation for agricultural production, no additional water would be available for newly reclaimed land. Some villages are located close to the desert, which makes it more difficult for villagers to expand arable land without an increased supply of water. Each of the nine surveyed villages had at least some development land (Table 7.7). One village (Kizil dong) had 2,200 mu of development land versus 1,464 mu of contracted land, while another village (Ustunki togra osteng) had only 120 mu of development land

Table 7.7 Village land areas: contracted, development and grassland, Awati County, 2008 (mu)

Town-ship	Village	Con-tract-ed land	De-velop-ment land (to-tal)	Devel-opment land (HHs)[1]	De-velop-ment land (vil-lage)[2]	Grass-land	Grass-land (HHs)	Grass-land (vil-lage)	Pri-vate plots
Bex erik	Ustunki imampaxa	4,900	1,980	0	1,980	2,000	0	2,000	370
Bex erik	Towenki dong huxlak	1,800	120	120	0	0	0	0	100
Bex erik	Ustunki hojiwaska	2,180	300	300	0	1,200	0	1,200	250
Horiqol	Kizil dong	1,464	2,200	2,200	0	16,200	15,000	1,200	100
Horiqol	Raidang	3,916	820	0	820	0	0	0	0
Horiqol	Kum erik	4,000	150	0	150	0	0	0	120
Yengi erik	Su yaydi	6,200	2,000	2,000	0	0	0	0	680
Yengi erik	Ustunki togra osteng	3,140	120	0	120	0	0	0	0
Yengi erik	Latkilik	2,883	209	209	0	250	250	0	350

Source: XJAU and ISS Household and Village Survey (December 2008).

Notes:
1 HH = Household.
2 In some cases the development land is controlled by HHs, in others by the Village Committee.

versus 3,140 mu of contracted land. In some villages development land is controlled by households, while in others by village committees, which rent out the land to households. Grassland is relatively scarce, and only four out of the nine villages reported having grassland. However, Kizil dong is an exception with 16,200 mu of grassland versus 3,664 mu of contracted and development land combined. Furthermore, our survey findings suggest that local people consider soil salinity a problem, which is not surprising considering the local conditions of sandy soil, a near monoculture of cotton, and problems of water logging.

Severe soil salinisation was reported in Raidang Village by the village authorities, with 23.2 per cent of land being moderately saline (for the absolute figure of salinisation, see Table 7.8), and 71.7 per cent lightly saline. In Su yaydi Village soil salinisation was even worse, and nearly all arable land was reported to be saline, with 25.2 per cent in the severe, 40.3 per cent in the moderate and 35.2 per cent in the light categories. In other villages salinisation was much less serious; however, these reported data might actually be underestimated. Soil salinisation is generally seen by farmers as a serious problem, which could become worse if no water saving techniques are introduced. Farmers have used water leaching to extract salt from topsoil. However, the practice increases water use,

Table 7.8 Soil salinisation at the village level, Awati County, 2008

Township	Village	Agricul-tural area (mu)	Arable land (mu)	Land with salinisa-tion (mu)	Level of salinisation (mu)		
					Severe	Moderate	Light
Bex erik	Ustunki imampaxa	9,350	7,350	300	100	100	100
Bex erik	Towenki dong huxlak	3,930	2,730	300	10	290	0
Bex erik	Ustunki hojiwaska	2,020	2,020	50	20	30	0
Horiqol	Kizil dong	19,994	3,764	800	150	250	400
Horiqol	Raidang	4,988	4,988	4,736	0	1,160	3,576
Horiqol	Kum erik	4,270	4,270	150	150	0	0
Yengi erik	Su yaydi	9,040	8,980	9,040	2,260	3,616	3,164
Yengi erik	Ustunki togra osteng	3,260	3,260	0	0	0	0
Yengi erik	Latkilik	3,692	3,442	0	0	0	0

Source: XJAU and ISS Household and Village Survey (December 2008).

and thus in the long run may well aggravate the problem. While a precise analysis of water distribution, its relative scarcity and seasonal availability is beyond the scope of this chapter, our household and village survey indicated that development land usually had less water for irrigation than contracted land.[4] Furthermore, we found that six out of the nine surveyed villages were using groundwater to supplement surface irrigation water.

The long-term use of ground water has clearly affected the ground water level in the area, which, in some cases, is more than 100 metres deep (Table 7.9). Rapid deterioration of the water table over the past decade was reported during the village and household survey, and in some villages the change was as dramatic as from 2 to 60 metres or from 5 to 50 metres (Table 7.9). Such drastic change in the water table has further complicated the existing problems of water supply and distribution.

Table 7.9 Estimated groundwater levels in six surveyed villages

	1	2	3	4	5	6
Depth groundwater (metres)	140	120	85	60	50	40
Depth groundwater 10 years ago (metres)	–	0	35	2	5	20

Source: XJAU and ISS Household and Village Survey (December 2008).

Diversification and policy-induced change

In China's other regions, resource use has been intensified by small farmers since the initiation of the market reforms in the early 1980s, a process brought about by farmers' increased autonomy in agricultural production and marketing. However, this process has had negative environmental consequences for small landholding farms (Tilt 2008). In addition to intensive use of resources, many farmers in China, through participating in non-farm activities, such as rural-urban migration, have diversified their livelihoods and household income, effectively diminishing risks and increasing socio-economic gains for the household (Shi 2007). In Xinjiang, this process of livelihood diversification and intensive resource use has been much slower. Currently the attempt to diversify the local economy in the prefectures of southwestern Xinjiang through the production of more fruit, nuts and vegetables has been largely policy-driven rather than being attributed to the "push" factors of the market. The provincial, prefecture and county governments have pushed ahead programmes and policies, such as the recent "Fruit and Forest Planting around Tarim Basin" project, and the "6311" project in Awati County. This suggests an increasing awareness by regional and local authorities of the pressing need to diversify livelihoods and develop more high value-added agriculture in order to promote the growth of both agricultural production and farmers' income.

Under these policies, farmers are being strongly "advised" to practise inter-cropping of cotton or wheat with fruit and/or nut trees and massive technical assistance, seeds and credit facilities are being provided. This has caused a significant policy-induced response in the region's agricultural production. According to the XUAR government plan outlined in a document entitled "Facilitating Development of Forest and Fruit Industry in Xinjiang", issued in 2007, the fruit tree planting area was to be extended from 10 million mu in 2000 to 15 million mu by the end of 2010. The fruit tree planting area in southern Xinjiang was planned to reach 12 million mu by the end of 2010 with a total output of more than 10 million tonnes (CCPC-XUAR 2007). These plans were not fully materialised, however, with the fruit tree planting area in 2010 reaching 17 million mu but the total output only 8 million tonnes (FD-XUAR 2011).

Regional and local governments are promoting diversification and implementing the policies in earnest, particularly with regard to expanding the area of fruit tree planting. Government support since 2006 has not been confined to the production phase (such as through providing free fruit nurse trees, fertilisers and pesticides), but also extended to the marketing phase (for example, providing subsidies for large-scale fruit-processing enterprises) (Research Report by the Team for Moderation of Agriculture in South Xinjiang 2008, see also Chapter 10 for a detailed analysis of the more recent policies on subsidising agriculture, in particular, grain farmers). In addition, governments at different levels have provided direct subsidies for research institutions and agricultural extension services to work on high-yield, high-quality fruit tree varieties, and the regional government has invested 160 million yuan to set up a "special fund" for fruit tree

Table 7.10 Fruit production in Aksu, 2001–2009

Year	Apricots		Jujubes	
	Planted area (hectares)	Output (tonnes)	Planted area (hectares)	Output (tonnes)
2001	13,300	68,835	480	1,290
2004	27,457	160,728	9,574	2,194
2006	35,413	224,214	30,827	6,464
2008	39,297	299,341	66,593	34,903
2009	33,839	362,218	95,491	76,754

Source: Statistical Bureau of XUAR (2002, 2005, 2007, 2009, 2010).

research and development (FD-XUAR 2011). Table 7.10 shows the aggregate data on the planted acreage of apricot and jujube (though most of this is inter-cropped with cotton and to a lesser extent wheat), and their respective outputs. It demonstrates that production growth over the period 2001–2009 was spectacular, in particular during the latter half of the period. Similar trends are noted in the production of other fruits, as well as in the more traditional almond and walnut crops. In addition to fruit and nut production, the conversion of some farmland, especially in areas near cities, towns and suburban areas, into greenhouses for growing vegetables has been promoted in the southwestern prefectures of Xinjiang. Moreover, supporting facilities in the production chain have been constructed. For example, in Shache County, Kashgar Prefecture private investors were encouraged by the county government to set up a fruit processing company, which began operation in 2008 (Field notes, March 2008).

These developments confirm the hypothesis that in the rural development context of small landholding farms, such as those of Uyghur farmers in southwestern Xinjiang, growing cotton alone would not be sufficient to sustain household income. Therefore, diversifying rural livelihoods to also include temporary or permanent rural out-migration should be considered one option to increase income and reduce poverty. The findings of our research indicate that the government at various levels has been aware of the problem, and has taken actions to address it. In addition to migration, the government has promoted large-scale inter-cropping of cotton and wheat with fruit and nut trees. However, there is a potential downside with regard to the impact of such policies on resource use, increasing intensification and the implications for the environment. For example, over-application of pesticides in cotton production could negatively affect fruit and nut trees, which might, in turn, affect the quality of the tree products. Furthermore, the situation of water shortage in the semi-arid area could be exacerbated as irrigation is needed for cotton in June while for fruits and vegetables in the spring when water supply is tight due to the paucity of water-regulating dams and reservoirs upstream from the Yarkant River (Field notes, 24 March 2008).

In our fieldwork we asked a question about possible pesticide residues in the fruits or nuts produced in the inter-cropping cotton fields, but did not receive a satisfactory answer from the officials in charge of agricultural work.[5] This might suggest that there is little awareness among local officials and farmers alike of the potential environmental and health issues caused by intensive farming. Moreover, there may be a "fallacy of composition" problem, since it remains relatively unclear where the markets for the newly introduced fruits and nuts are, both domestically and internationally. Local officials in charge of agricultural work in the surveyed area of Xinjiang had little idea about the potential markets for their fruits and nuts. Instead of grounding their projections on sound evidence obtained through, for instance, some market research, they often assumed that there would be a market for the products within Xinjiang or in other parts of China. Answers, such as "in Xinjiang people should start eating more fruit", were based more on the officials' wishes than demand in the real market. Such uncertainties could only be increased when other nearby regions, such as Sichuan, start implementing similar diversification policies (Tilt 2008). Lack of information flow and coordinating mechanisms across regions could also result in oversupply of the new economic crops in time, reducing the positive effect of diversification on household income and village economy. Internationally, the export markets of several targeted fruits and nuts tend to have been dominated by countries such as Turkey.[6]

Conclusion

This chapter explores the relationship between low income and dependency on cotton production for small landholding Uyghur farmers in southwestern Xinjiang. The analysis of the combined primary data gathered during our household and village survey conducted in December 2008 and secondary data from the XUAR Statistical Bureau show that the majority of Uyghur farming households live on small landholdings of combined "contracted" and "development" land with scarce water resources. There are considerable differences in landholding within prefectures in the region, as well as within and across ethnic groups. These findings indicate some of the constraints on rural development and livelihoods imposed by the region's less than favourable natural endowments, and that widening income inequalities are, in part, due to the increasingly differentiated landholdings. We have shown that in Xinjiang's specific context, growing cotton alone can no longer adequately improve income and sustain livelihoods for rural households. This constitutes a strong "push" factor for greater diversification.

Rural households' heavy dependence on agricultural production for income is also related to the limited rural out-migration and a weak non-farm economy in most of Xinjiang. While off-farm productive activities and their contribution to rural income are rather marginal, our research finds that these strategies (e.g. raising sheep) are still considered important by local farmers. Cotton is seen as a strategic crop in China, particularly in Xinjiang, which led to the substantial expansion of its sown area in the region up till 2009. This, however, was achieved at the expense of grain production. Since then, the issue of regional food security (particularly with regard to wheat) has come to the forefront, and grain production has started to be emphasised, subsidised and as a result, increased.

In addition, with market liberalisation, small-scale Uyghur farmers have gained more autonomy in determining what to grow. However, high volatility in the cotton price combined with rising input prices during the past decade has generated high risk and uncertainty, and negatively impacted on rural households' income and livelihoods. In the meantime, markets for other agricultural commodities, such as vegetables, fruits and nuts, have emerged (at least partially) and therefore have served as "pull" factors for farmers to diversify into growing such cash crops.

In this context, the Xinjiang regional government has started a massive campaign to promote the inter-cropping of fruit (apricot and jujube) and nut (almond and walnut) trees, and the conversion of some farmland close to cities and towns into greenhouses for vegetable production. This campaign is supported with subsidised (or sometimes free) seeds, technical assistance and credit facilities (see also Chapter 10 of this volume). The shift towards a more diversified agricultural production has been underway since the mid-2000s, with particularly strong growth in jujube production in Aksu and Kashgar prefectures. This trend was further evidenced during our fieldwork through the household and village survey in Awati County in December 2008. As discussed above, this largely policy-induced diversification could open new avenues for small farmers to make specific decisions, diversify livelihoods and reduce dependency on cotton. It could also stimulate private investments in processing facilities and the development of markets for the new produce. However, our research also suggests that some potential problems could result from this massive campaign, and that these problems have not yet come to the attention of policy-makers and local farmers alike. The inter-cropping of fruit and nut trees with cotton has limitations as the crops have different water needs in the same season or across seasons, which potentially could cause tensions and difficulties in the production and management of the crops. There is also a greater need for expensive drip irrigation to counter increased pressure on scarce water resources. Furthermore, the use of pesticides on cotton might negatively affect fruit and nut trees growing in the same field. Finally, there is the possible risk of the "fallacy of composition" effect, as it remains unclear where the markets for all these (largely unprocessed) new commodities are. There has already been some public and private investment in fruit processing enterprises, and there could also be more rigorous efforts to promote the local products at the local, regional and national markets. However, similar processes of agricultural diversification towards fruits, nuts, spices and vegetables are taking place in many other parts of China, which might lead to increased market competition or even oversupply. Thus, it remains to be seen whether this diversification strategy in Xinjiang will succeed in reducing single crop dependency, increasing farmers' income and sustaining livelihoods.

Acknowledgements

The empirical research is part of the collaborative project "Changing Livelihood Strategies in Rural Xinjiang: Cotton Production, the Environment and Poverty Reduction" (Project No. 07CDP028: 2007-2011), jointly financed by the Royal

Dutch Academy of Arts and Sciences and the Chinese Ministry of Science and Technology. This project is executed by the International Institute of Social Studies in The Netherlands (Erasmus University Rotterdam), in cooperation with Xinjiang Agricultural University, in particular its College of Economics and Management, with support from Nanjing Agricultural University (The Fundamental Research Funds for the Central Universities [KYJ200902] and the Programme for New Century Excellent Talents in Universities).

Notes

1 The administrative status of XUAR is equivalent to that of provinces in China.
2 One mu is equivalent to 1/15 of a hectare.
3 There may be various reasons for these differences; for example, village committees might deliberately underestimate their land resources, while households might "illegally" use more land.
4 Household and Village Survey Report, XAU and ISS, Mimeo, June 2009.
5 Officials claimed that farmers spread pesticide as close to the ground as possible.
6 Personal communication with Dr Murat Arsel in ISS, who participated in the field work in Shache County, Kashgar Prefecture (March 2008).

References

Awudu, Abdulai and Anna CroleRees (2001), Determinants of income diversification amongst rural households in Southern Mali. *Food Policy* 26: 437–452.

Becquelin, Nicolas (2000), Xinjiang in the nineties. *The China Journal* 44: 65–90.

Becquelin, Nicolas (2004), Staged development in Xinjiang. *The China Quarterly* 178: 358–378.

Carter, Michael R. (1997), Environment, technology, and the social articulation of risk in West African agriculture. *Economic Development and Cultural Change* 45(3): 557–591.

Chai, Jun, Jing Chen, Zhiqing Jiang and Kunling Chen (2004), Causes of regional poverty and direction of investment in Xinjiang China. In James Laurenceson, Kam Ki Tang and Scott Waldron (eds), *Proceedings of the 16th Annual Conference of the Association for Chinese Economics Studies*. Brisbane, Australia, 19–20 July: Australian Association of Chinese Economic Studies, pp. 1–20.

Chinese Communist Party Committee of Xinjiang Uyghur Autonomous Region (CCPC-XUAR) (2007), *Zizhiqu dangwei zizhiqu renming zhengfu guanyu jiakuai tese linguoye fazhan de yijian* [The opinion of CCPC and government of XUAR on expediting characteristic development of the forestry and fruit industries]. Available at: www.xjlyt.gov. cn/Get/zcxwj/170436869.htm (accessed 23 September 2011).

Davis, Junior and Douglas Pearce (2001), The rural non-farm economy in Central and Eastern Europe. In Zvi Lerman and Csaba Csáki (eds), *The Challenge of Rural Development in the EU Accession Process*. Washington, DC: The World Bank.

Démurger, Sylvie, Martin Fournier and Weiyong Yang (2010), Rural households' decisions towards income diversification: Evidence from a township in northern China. *China Economic Review* 21(1): 32–44.

Ellis, Frank (1998), Household strategies and rural livelihood diversification. *Journal of Development Studies* 35(1): 1–38.

Forest Department of XUAR (FD-XUAR) (2011), *Tuchu kexue fazhan zhuti, jiakuai zhuanbian fazhan fangshi, quanmian tuijin Xinjiang linye kuayue fazhan* [To emphasise the theme of scientific development, to expedite the change of the development mode, and to promote Xinjiang forestry spanning development comprehensively]. Available at: www.xjxnw.com (accessed 23 September 2011).

Heilig, Gerhard K., Ming Zhang, Hualuo Long, Xiubin Li and Xiuqin Wu (2005), Poverty alleviation in China: A lesson for the developing world? Paper presented at the International Conference on the Western Development and Sustainable Development, Urumqi, China, August 2–4.

Ho, Peter (2009), Land markets, property and disputes in China. In Max Spoor (ed.), *The Political Economy of Rural Livelihoods in Transition Economies: Land, Peasants and Rural Poverty*. London: Routledge, pp. 200–224.

Ho, Peter and Max Spoor (2006). Whose land? The political economy of land titling in transition economies. *Land Use Policy* 23(4): 580–587.

National Bureau of Statistics of China (NBSC) (2007), *Zhongtuo tongji nianjian 2007* [China statistical yearbook 2007]. Beijing: Zhongguo tongji chubanshe.

Research Report by the Team for Moderation of Agriculture in South Xinjiang (2008), *Guanyu nanjiang linguoye fazhan de diaoyan baogao* [Research report on the development of the fruit tree industry in south Xinjiang]. Available at: www.xjnb.gov.cn/news/Show.asp?id=8944 (accessed 23 September 2011).

Rosenzweig, Marc R. and Hans P. Binswanger (1993), Wealth, weather risk and the composition and profitability of agricultural investments. *The Economic Journal* 103: 56–78.

Shi, Xiaoping (2007), Away from the farm: The impact of off-farm employment on farm production, factor market development and sustainable land use in Jiangxi Province, P.R. China. Ph.D. thesis, Institute of Social Studies, The Hague.

Shi, Xiaoping, Heerink Nico and Futian Qu (2007), Choices between different off-farm employment sub-categories: An empirical analysis for Jiangxi Province, China. *China Economic Review* 18(4): 438–455.

Spoor, Max and Xiaoping Shi (2009), Cotton and rural income development in Xinjiang. In Max Spoor (ed.), *The Political Economy of Rural Livelihoods in Transition Economies: Land, Peasants and Rural Poverty in Transition*. London: Routledge, pp. 225–243.

Spoor, Max, Xiaoping Shi and Chunling Pu (2010), Shifting livelihood strategies of small cotton farmers in southern Xinjiang. In Volker Beckman, Nguyen Huu Dung, Xiaoping Shi, Max Spoor and Justus Wesseler (eds), *Economic Transition and Natural Resources Management in East and Southeast Asia*. Maastricht: Shaker Publications. pp. 221–239.

Statistics Bureau of XUAR (various years from 2002–2010), *Xinjiang tongji nianjian 2002 nian* [Xinjiang statistical yearbook]. Urumqi and Beijing: Zhongguo tongji chubanshe.

Sun, Fenglan (2009), Researching Xinjiang fruit tree programme from the perspective of sustainable development. Unpublished Ph.D. thesis, Urumqi, China: Xinjiang University.

Tilt, Bryan (2008), Smallholders and the "household responsibility system": Adapting to institutional change in Chinese agriculture. *Human Ecology* 36: 189–199.

Unger, Jonathan (2002), *The Transformation of Rural China*. New York: M.E. Sharpe.

Wouterse, Fleur and J. Edward Taylor (2008), Migration and income diversification: Evidence from Burkina Faso. *World Development* 30(4): 625–640.

8 Rural finance and development in China

The state of the art and ways forward

Heather Xiaoquan Zhang and
Nicholas Loubere

Introduction

Recent research has highlighted the importance of developing comprehensive and accessible financial systems, and allocating scarce resources in rural areas as a means of promoting socio-economic development (Brandt *et al.* 2001; Nyberg and Rozelle 1999; Zhang *et al.* 2012). Financial intermediaries have also been linked to increasing rural income, encouraging entrepreneurship, and improving rural livelihoods through the provision of resources for investment in farm, off-farm and non-farm activities, rural industries, human capital (e.g. education and healthcare), and/or for consumption purposes such as housing (Ong 2011; Pan *et al.* 2009; see also Chapter 7 in this collection). Moreover, with the popularisation of the global microfinance movement in international development since the 1970s, the concept of financial inclusion – the argument that access to financial services is a basic right – has gained popularity, and increased access to financial services has been credited with having a variety of benefits (both financial and social) for rural individuals, households and communities (Helms 2006; United Nations 2006).

There can be no doubt that rural finance has played an important role in the transformative development of rural China over the past three decades and more. Financial services have expanded and diversified during this time, which has facilitated rural industrialisation through investment in township and village enterprises (TVEs), the promotion of local entrepreneurial and sideline businesses, agricultural intensification and mechanisation, and rural to urban migration through the provision of remittances transfer services (Cheng 2006; Tsai 2002; Zhou and Takeuchi 2010). While there is a growing body of research on the development of rural finance in China, this literature tends to be from the disciplinary perspectives of economics and finance, and is more concerned with macro-level issues related to the system as a whole or the functioning of rural financial service providers. Less academic and policy attention has been paid to the experiences and perspectives of farmers and other rural actors as service users, or the impact that changes in the provision of rural financial services have had on the lives and livelihoods of local people. In this chapter we critically review the existing literature on rural finance in relation to and against a background of broader rural development policies in China, in order to gain a better understanding of the current state of the art, and to identify approaches and areas that future research can adopt and engage with.

In the following, we first delineate the historical context by mapping out the development trajectory of rural financial services and institutions since the establishment of the People's Republic of China (PRC) in 1949. We then provide a critical review of the current research on rural finance in China, identifying some of its strengths and weaknesses, and proposing fresh conceptual and methodological approaches that can be applied in future research. We conclude by highlighting our central argument as well as the need to focus on the role that financial services play in the construction and diversification of livelihoods, and rural development in China.

Mapping rural financial trajectories and contours in China since 1949

The recent transformation of China's rural financial landscape with the emergence of new institutions and services must be understood in the socio-historical context within which changes to financial policies and institutional structures have taken place. In order to fully understand the relationship between rural finance and socio-economic development, and the implications this has for rural livelihoods, we first provide a historical overview of financial service development in rural China since the founding of the PRC.

The pre-reform period

The Chinese Communist Party (CCP) began restructuring the rural financial system and practice through the introduction of rural credit cooperatives (RCCs) in CCP-controlled areas before 1949.[1] In the 1950s, shortly after coming to power, the CCP further restructured the rural financial system. The Agricultural Bank of China (ABC) was established to finance agricultural production and the RCC network was extended nationwide to become the main financial service provider in rural areas. By the mid-1950s the number of RCC branches had increased to over 103,000 and more than 100 million rural households were members (Cheng 2006: 26). However, with the rapid agricultural collectivisation after the mid-1950s, control over RCCs swiftly shifted from the members to the much larger people's communes, which, together with the supply and marketing cooperatives, incorporated RCCs into a single system (Zhao 2011). Following the failed Great Leap Forward (GLF) in 1958, and with the implementation of the economic readjustment policies and consolidation of a three-tiered (commune, brigade and team) collective agricultural system in the early 1960s, management of some of the RCCs was handed to the production brigades until the Cultural Revolution of the 1970s when the People's Bank of China (PBC) took over their administrative duties. Meanwhile, the ABC merged with the PBC during the GLF and was only re-established after the initiation of the reforms in the late 1970s (Herrmann-Pillath 2009).

Under the system of collectivised agriculture, the Chinese rural economy was less diverse and rural people were paid largely in kind (e.g. grain) through the commune's work point remuneration system (Riskin 2009). As a result, rural people were short of cash, and the ideological rigidity of the time largely forbade private entrepreneurship and discouraged most collective efforts to diversify local economies and livelihoods. Within an overall policy framework favouring urban heavy industry over agriculture and the rural sector, RCCs became one of the institutional mechanisms through which the transfer of rural resources (including rural household deposits) to urban areas and industries systematically took place – for example through policies mandating that RCCs place deposits in the PBC (Cheng 2006; Herrmann-Pillath 2009; Tam 1988). At the same time, however, RCCs also provided the financial support (e.g. the necessary start-up and operational capital) for an emerging sector of rural enterprises, especially in relatively better-off areas with stronger collective entities. These rural enterprises, which later become known as TVEs, generated extra cash income for both the collectives and rural households. While TVEs did not receive as much support as larger state-owned enterprises, they did manage to tap into the RCCs for loans. With rapid rural industrialisation since the early 1980s, RCCs continued to use pooled local savings to support local government budgets and TVEs, but were found by some researchers to be reluctant to lend to private individuals and households to initiate small business ventures (Ong 2011; Tsai 2004).

Informal finance for the purpose of investment was also constrained because of the restrictions on almost all forms of private economic and financial activities, the predominance of subsistence agriculture, and a largely mono-model of livelihood during this period. Nevertheless, in some areas rural people still set up rotating savings and credit associations (ROSCAs) to provide interest-free mutual help in meeting the financial needs of local people for ceremonial events, such as weddings and funerals, or during household crises, such as supplementing income during the illness of a family member, as opposed to investment in diverse livelihood activities and entrepreneurial ventures (Hu 2003; Tsai 2004).

The post-reform period

Since the initiation of the reforms with agricultural decollectivisation and the introduction of the household responsibility system in the late 1970s, China's rural financial system has changed dramatically. In 1979, the central government made the PBC the country's central bank responsible for setting national monetary policy and regulating the financial sector, and the ABC was demerged out and restructured to become one of the four major banks under the administration of the PBC. The ABC was redefined as both a policy and commercial bank,[2] and it also took over the governance of the RCCs from the PBC, given the changing nature of both institutions. These reforms were also meant to re-establish the cooperative nature of RCCs to meet the increasing credit needs of farmers, which went hand in hand with rapidly diversifying rural livelihoods and the increase in farmers' income in the first half of the 1980s. However, this restructuring failed to meet the designed goal; while rural savings deposited in the RCCs increased rapidly from 16.6 billion yuan[3] in 1978 to 214.5 billion yuan in 1990 (Cheng 2006: 27), RCCs were required to transfer 30 per cent of these savings to the ABC at low interest rates. Some researchers have pointed out that in the 1980s the RCCs' deposits actually became the largest source of funds for the ABC, representing some 50 per cent of the latter's total savings (Tam 1988; Watson 2003: 67). Drained of their resources, the RCCs were only able to lend 50 per cent of their total savings amount (Cheng 2006: 27), most of which went to the TVEs within a wider policy environment that encouraged the expansion of TVEs, rural industrialisation, small town development and *in-situ* urbanisation.

As formal public and collective financial institutions, the ABC and RCCs were also required to provide loans at very low interest rates to support this rural industrialisation strategy. This was evidenced by the fact that between 1985 and 1990, even though the RCCs expanded their loan provision tremendously from 4.5 billion yuan to 141.3 billion yuan and the ABC registered rapid growth in loans from 168.8 billion yuan to 377.4 billion yuan, both institutions were loss-making (Cheng 2006: 27; Tam 1988). While the strong government support for the TVE sector can be considered a success story of state-led rural industrialisation – given the role of TVEs in driving China's miraculous economic growth for more than a decade after the mid-1980s (Bateman 2010) – the strategy also led to some unintended outcomes. First, it, in a sense, contributed to the widening inequalities within rural areas and between coastal and inland regions since the eastern coastal region, with its booming TVE sector, received the bulk of government support in the form of subsidised loans, while the less developed inland central and western regions shared much less in the financial resources. Second, the unsatisfactory performance of the two leading financial institutions in rural areas also contributed to dampened incentives to further expand and diversify their products and services for the rural population.

In the second half of the 1980s, two important structural changes to the rural financial system occurred, resulting in increased rural capital outflow. First, the ABC was allowed to pursue profitable commercial lending opportunities, most of which were in urban areas, by using rural deposits (Tam 1988). This pursuit of profits also saw the declining presence of the ABC in rural areas. Second, in 1986, the Postal Savings and Remittance Bureau (PSRB) was established, offering savings and remittance transfer services through the China Post network. Since the PSRB was not a bank at that time, it reached a special agreement with the PBC whereby the PSRB could store funds at the Central Bank at preferential interest rates. This enabled the PSRB to provide its customers with higher interest rates for their savings, resulting in the rapid growth of PSRB deposits from 128.8 billion yuan in 1996 to 442.1 billion yuan in 2002. While most PSRB funds were deposited by rural households, its pot allocated by the PBC for rural lending was small (Cheng 2006: 33; Ong 2009a: 53).

In other words, rural deposits in the PSRB were not used locally. This capital flow from rural to urban areas through the RCCs, the ABC and the PSRB occurred despite the intention to provide increasing numbers of migrant workers in Chinese towns and cities with improved services to remit money back to their rural origins. As such, the newly established financial institutions continued the earlier policy effect of channelling rural financial resources to feed into urban development and industrialisation.

Meanwhile, rural people continued to rely on semi-formal and informal finance to meet their needs, which, in turn, drove the expansion and diversification of such services. In the early 1980s, the Ministry of Agriculture (MOA) introduced another network of financial providers known as rural cooperative foundations (RCFs) (Nyberg and Rozelle 1999) to ease the severe shortage of capital and financial services in the countryside. The RCFs became an immediate success – attracting deposits of 10 billion yuan by the end of the decade despite their semi-formal status (Cheng 2006: 28; Tsai 2004).[4] Informal providers such as ROSCAs, pawnshops and even loan sharks also made a dramatic return to rural China. Faced with difficulties in accessing formal finance for loans, rural people have also relied heavily on their social networks, e.g. families, kin (often on the man's side but increasingly on the woman's side as well), fellow villagers and friends, etc., for loans or pooled funds for a variety of purposes, e.g. economic, socio-cultural and human investment, consumption, start-up capital for microbusinesses, children's education, medical expenses, house-building, ceremonial events, and so forth. Some researchers thus estimate that informal finance has become the largest source of lending capital in rural China since the reform began (Hu 2003; Tsai 2004; Turvey and Kong 2010; Zhao 2011).

The 1980s also saw the first attempts at microfinance[5] with the incorporation of microcredit based on the Grameen Bank joint-liability lending method into some small-scale projects run by international development agencies and non-profit or non-governmental organisations (NPOs/NGOs), such as the United Nations Development Fund for Women, the International Fund for Agricultural Development, and others. These projects, initially relying on exogenous sources (e.g. grants) to fund their activities, were often run in coordination with local authorities and aimed to reduce poverty in rural areas (He *et al.* 2009). In 1986, the central government started its own subsidised poverty alleviation microloan programme (*guojia fupin tiexi daikuan*) in rural areas within its overall poverty reduction strategy. These loans had interest rates set as low as 2.88 per cent and subsidies were paid for by the Central Treasury (Park and Ren 2001: 43). The poverty alleviation microloan scheme was further expanded after 1996 as part of the 8-7 National Poverty Reduction Programme (*guojia baqi fupin gongjian jihua*)[6] to become one of the largest microcredit programmes in the world (Park and Ren 2001; Park and Wang 2010).

The 1990s brought more change through the official restructuring and classification of rural finance providers into policy, commercial and cooperative institutions. The Agricultural Development Bank of China (ADBC) was created in 1994 to take over the policy lending duties of the ABC, which also included the official microcredit programmes. The RCCs, which had been under the governance of the ABC after the late 1970s, demerged, with their administration transferred to county units, which became directly responsible to the PBC (Cheng 2006; Zhao 2011). Such reforms also marked a shift in the operating principles of the financial intermediaries. The RCCs, as cooperative institutions, were expected to be more responsive to the needs of farmers and small enterprises. As the ADBC started shouldering the bulk of policy lending duties, the ABC was increasingly engaged in profitable commercial endeavours, which, however, were better achieved in urban areas. This led to the ABC's further retreat from rural areas, and by the end of the 1990s the bank closed almost all its township- and village-level and many county-level branches (Li *et al.* 2011; Ong 2009b). Meanwhile, the PSRB continued expanding into both urban and rural areas (Cheng 2006).

In 1994, a group of researchers from the Chinese Academy of Social Sciences' Rural Development Institute established the Funding the Poor Cooperative (FPC) with support from the Ford Foundation and the Grameen Trust. Although some small-scale microcredit projects had been initiated in the 1980s, the FPC was the first purpose-run microfinance institution (MFI) in China. Throughout the 1990s, NPO/NGO-style MFIs modelled on the Grameen group-lending practice gained popularity and by the end of the decade there were more than 200 such MFIs nationally (He *et al.* 2009; Jia 2008; Tsai 2004). These MFIs, however, are not registered as formal financial institutions, and are thus not considered a constituent of the financial market subject to government supervision and regulation. As such, they tend to play a complementary role to the official poverty reduction strategy by providing microloans for low-income groups in some rural areas.

After 1996, the government-subsidised poverty alleviation microloan programme was expanded and its management changed hands from the ADBC to the ABC.[7] The ABC was required to allocate the microloan quotas to the township and village Poverty Alleviation Offices (PAOs) – under the auspices of the State Council's PAO – which were then responsible for organising Grameen-style lending groups of about five people each, and disbursing the loans in accordance with the quotas. It is reported, however, that these subsidised loans often missed the target groups, and instead were captured by more powerful local elites, e.g. officials and better-off groups, to either promote local development projects, e.g. infrastructure and TVEs, or serve self-interests not necessarily related to the poverty reduction objectives (Ong 2011). Moreover, instead of demanding repayments by stringently applying penalties, which could cause indebtedness, distress, and even crisis for individuals and families of low income groups, thus aggravating poverty as documented in many other developing and transitional contexts (Bateman 2012; Taylor 2011, 2012), the poverty alleviation microloan programme did not forcefully enforce repayment rules. With policy goals frequently overriding commercial considerations, these loans tended to become outstanding with repayment rates sometimes as low as 50 per cent, and thus became a liability for the ABC (Ong 2011; Park and Ren 2001: 43).

The end of the 1990s was a turbulent time for rural finance in China, which went hand in hand with serious emerging development challenges, namely the three rural issues (*san nong wenti*),[8] the state's continued neglect of these issues and retreat from its support for agriculture and rural areas. In the financial sector, with the exception of the PSRB, other rural financial institutions were considered commercially "unsustainable" because of their policy lending practices and loss-making outcomes, and thus subject to further "restructuring" and "overhauls" in an increasingly neoliberal-dominated climate in tandem with substantially reduced central government support for agriculture, which had been partly provided through subsidised financial service provision. The existing financial system was seen as incompatible with the commercial banks' core objectives of making and maximising profits, or their "efficiency" and "competitiveness". The idea of egalitarianism was further abandoned in the overall trend of privatisation and the promotion of a free market economy (Bateman 2010). All this led to further withdrawal of the existing financial institutions from the "unprofitable" and "inefficient" rural sector. About 18,000 RCFs, which had five million clients, were either closed down or merged with RCCs, triggering local campaigns and protests (Tsai 2004). Furthermore, many RCCs, especially village-level branches, were shut down or consolidated through merging with other "more financially successful" RCCs, and the total number of RCC branches fell from about 50,000 to 33,020 by the beginning of the twenty-first century (Cheng 2006: 31; Tsai 2004; Wen 2009).

These reductions in RCC branch numbers and services, along with the ABC's retreat from townships and villages, represented a significant retraction of the rural financial sector and substantially hindered access (e.g. through increased travelling distances) to financial information, services and institutions for a number of rural actors, especially farmers.[9] Under such circumstances, the extensive PSRB network became even more popular. Meanwhile, the RCCs continued to channel rural household deposits into local governments and TVEs, most of which had changed from collective to private or semi-private entities by the turn of the new century (Chen et al. 2009). At the same time, the government poverty alleviation microloan programme tended to be captured by local elites who had wider access to information, better connections, and more resources and power to secure such loans than the targeted population (i.e. low-income groups), resulting in funds being directed away from their designed goals (Ong 2011). For these reasons, the majority of rural households and microenterprises continued to rely on informal sources to meet their credit needs (Tsai 2004). All this also contributed to the problem of widening inequalities both across urban-rural areas and within rural localities.

Since the early 2000s, there have been two divergent trends in Chinese rural finance. First, the continued exacerbation of the three rural issues and increasing social discontent in the countryside have led to serious concerns within the central government about potential social instability and its own political legitimacy. This prompted the Hu-Wen leadership to pay greater attention to the rural development problems. For example, the three rural issues have been featured in every Number One Document issued by the central government at the beginning of each year since 2004, which has delivered a message of stronger political will to deal with the problems. Specific measures have since been taken in an attempt to reverse the trend of rural China lagging further behind urban areas due to a range of unfavourable policies at both the macro- and micro-levels. Of these measures, the most prominent are the nationwide abolition of the agricultural tax in 2006, the provision of subsidies for agriculture and farmers since the mid-2000s within a new discourse of "industry supporting agriculture" (see Chapter 10 of this collection for a detailed analysis of the new "agricultural subsidies" policy), the launch of the "construction of a new countryside" movement at the end of 2005, the stress on "urban-rural integration" since 2007 (Fan 2006; Veeck and Shui 2011; Zhang 2009a, 2009b), and, in more recent years, the introduction and establishment of basic social security schemes for migrant workers and a welfare system in rural areas (Brown *et al.* 2009; Watson 2009; Zhang 2009c. See also Chapters 2 and 3 in this book for in-depth analyses of the development of the new rural pension scheme, and of the social protection programmes for migrant workers and the associated challenges).

Within this context, the government again attempted to reform the RCCs in order to better support their rural members. Along with various changes to the RCC structure,[10] a large part of the RCC debt from the non-performing loans was written off and the PBC was required to subsidise a new RCC microloan programme aimed at promoting rural microenterprises and further diversifying livelihoods. The subsidised RCC microloan not only offers lower interest rates,[11] but is also expected to be accessible to low-income households without collateral (Ong 2011). Another important development was the transformation of the PSRB into the Postal Savings Bank of China (PSBC) in 2007 with the ability to provide loans in both urban and rural settings. The PSBC national network has been mandated to redirect investment capital back into rural areas by providing microcredit (for rural individuals, households and microenterprises) and wholesale loans (for MFIs and private commercial institutions) (Du 2008b). Additionally, the government poverty alleviation microloan programme has seen continued expansion, and in recent years the urban employment promotion microloan programme has been extended to rural areas, providing microcredit at zero per cent interest subsidised by the Central Treasury in an effort to generate employment opportunities and increase income for a number of rural actors, such as migrant returnees and local farmers.[12] These initiatives have been created and expanded in an attempt to more effectively address the three rural issues, in contrast to the earlier neoliberal policy discourse prioritising "financial sustainability" and "efficiency" through the pursuit of larger profits (see also Chapter 5 of this volume for a critical discussion of such a discourse related to the restructuring of China's construction industry).

In the meantime, the growing domination of a global neoliberal ideology, particularly with regard to microfinance,[13] has also impacted policy-making in China. In 2005, the PBC piloted the operation of profit-oriented private microloan companies (MLCs) in rural China; in 2006, the China Banking Regulatory

Commission (CBRC) piloted private village and township banks (VTBs); and in 2007 the CBRC approved the piloting of rural mutual credit cooperatives (RMCCs), which are the equivalent of ROSCAs, but, unlike the latter, officially recognised and regulated. While different rules apply to MLCs and VTBs, the two emerging rural financial institutions can lend at up to four times the PBC basic lending rate – much higher than the 2.3 times the basic rate allowed for state-owned financial institutions. However, current rules forbid MLCs and VTBs from operating beyond their home counties, and they cannot link up to central administrative units at higher levels in order to prevent the type of rural capital outflow discussed earlier (Du 2008b; He *et al.* 2009).

The entry of the new actors into the rural financial sector has created new opportunities for private financial institutions, local investors and global capital – represented by international commercial banks – to tap into China's rural cash reserves. For instance, since 2008, major international players, such as the Hong Kong and Shanghai Banking Corporation (HSBC), the Bank of East Asia (BEA) and Standard Chartered Bank have set up VTBs, and CitiBank has invested in MLCs. Between 2008 and 2012, an increasing number of VTBs and over 4,000 MLCs were established nationwide (Wang and Wang 2012). In a reversal of earlier practices, the ABC has started reopening some of its closed township-level branches, while other state-owned banks have begun investing in VTBs and MLCs (Du 2008a) though with different proclaimed objectives, e.g. within the wider framework of urban-rural integration – a crucial part of which is the extension of financial services and institutions to rural areas. The increased competition caused by the growing number of providers backed by international and private capital threatens the RCCs' position as the leading rural financial institution, and the RCCs, in response, have become increasingly profit-driven.[14] This has resulted in greater marketisation of the rural financial sector, which is increasingly prioritising profit-making over considerations of financial inclusion and widening access.

These two trends (subsidised poverty lending versus commercialisation) have created a complex, dynamic but often fragmented financial landscape composed of an increasing number of players with diverse and sometimes conflicting objectives, providing a variety of financial services and products to different rural actors. For instance, Cheng (2006) notes that the RCCs should meet the central government's mandate of providing support for rural actors through policy loans. At the same time, the government expects the RCCs to be financially independent, i.e. responsible for their own profits and losses. To achieve this, the RCCs must operate on a for-profit basis. Thus, there is clear inconsistency between the political and social goals, on the one hand, and the market-oriented demands, on the other. Without strong government fiscal support and transfers, the RCCs tend to operate more as a commercial entity regardless of their officially defined duties, and this is particularly true in the context of growing competition in the rural financial market. Furthermore, it is, at this stage, still unclear whether or how this increasingly complex rural financial market, with its wide range of financial products and services, has been effectively regulated by the state to protect rural clients, particularly small-scale farmers, microenterprises and vulnerable social groups (e.g. low-income individuals and families, and the elderly) from falling victim to the unbridled profit-seeking malpractices and even fraud as witnessed in almost all parts of the world.

Research on rural finance in China: the current state of the art

Our analysis above shows that China's rural financial system has undergone dramatic changes during the past few decades, which have been closely associated with the implementation of, or shifts in, national development strategies in general, and rural policies in particular. These changes have impacted rural livelihoods in diverse ways. Given this, it is unsurprising that there is a considerable, and still growing, body of research in both English and Chinese examining the role of China's financial system in rural development. However, a careful scrutiny of current scholarship reveals that, with a few exceptions (e.g. Bislev 2012; Zhang *et al.* 2012), most work is from the disciplinary perspectives of economics, finance or, to a much lesser extent, political economy, that are mainly interested in macro-level issues related to the provision of rural finance and/or specific elements related to the environment within which rural financial institutions operate. Comparatively, much less effort has been made through the application of micro-level sociological and anthropological approaches that may shed light on the economic and socio-cultural processes, practices and dynamics involved in local actors' accessing and using the financial information, products and services. There has been limited representation of the voices and perspectives of local people in terms of the relevance of rural finance to their livelihoods, their dealings and negotiations with institutional actors (e.g. government and private financial service providers, and NPOs or NGOs), and the ways in which access to formal and informal finance may have shaped their livelihood choices, strategies, trajectories and outcomes. In this section we critically review current scholarship on rural finance in China in order to identify some of its strengths and weaknesses, the main assumptions underlying both research and policy-making, and areas where our understanding is relatively less developed, necessitating the exploration of new approaches that can direct future research.

Financial institutions and service provision

Current research has paid considerable attention to the functioning of China's rural financial markets (Findlay *et al.* 2003; Meyer and Nagarajan 2000; Organisation for Economic Co-operation and Development, hereafter OECD 2003), the role that rural finance has played in economic growth (Nyberg and Rozelle 1999; Ong 2011), rural finance and poverty alleviation (Brandt *et al.* 2001; Zhu *et al.* 2002), with some studies also looking at the development of informal finance (Li and Hsu 2009; Tsai 2002; Zhou and Takeuchi 2010), and microfinance in China (Du 2008b; He *et al.* 2009; Montgomery and Weiss 2006;

Park and Ren 2001; Tsai 2004). Special attention has also been paid to how regulatory reforms have changed the institutional environment for financial service providers, for instance, the differentiation between policy, commercial and cooperative financial intermediaries (Chen *et al.* 2009), and how policies have either facilitated or constrained the expansion and diversification of the rural financial industry (Kwong 2011; Ma 2003; Sun 2008; Thompson 2003). Most commentators tend to consider the current state of China's financial system as "weak" or "underdeveloped", and then attribute this mainly to "unwanted" government interventions, which have distorted the market (e.g. through subsidies) and a legal framework that restricts financial service providers in a number of ways (Farrell and Lund 2006; OECD 2003).

There has been significant interest in examining the operation and functioning of, and the overall structural changes to, rural financial intermediaries. For example, the RCCs, which have the widest network and outreach in rural China, tend to be the focus of many studies, particularly regarding the reforms made over the past few decades to their structure and governance, their regulatory environment, the institutional factors contributing to the RCC crisis in the late 1990s, and the ongoing expansion of RCC-provided microcredit services (Cheng 2006; Ong 2009a; Wang 2003; Xie 2003). Similarly, the ABC and its role in rural China are the focus of much attention, especially with regard to the bank's relationship with the RCCs in the 1980s and 1990s, its systemic shift from a policy bank to a state-owned commercial bank in the early 1990s, its retreat from the countryside in the mid-late 1990s and subsequent return, its responsibility to implement the central government's mandate of addressing the rural development issue, and so forth (Cheng 2006; Du 2008a; Ong 2011; Park and Ren 2001; Park and Wang 2010; Tam 1988). Additionally, there are some good accounts of the regulatory environment, institutional structures, and current outreach of the new players that have come onto the stage since 2005, such as the PSBC, VTBs, MLCs and RMCCs (Cheng 2006; Du 2008b; He *et al.* 2009; Ong 2011; Sun 2011), but as of yet there has been limited empirical investigation into how these new actors operate at the local level, how they – their presence and practices, products and services – have been received, used and perceived by local people, and the impact that they are having on rural livelihoods and development. Finally, there is some fine empirically-based research on informal finance, mainly focusing on the classification of its types, the operation of the system, and the practices of pooling financial capital through informal social networks, both historically and today (Hu 2003; Li and Hsu 2009; Tsai 2000, 2002, 2004; Zhang *et al.* 2012; Zhao 2011), in an attempt to understand how rural people have dealt with credit constraints, and sustained and diversified their livelihoods through informal lending and borrowing.

Much of the existing research seeks to provide policy recommendations that are increasingly informed by a neoliberal agenda that has started dominating economic and financial research on China. These include, for example, a discourse diagnosing the problem related to China's rural financial institutions as "unsustainable" and "inefficient", and providing prescriptions of greater "market liberalisation" through further privatisation of existing financial institutions (e.g. the RCCs) and deregulation of the financial market. The advocacy for further commercialisation and financialisation of microfinance typifies this trend. These recommendations are made on the grounds that state subsidies for the agricultural sector create distortions, thus worsening the existing "unsustainability" and "inefficiency" of China's rural financial system as a whole. Furthermore, government actions in the form of monitoring and regulating the financial sector have been under increasing attack and are frequently framed in negative terms, e.g. as inhibiting free market operation, prohibiting competition, preventing the market's automatic optimal allocation of resources, discouraging entrepreneurship and, thus, hindering economic growth and development (OECD 2003). Therefore, much research in the field, implicitly or explicitly, advocates further financial market liberalisation with regard to, for instance, interest rates, services, institutional practices, ownership forms, consolidation of providers, geographical limitations, and so forth (Du 2008b). More controversial is the political pressure and lobbying efforts by powerful private and corporate interests for full-scale privatisation through fundamental property rights changes, particularly regarding collectively-owned agricultural land, which, according to such logic, would provide a form of collateral for loans, thus enabling the release of capital locked up in land for farmers to invest in larger-scale agribusiness and other productive assets (OECD 2003).[15]

These policy recommendations mirror the wider, increasingly dominant ideology of neoliberalism in global finance research and policy-making, which largely underpins the fundamental shift from promoting agricultural development through state actions – e.g. government-subsidised lending to farmers as witnessed in post-Second World War Europe or non-profit microloans aimed at poverty alleviation in the 1970s and 1980s – to the present-day profit-seeking "financial systems approach" particularly related to microcredit schemes (Adams *et al.* 1984; Aitken 2013; Bateman 2012; Bateman and Chang 2012; Hulme 2008; Robinson 2008). In the context of China's financial system development, however, more complexities are involved with respect to ideological and policy directions. On the one hand, the extension of financial institutions and services to rural areas and their subsequent diversification and expansion have been strongly state-led as opposed to a *laissez-faire* market approach, which contradicts the predominant neoliberal market orthodoxy. On the other hand, the provision of rural finance, especially the supposedly non-profit types (e.g. NPO/NGO and government-subsidised microcredit), has become increasingly commercialised and dominated by a neoliberal discourse, which is also reflected in the growing body of research in the field taking the "financial systems approach" as a point of departure. Added to this complexity is the fact that the extension, diversification and expansion of rural finance during the past decade or so have been intertwined in complex ways with, and constituted an important part of, the Chinese central government's policy initiatives to address more effectively the rural issues and to alter the dualistic structure between urban and rural economy and society in the wider context of China's political economy of development.

All this makes the attempt to box China's dynamic rural financial landscape in a single "ism" overly simplistic. The situation, therefore, calls for the identification and application of more appropriate and sophisticated conceptual, analytical and methodological approaches.

Impact and implications

Apart from the institutional perspectives identified above, some research has started paying attention to the impact of rural finance on diverse actors. This research, however, also tends to lean on the disciplinary perspective of economics combined with a discourse centring on the supply and demand of financial services and products, i.e. an analysis of the demand that different rural actors have for financial services (especially credit). The main argument put forward is that the market reforms have brought about increasing demand for credit from individuals, households, communities and enterprises, but supply by the formal financial sector has fallen far short, causing credit constraints and the formation of a large and diverse curb market (Cheng 2006; Du 2004; Unger 2002). For example, the OECD (2003: 7) estimated that only 16 per cent of Chinese farmers sought formal credit due to difficulties in meeting lenders' threshold requirements (e.g. for collateral or a guarantor), and that formal financial institutions were reluctant to lend to small businesses also because of the high transaction cost involved. It was estimated that more than 70 per cent of loans for rural people were obtained through informal channels (ibid.: 7). Most studies attribute such a state to a restrictive policy environment created through unwanted government interventions as discussed above, and recommend further liberalisation and deregulation of the financial market in order to meet demand (Du 2004; Feder *et al.* 1989; He 2008). At the same time, however, some researchers argue that the Chinese credit constraints are not universally or evenly observed across time and space, pointing to survey data that show widespread and sometimes concurrent use of both formal and informal sources (Park and Ren 2001; Tsai 2004; Zhou and Takeuchi 2010). Other studies contest the predominant view that low-income rural households have high demand for loans by showing that many such households have actually decided not to participate in credit programmes based on careful calculation of potential risks and returns (Park and Ren 2001; Turvey and Kong 2010). Still others have begun investigating, in greater detail through micro-level research, individuals' and households' awareness of, and access to financial information and services as *vital livelihood resources*, their selection of the type and provider of products and services (formal and/or informal), as well as their borrowing behaviours (Tsai 2004; Xu 2009; Zhang 2008; Zhang *et al.* 2012; Zhao 2011), revealing dynamism, diversity and heterogeneity in individual and household preferences, practices and goals with regard to lending and borrowing.

Investigation into the use of finance constitutes another aspect of impact-oriented research. The majority of studies in this area focus on the use of credit, with a very small minority looking into savings or other financial

services, such as remittance transfers or insurance products (Fleisher *et al.*
1994; Zhang 2013; Zhao 2011). Rural households are found to have used loans
for productive purposes (e.g. input and investment in agriculture[16] or non-farm
activities such as microenterprises), and/or for consumption purposes, such as
children's education, healthcare,[17] house construction, consumer durables,
weddings, funerals, and daily necessities – though the boundaries between
productive investment and non-productive consumption are often blurred
since the latter can also be considered investment in human and/or social
capital and is therefore "productive" in socio-cultural as well as economic
senses. In existing research, borrowed capital used to help individuals and
families survive due to poor harvests or other contingencies is conceptualised
as "consumption smoothing" (Park *et al.* 2003; Unger 2002; Zhou and Takeuchi
2010). This notion and the associated dichotomy of loan use between "productive investment" and "consumption smoothing", however, have recently been
questioned by critics, particularly in relation to debates surrounding microfinance (Taylor 2012). Interestingly, in China, unlike elsewhere, loan provision
and use for "consumption smoothing" tend to be more positively framed – as a
result of the outreach of rural financial services, as well as of rural people's
increased awareness of, and access to them. The heterogeneous and multiple
uses of loans in diverse household livelihood strategies (e.g. engaging simultaneously in farm, off-farm and non-farm activities, and/or through rural-urban
migration), have, to some extent, been explored in this research (Kumar *et al.*
2013; Xu 2009).

Generally speaking, only limited research has examined how access to financial information, services and intermediaries may have impacted rural livelihoods from the perspective of local actors through in-depth fieldwork in
Chinese villages. That being said, some studies have made such an attempt by
applying econometric methods, and found that easier access to financial intermediaries has resulted in increased income and/or consumption (Li *et al.* 2011;
Pan *et al.* 2009; Park and Ren 2001). It has also been reported that access to,
and use of, financial intermediaries and their services, and the negotiations
surrounding these may have broader societal implications, e.g. for the gendered
division of labour and/or female empowerment (Bislev 2012; Tsai 2000; Tsien
2002). Some researchers have observed that access to information and subsidised loans provided by NGO/NPO or government microfinance schemes is
differentiated based on existing social relations, power and emerging social
stratification in rural society – a phenomenon known as "elite capture" (Bislev
2012; Tsai 2000; Unger 2002; Zhang *et al.* 2012). Overall, due to the general
neoliberal orientation of most existing research in the China Studies field, the
literature on China's rural finance in general, and microfinance in particular,
has not engaged with the wider global debates over microfinance and the
impact of its financialisation on rural livelihoods, especially with regard to poor
people. In this debate, researchers have provided evidence that in many developing and post-socialist societies, such as India and Bosnia, the increasingly
commercialised microfinance industry has caused widespread risk, severe debt,

distress and crisis at individual, household, community and societal levels, with the impact on livelihoods being highly differentiated by caste, class, gender, ethnicity, and so forth (Bateman *et al.* 2012; Taylor 2011, 2012). This research has gone beyond a mere description and analysis of rural people's livelihood distress and suffering to question fundamentally the theoretical reasoning, logic and ideological pillars of neoliberal assumptions (Aitken 2013; Bateman 2010, 2012; Taylor 2011, 2012). The non-engagement with this global debate suggests an urgent need to apply critical theories and develop more reflexive perspectives in studies on China's rural finance in general and microfinance in particular.

Ways forward

As discussed above, overall, research on rural finance in China, while expanding, has fallen short on the empirical front that is solidly grounded in detailed ethnographic fieldwork. As Professor Peter Nolan at Cambridge University points out:

> There is painfully little in-depth scholarly research on China that uses fieldwork and case studies. This is especially true in the rural sector. Research in the Chinese countryside is exceptionally demanding. However, it is only through such research that the challenges facing China's policy makers can be fully understood.
>
> (2011: xv)

The scenario described by Nolan prompts us to think more deeply about searching for more fruitful conceptual frameworks, which may allow us to effectively address some of the key lacunae in current research that we have identified, and guide fieldwork and qualitative data collection and analysis. Here we propose that the livelihoods approach combined with an actor-oriented perspective holds such a potential on the grounds that these approaches, as both a critique of and an alternative to the prevailing institution-centred but "people-less" research (Long 2001: 1) manifest in existing studies on China's rural finance, stress the importance of examining "the real worlds" of local people by "trying to understand things from local perspectives" (Scoones 2009: 172), and by providing insight into "the self-organising practices of those inhabiting, experiencing and transforming the contours and details of the social landscape" (Long 2001: 1).

The livelihoods approach has gained prominence in development studies in general, and agricultural and rural development in particular, since the early 1990s with the publication of Robert Chambers and Gordon Conway's influential work that defines the notion as "a livelihood comprises people, their capabilities and their means of living, including food, income and assets" (1992: i). Professor Norman Long and his colleagues at Wageningen University in the Netherlands further developed and broadened the concept. According to Long:

> A livelihood best expresses the idea of individuals or groups striving to make a living, attempting to meet their various consumption and economic necessities, coping with uncertainties, responding to new opportunities, and choosing between different value positions.
>
> (1997: 11)

These definitions highlight the importance of not only the economic, but also non-material dimensions, including capabilities (cf. Sen 1984, 1985, 1987) and socio-cultural practices and value systems in understanding how people make and sustain a living (Long 2001).

In a wider historical context, where development policy-making tended to be dominated by top-down approaches, development thinking by economists embedded in classic or neoclassic traditions, and research methodology has leant heavily on positivist epistemological underpinnings obsessed with imitating the methods used in "hard science" and quantifying social data in order to seek "objective truth", the livelihoods approach has brought about alternative conceptual and methodological perspectives by placing local people and their agency right at the centre of social inquiry. It emphasises the socially constructed nature of knowledge and reality (e.g. through processes of social interactions, meaning generation, interpretation and negotiations between different actors involved). As such, it highlights the holistic and intertwined nature of livelihoods, and aims to understand the complex social interactions and relationships that are involved in making a living as part of individuals' and social groups' lifeworlds (Long 2001; Scoones 2009). Such a deep and nuanced understanding, the livelihood approach maintains, can only be gained through applying in-depth qualitative research methodologies, which take full account of the local context where diverse actors interact, negotiate, and deal with each other and with external agents in their daily livelihood struggles for their own interests, and to maintain and sustain their cultures, traditions and ways of life. In so doing, the local actors give meanings to their actions and make sense of their lifeworlds (Long 2001).

Despite the rise of the livelihood perspective and acknowledgement of its advantages as an analytical framework (as discussed above), it also faces some particular challenges. These include four interlocking aspects (Scoones 2009): (1) its frequent failure to connect what is observed at the local level with processes and politics on a larger scale (e.g. globalising forces, national policies and power relations); (2) its awkwardness, while focusing on individual human action, in dealing seriously with structural conditions and constraints; (3) its insufficient attention to longer-term change and dynamics due to its overwhelming concern with short-term coping and adaptation (e.g. with regard to climate change); and, (4), finally, its susceptibility to "multiple purposes and ends" (e.g. the possibility of being used or even hijacked by neoliberalism through an exclusive focus on individuals). Therefore, Scoones points to the need to pay closer attention to the "knowledge politics" (ibid.: 185) manifest in, for instance, how problems are framed and interpreted through discourses, power and domination on different levels and at different scales. Only when the livelihood perspective fully confronts such challenges, we believe, can it serve as a deep and sound analytical and methodological tool, and, in our particular case, aid in the exploration, examination and explanation of the complex relationships between rural finance and socio-economic development in China.

Conclusion

This chapter examines the links between rural finance, development and livelihoods in China. It charts the institutional trajectory and contours of rural financial development since the founding of the PRC. We show that China's rural financial system has, at different times, experienced either expansion and diversification, or contraction, with key players retreating from rural areas as a result of major ideological and policy shifts. These changes have had various impacts on the ways in which different rural actors access and utilise financial services, which, in turn, has implications for rural livelihoods. For instance, agricultural decollectivisation in the late 1970s and early 1980s led to a more dynamic rural economy, thus higher demand for financial services in general, and credit in particular, resulting in increased lending to individuals, households and microenterprises by formal providers as well as from informal sources. This played an important role in the dramatic rise of TVEs from the mid-1980s throughout the 1990s. At the same time, the establishment of the PSRB allowed rural households increased access to secure savings and remittance transfer services, which have facilitated rural to urban migration that has fundamentally transformed China's post-reform urban and rural development landscapes. The rise of both governmental and non-governmental microcredit after the second half of the 1980s further facilitated credit accessibility for some disadvantaged groups, even though it may have benefited local elites more than others. The retraction of the rural financial system at the end of the 1990s led to reduced access of farmers to formal financial services, especially at the village level. Over the past decade China's rural financial sector has been rapidly expanding and diversifying, both in terms of government-subsidised financial services and products in support of rural people, and commercial financial institutions seeking greater profits and returns on investment in rural areas.

We demonstrate that rural finance has played a vital role in diversifying and sustaining livelihoods over the past few decades within the context of the changing policy environment and priorities. Through a critical review of existing research in the field we show that, while considerable scholarship has been generated on the topic, this research: (1) tends to be predominantly from the disciplinary perspectives of economics and finance; (2) focuses on the macro-financial systemic and institutional change with much less attention being paid to the socio-cultural processes, practices and negotiations at the local level; (3) tends to apply quantitative survey or econometric methodologies underpinned by positivist epistemological assumptions, with much less research using in-depth, qualitative ethnographic fieldwork methods; and (4) tends to take for granted "China exceptionalism" manifest in the under-engagement with global theoretical and policy debates over the role of the state with regard to whether and how national financial markets should operate and be regulated in general, and microfinance in particular.

We, therefore, argue that the livelihoods approach, which is frequently applied in the field of development studies (particularly agricultural and rural development), can potentially serve as a conceptual and methodological tool to deepen our understanding of the links between rural finance, development and livelihoods in China, given its focus on human action at the local level, and its emphasis on representing and understanding the experiences and perspectives of local actors through micro-level telescopic qualitative studies. At the same time, we fully take account of Scoone's (2009) constructive critique of the livelihoods approach and suggest that the ways forward for researching the relationship between rural finance, livelihoods and development in China are to engage more actively with global theoretical and policy debates (e.g. on microfinance and its increasing commercialisation), and to employ a strengthened livelihoods perspective, which deals with power and politics, connects the micro-process with macro-forces, incorporates a dynamic dimension of long-run change, and demonstrates greater awareness of knowledge and its social and political construction associated with discourse, power and domination.

Ultimately, this chapter aims to build on the existing body of research on the rural financial system, institutions and policy in China, while also shifting gears to place rural people at the centre of social enquiry. Aminur Rahman, a microfinance specialist at the Canadian International Development Agency, commented that the global microfinance discourse has become increasingly fascinated "with the mechanics of microfinance, with the vehicle. There is less and less concern about the passengers and their destination" (cited in Hospes and Lont 2004: 3). This, in a sense, also reflects the reality of research on rural finance in China thus far. While it is imperative to understand the institutional changes relating to China's rural finance, it is of equal importance that we understand how such changes have shaped livelihood choices and strategies, and the lifeworlds of local people, as well as the ways in which rural people have interacted with financial institutions, negotiated their access to and command of financial resources, and how these actions may have, in turn, reshaped both the institutions and their own livelihood trajectories and outcomes. Future research, therefore, should start addressing a new set of questions that will allow for a more comprehensive and holistic understanding of how rural actors creatively construct, diversify and sustain their livelihoods, and the role that rural finance plays in these processes.

Notes

1 As cooperative institutions, RCCs were initially owned by rural households (as members) and provided both savings and loans for small agricultural producers. Politically and ideologically, RCCs were established to protect peasants from the usurious money-lending practices that were commonplace under the Nationalist government, and therefore can be considered an initial social policy intervention aimed at improving rural welfare and achieving greater equality rather than a mere financial intermediary (Cheng 2006; Herrmann-Pillath 2009).

2 Policy banks are not profit-oriented but instead provide loans for policy objectives (e.g. poverty reduction). Commercial banks are expected to be profit-oriented and financially sustainable. Cooperative institutions, typified in the case of the RCCs, in contrast, are mutually owned and should meet the needs of their members (Chen *et al.* 2009).

3 The exchange rate of US dollar to Chinese yuan (RMB) is about 1:6 in 2014. The US dollar was much stronger in the 1970s–1990s.

4 Because RCFs were sanctioned by the MOA, a government ministry rather than a state financial regulator, the PBC did not recognise them as formal financial institutions. Thus, despite their association with the MOA, RCFs fell into a legal grey zone with only a semi-formal status.

5 Aitken (2013: 474) defines microfinance as "a form of credit offered to the 'very poor' as a way to generate income from micro-enterprises and, by extension, to reduce poverty among those most disenfranchised in the global economy."

6 The 8-7 National Poverty Reduction Programme was named for its declared targets of lifting 80 million rural people out of poverty in seven years (1994–2000) (Tsai 2004).

7 The fact that the ABC, a commercial bank, took over the responsibility of the poverty alleviation microloan programme illustrates the often blurred category boundaries between policy, commercial and cooperative financial institutions.

8 The *san nong wenti* refers to development problems related to agriculture (*nongye*), rural areas (*nongcun*) and farmers (*nongmin*). These problems became increasingly serious in the late 1980s and throughout the 1990s. For more detailed discussions, see Christiansen and Zhang (2009), and Zhang (2009a).

9 In Loubere's 2012–2013 fieldwork in a village in Jiangxi Province, local people said that the village had an RCC branch in the 1990s. Since its closure at the end of the decade, villagers had to travel 10 kilometres in order to use the services provided by the township branch.

10 After 2003, the RCCs were put under the administration of provincial unions and three different RCC models were introduced: rural credit cooperatives, rural cooperative banks and rural commercial banks (Ong 2009b).

11 Normally RCCs and state-owned financial institutions are allowed to charge 0.9–2.3 times the basic interest rate set by the PBC (Du 2008a: 24).

12 Data gathered during field work in 2012 and 2013.

13 Microfinance in the global context has witnessed a significant shift from NPO-style loans aimed at tackling rural poverty and improving livelihoods towards market-oriented for-profit goals, known as "the financial systems approach". For a critical analysis of this trend, see Bateman (2012), Bateman and Chang (2012), Hulme (2008), and Robinson (2008).

14 Data from interviews with RCC managers and government officials during the 2012–2013 fieldwork in Jiangxi Province.

15 For a counter-argument, see Zhang and Donaldson (2013).

16 Recent global debates over the efficacy of microfinance point out that, in some development contexts, farming does not produce high enough profit margins to allow rural clients to repay high-interest loans from commercialised MFIs (Harper 2012;

Marr 2012). However, such a conclusion has not yet been proven with empirical evidence drawn from the Chinese context.

17 The fact that many farming households have to borrow money for their children's education and/or healthcare for family members points to an important aspect of the three rural issues, i.e. the underdeveloped social safety net. The issue started to attract increasing attention from the central government in the early 2000s, and greater efforts have been made to establish a rural welfare system with the support of substantial central government fiscal transfers combined with matching local authorities' expenditures and individual contributions. See also Chapters 2 and 3 in this book for more detailed discussions.

References

Adams, Dale W., Douglas H. Graham and J.D. von Pischke (eds) (1984), *Undermining Rural Development with Cheap Credit*. Boulder, CO: Westview Press.

Aitken, Rob (2013), The financialisation of micro-credit. *Development and Change* 44(3): 473–499.

Bateman, Milford (2010), *Why Doesn't Microfinance Work?: The Destructive Rise of Local Neoliberalism*. London: Zed Books.

Bateman, Milford (2012), The role of microfinance in contemporary rural development finance policy and practice: Imposing neoliberalism as "best practice". *Journal of Agrarian Change* 12(4): 587–600.

Bateman, Milford and Ha-Joon Chang (2012), Microfinance and the illusion of development: From hubris to nemesis in thirty years. *World Economic Review* 1: 13–36.

Bateman, Milford, Dean Sinković and Marinko Škare (2012), The contribution of the microfinance model to Bosnia's post-war reconstruction and development: How to destroy an economy and society without really trying. OFSE Working Paper No. 36. Juraj Dobrila Pula University, Pula, Croatia.

Bislev, Ane (2012), Embedded microcredit: Creating village cohesion on the basis of existing social networks. In Ane Bislev and Stig Thøgersen (eds), *Organising Rural China, Rural China Organising*. Plymouth: Lexington Books, pp. 189–204.

Brandt, Loren, Albert Park and Sangui Wang (2001), Are China's financial reforms leaving the poor behind? In *Financial Sector Reform in China*. Cambridge, MA: Harvard University, JFK School of Government, pp. 1–46.

Brown, Philip H., Alan de Brauw and Yang Du (2009), Understanding variation in the design of China's new co-operative medical system. *The China Quarterly* 198: 304–329.

Chambers, Robert and Gordon Conway (1992), Sustainable rural livelihoods: Practical concepts for the 21st century. *IDS Discussion Paper 296*.

Chen, Xiwen, Yang Zhao, Jianbo Chen and Dan Luo (2009), *Zhongguo nongcun zhidu bianqian 60 nian* [60 years of rural systemic change in China]. Beijing: Renmin chubanshe.

Cheng, Yuk-shing (2006), China's reform of rural credit cooperatives: Progress and limitations. *Chinese Economy* 39: 25–40.

Christiansen, Flemming and Heather Xiaoquan Zhang (2009), The political economy of rural development in China: Reflections on current rural policy. *Duisburg Working Papers on East Asian Studies 81*.

Du, Xiaoshan (2008a), The current supply of microfinance services in China. In *World Microfinance Forum Geneva: Microfinance in China*. Geneva, Switzerland, pp. 22–31.

Du, Xiaoshan (2008b), The current situation and future prospects for microfinance in China. In *World Microfinance Forum Geneva: Microfinance in China*. Geneva, Switzerland, pp. 2–9.

Du, Zhixiong (2004), Credit demand of rural enterprise and loan supply in China: Report on data processing results of two surveys. *Chinese Economy* 37(5): 37–58.

Fan, C. Cindy (2006), China's Eleventh Five-year Plan (2006–2010): From "getting rich first" to "common prosperity". *Eurasian Geography and Economics* 47(6): 708–723.

Farrell, Diana and Susan Lund (2006), Putting China's capital to work: The value of financial system reform. *Far Eastern Economic Review*. Available at: www.mckinsey.com/Insights/MGI/In_the_news/Putting_Chinas_capital_to_work (accessed 29 September 2012).

Feder, Gershon, Lawrence J. Lau and Justin Y. Lin (1989), Agricultural credit and farm performance in China. *Journal of Comparative Economics* 13(4): 508–526.

Findlay, Christopher C., Enjiang Cheng and Andrew Watson (2003), *Rural Financial Markets in China*. Canberra: Asia Pacific Press.

Fleisher, Belton M., Yunhua Liu and Hongyi Li (1994), Financial intermediation, inflation, and capital formation in rural China. *China Economic Review* 5(1): 101–115.

Harper, Malcolm (2012), Microfinance interest rates and client returns. *Journal of Agrarian Change* 12(4): 564–574.

He, Guangwen (2008), An analysis of microfinance demand in China. In *World Microfinance Forum Geneva: Microfinance in China*. Geneva, Switzerland, pp. 16–21.

He, Guangwen, Xiaoshan Du, Chengyu Bai and Zhanwu Li (2009), *China Microfinance Industry Assessment Report*. China Association of Microfinance. Available at: http://files.chwsda.webnode.com/200000073-aed4cafceb/Industry%20Assessment%20Report.pdf (accessed 29 September 2012).

Helms, Brigit (2006), *Access for All: Building Inclusive Financial Systems*. Washington, DC: World Bank.

Herrmann-Pillath, Carsten (2009), Credit cooperatives. In David Pong (ed.), *Encyclopedia of Modern China*, vol. 3. Detroit, MI: Gale, Cengage Learning, pp. 307–308.

Hospes, Otto and Hotze Lont (2004), Introduction. In Hotze Lont and Otto Hospes (eds), *Livelihood and Microfinance: Anthropological and Sociological Perspectives on Savings and Debt*. Delft, Netherlands: Eburon, pp. 3–24.

Hu, Biliang (2003), Active informal financing in rural China: A case study of rotating savings and credit associations in a Chinese village. In OECD (ed.), *Rural Finance and Credit Infrastructure in China*. Paris: OECD, pp. 237–255.

Hulme, David (2008), The story of Grameen: From subsidised microcredit to market based microfinance. In David Hulme and Thankom Arun (eds), *Microfinance: A Reader*. London: Routledge, pp. 163–170.

Jia, Xiqin (2008), *Xiao'e xindai de guoji jingyan dui woguo nongcun jinrong fazhan de qishi* [International experience of microfinance and the revelations to rural finance in China]. *Guangdong guangbo dianshi daxue xuebao* 17(6): 70–73.

Kumar, Chandra S., Calum G. Turvey and Jaclyn D. Kropp (2013), The impact of credit constraints on farm households: Survey results from India and China. *Applied Economic Perspectives and Policy* 35(3): 508–527.

Kwong, Charles C.L. (2011), China's banking reform: The remaining agenda. *Global Economic Review* 40(2): 161–178.

Li, Jianjun and Sara Hsu (eds) (2009), *Informal Finance in China: American and Chinese Perspectives*. Oxford: Oxford University Press.

Li, Xia, Christopher Gan and Baiding Hu (2011), The welfare impact of microcredit on rural households in China. *The Journal of Socio-Economics* 40(4): 404–411.

Long, Norman (1997), Agency and constraint, perception and practices. A theoretical position. In Norman Long and Henk de Haan (eds), *Images and Realities of Rural Life.* Assen, Netherlands: Uitgeverij Van Gorcum, pp. 1–20.

Long, Norman (2001), *Development Sociology: Actor Perspectives.* London: Routledge.

Ma, Xiaohe (2003), The difficulties and policy reform in China's rural finance. In OECD (ed.), *Rural Finance and Credit Infrastructure in China.* Paris: OECD, pp. 87–96.

Marr, Ana (2012), Effectiveness of rural microfinance: What we know and what we need to know. *Journal of Agrarian Change* 12(4): 555–563.

Meyer, Richard L. and Geetha Nagarajan (2000), *Rural Financial Markets in Asia: Policies, Paradigms, and Performance.* Oxford: Oxford University Press.

Montgomery, Heather and John Weiss (2006), Modalities of microfinance delivery in Asia and Latin America: Lessons for China. *China and World Economy* 14(1): 30–43.

Nolan, Peter (2011), Foreword. In Yuepeng Zhao, *China's Rural Financial System: Households' Demand for Credit and Recent Reforms.* New York: Routledge, pp. xii–xvi.

Nyberg, Albert and Scott Rozelle (1999), *Accelerating China's Rural Transformation.* Washington, DC: World Bank.

OECD (2003), *Rural Finance and Credit Infrastructure in China.* Paris: OECD.

Ong, Lynette (2009a), Gold in China's rural hills. *Far Eastern Economic Review*: 48–51.

Ong, Lynette (2009b), Agricultural banking. In David Pong (ed.), *Encyclopedia of Modern China*, vol. 3. Detroit, MI: Gale, Cengage Learning, pp. 313–314.

Ong, Lynette (2011), Greasing the wheels of development: Rural credit in China. In Björn Alpermann (ed.), *Politics and Markets in Rural China.* London: Routledge, pp. 48–68.

Pan, Suwen, Roderick M. Rejesus and Xiurong He (2009), Does financial intermediation development increase per capita income in rural China? *China and World Economy* 17(4): 72–87.

Park, Albert and Changqing Ren (2001), Microfinance with Chinese characteristics. *World Development* 29(1): 39–62.

Park, Albert, Changqing Ren and Sangui Wang (2003), Microfinance, poverty alleviation, and financial reform in China. In OECD (ed.), *Rural Finance and Credit Infrastructure in China.* Paris: OECD, pp. 256–270.

Park, Albert and Sangui Wang (2010), Community-based development and poverty alleviation: An evaluation of China's poor village investment programme. *Journal of Public Economics* 94(9–10): 790–799.

Riskin, Carl (2009), Great Leap Forward. In David Pong (ed.), *Encyclopedia of Modern China*, vol. 3. Detroit, MI: Gale, Cengage Learning, pp. 304–307.

Robinson, Marguerite S. (2008), Supply and demand in microfinance: The case for a financial systems approach. In David Hulme and Thankom Arun (eds), *Microfinance: A Reader.* London: Routledge, pp. 45–64.

Scoones, Ian (2009), Livelihoods perspectives and rural development. *Journal of Peasant Studies* 36(1): 171–196.

Sen, Amartya (1984), *Resources, Values and Development.* Oxford: Basil Blackwell.

Sen, Amartya (1985), Well-being, agency and freedom. *The Journal of Philosophy* 132(4): 169–221.

Sen, Amartya (1987), The Standard of Living. The Tanner Lectures, Clare Hall, Cambridge: Cambridge University Press.

Sun, Bingyao (2011), *Nongcun hezuo jinrong qianyan wenti zongshu* [A review of recent rural cooperative finance issues]. *Zonghe nongxie* 2: 8–20.

Sun, Tongquan (2008), The policy and legal framework for microfinance in China. In *World Microfinance Forum Geneva: Microfinance in China*, Geneva, Switzerland, pp. 10–15.

Tam, On-Kit (1988), Rural finance in China. *The China Quarterly* 113: 60–76.

Taylor, Marcus (2011), Freedom from poverty is not for free: Rural development and the microfinance crisis in Andhra Pradesh, India. *Journal of Agrarian Change* 11(4): 484–504.

Taylor, Marcus (2012), The antinomies of "financial inclusion": Debt, distress and the workings of Indian microfinance. *Journal of Agrarian Change* 12(4): 601–610.

Thompson, John (2003), Financial system and financial regulatory policies in China and their impact on rural finance reform. In OECD (ed.), *Rural Finance and Credit Infrastructure in China*. Paris: OECD, pp. 67–84.

Tsai, Kellee S. (2000), Banquet banking: Gender and rotating savings and credit associations in South China. *The China Quarterly* 161: 142–170.

Tsai, Kellee S. (2002), *Back-Alley Banking: Private Entrepreneurs in China*. Ithaca, NY: Cornell University Press.

Tsai, Kellee S. (2004), Imperfect substitutes: The local political economy of informal finance and microfinance in rural China and India. *World Development* 32(9): 1487–1507.

Tsien, Sarah (2002), Women, family and microfinance in China. Unpublished dissertation, Harvard University. Available at: www.microfinancegateway.org/gm/document-1.9.26388/27825_file_Women_MicrofinanceinChina1.pdf (accessed 9 January 2013).

Turvey, Calum G. and Rong Kong (2010), Informal lending amongst friends and relatives: Can microcredit compete in rural China? *China Economic Review* 21(4): 544–556.

Unger, Jonathan (2002), Poverty, credit and microcredit in rural China. *Development Bulletin* 57: 23–26.

United Nations (2006), *Building Inclusive Financial Sectors for Development*. Washington, DC: United Nations.

Veeck, Gregory and Wei Shui (2011), China's quiet agricultural revolution: Policy and programmes of the new millennium. *Eurasian Geography and Economics* 52(2): 242–263.

Wang, Wenjun (2003), The regulatory framework for rural credit cooperatives: The role of Chinese supervisory authorities. In OECD (ed.), *Rural Finance and Credit Infrastructure in China*. Paris: OECD, pp. 129–137.

Wang, Yu and Peiwei Wang (2012), *Woguo xiao'e daikuan gongsi shuliang tipo 4,000 jia congye renyuan 4.4 wan* [The number of microloan companies in China exceeds 4,000 and employs 44,000 people]. Available at: www.gov.cn/jrzg/2012-01/09/content_2040528.htm (accessed 30 April 2012).

Watson, Andrew (2003), Financing farmers: The reform of rural credit cooperatives and provision of financial services to farmers. In Christopher C. Findlay, Enjiang Cheng and Andrew Watson (eds), *Rural Financial Markets in China*. Canberra: Asia Pacific Press, pp. 63–88.

Watson, Andrew (2009), Social security for migrant workers: Providing for old age. *Journal of Current Chinese Affairs* 38(4): 85–115.

Wen, Tiejun (2009), *Nongcun hezuo jijinhui de xingshuaishi* [The rise and fall of the rural cooperative foundations]. *Zhongguo laoqu jianshe* 9: 17–19.

Xie, Ping (2003), Reforms of China's rural credit cooperatives and policy options. *China Economic Review* 14(4): 434–442.

Xu, Lanlan (2009), Providing financial services to those in need?: Challenges and experiences in rural China. Unpublished dissertation, City University of Hong Kong, Available at: http://libque.cityu.edu.hk/handle/2031/6148 (accessed 9 January 2013).

Zhang, Forrest Q. and John A. Donaldson (2013), China's agrarian reform and the privatisation of land: A contrarian view. *Journal of Contemporary China* 22(80): 255–272.

Zhang, Guibin (2008), The choice of formal or informal finance: Evidence from Chengdu, China. *China Economic Review* 19(4): 659–678.

Zhang, Heather Xiaoquan (2009a), Three rural issues. In David Pong (ed.), *Encyclopedia of Modern China*, vol. 3. Detroit, MI: Gale, Cengage Learning, pp. 316–317.

Zhang, Heather Xiaoquan (guest editor) (2009b), Transforming rural China: Beyond the urban bias? *Journal of Current Chinese Affairs* 38(4).

Zhang, Heather Xiaoquan (2009c), Social policy programmes. In David Pong (ed.), *Encyclopedia of Modern China*, vol. 3. Detroit, MI: Gale, Cengage Learning, pp. 430–432.

Zhang, Heather Xiaoquan (2013), Chinese cities and mobile livelihoods: Migration, risk and social networks. In Fulong Wu, Fangzhu Zhang and Chris Webster (eds), *Rural Migrants in Urban China*. London: Routledge, pp. 35–50.

Zhang, Yanlong, Nan Lin and Ting Li (2012), Markets or networks: Households' choice of financial intermediary in Western China. *Social Networks* 34(4): 670–681.

Zhao, Yuepeng (2011), *China's Rural Financial System: Households' Demand for Credit and Recent Reforms*. New York: Routledge.

Zhou, Li and Hiroki Takeuchi (2010), Informal lenders and rural finance in China: A report from the field. *Modern China* 36(3): 302–328.

Zhu, Ling, Zhongyi Jiang and Joachim Von Braun (2002), Credit systems for the rural poor in the economic transition of China: Institutions, outreach, and policy options. In Manfred Zeller and Richard L. Meyer (eds), *The Triangle of Microfinance: Financial Sustainability, Outreach, and Impact*. Washington DC: International Food Policy Research Institute, pp. 341–360.

9 The effects of political recentralisation on rural livelihoods in Anhui, China

Graeme Smith

Introduction

Many attempts to encourage rural development focus on political decentralisation as a panacea for economic stagnation and corruption (Cross and Kutengale 2005), with decentralisation taken as an essential first step for "good governance" by many development economists (Ahmad and Brosio 2009). However, in recent years China's policy-makers, faced with a local state that is often unable to deliver basic services, have reversed their earlier experiments with decentralisation, and embarked on a piecemeal strategy of political recentralisation to ensure that their policies are implemented. In this chapter, I examine the lowest formal level of government administration, the townships, which have been both the target and the agent of this recentralisation project. The starting point of this chapter is the perspective of township government officials and rural residents. From this starting point, I examine the often unintended effects of recent reforms on the livelihoods of rural residents.

Previous authors have accurately described township governments as hollow "administrative shells" (Kennedy 2007; Li 2007) with limited ability to raise revenue and provide basic services for rural residents. This is attributed to the tax-for-fee reform of the 1990s, and the abolition of agricultural taxes in 2006.[1] While the abolition of agricultural taxes has been welcomed by farmers (see Chapter 10 in this book), initial studies have indicated that poorer, agriculture-dependent counties and townships have been hard hit by the reforms, with central government compensation in the form of transfers insufficient to compensate for the loss in local revenues, resulting in a rise in inequality across regions and social groups (Shue and Wong 2007; Wong 2009). However, the more subtle long-term effects on rural livelihoods of political recentralisation, which has accompanied the reforms, have not been elucidated. The centralisation of township government agencies provides an opportunity to observe the response of local interests to this shift in the dynamics of political power. Rather than perceiving it as a smoothly implemented top-down reform, this chapter explores how local power nexuses have negotiated these changes, making use of formal and informal mechanisms to maintain a degree of control over nominally centralised agencies. The reforms have had unintended consequences, not always to the benefit of rural residents.

This chapter draws upon fieldwork conducted in 16 townships in a relatively well-off county in Anhui Province, which is referred to as Benghai, between 2004 and 2008.[2] When agricultural taxes were abolished in 2006, the impact on government revenue was negligible, as the different agricultural taxes had accounted for less than 10 per cent of the county's revenue. The county is located in central China and GDP per capita in 2008 was slightly higher than the provincial average. Benghai ranks in the top five in the province in terms of government revenues, meaning that the county government is in a position to provide services to rural residents, if it chooses to do so. Industrial output accounted for nearly two-thirds of GDP in 2000 (Smith 2009). From 2004 to 2008, I spent 21 months in Benghai County, working in the county government on poverty alleviation projects related to agriculture, education and forestry. As a result, I worked closely with township and county government officials on a daily basis, allowing me to obtain information beyond the scope of formal interviews.

A survey of 95 township government staff in all 16 townships was conducted with the assistance of staff from the Ministry of Agriculture between January and March 2006. Extensive follow-up interviews with township staff and ordinary farmers were conducted. Interviews were conducted either at my residence in the county seat, or at the residences of the interviewees. These semi-structured interviews provided a more nuanced picture of the behaviours of the interviewees, allowed them to frame and discuss issues in their own terms, and to construct their own narratives of their experiences with the local government.

This chapter also draws upon the work of three Chinese researchers who examine the day-to-day workings of township governments. Shukai Zhao, from the State Council's Development Research Centre, surveyed 20 township governments in 10 different provinces during the mid-2000s, spending considerable time in each township, and inviting all of the township Party secretaries to Beijing for in-depth discussions (Zhao 2007). Wenfeng Gu, a sociologist, was posted by the Henan provincial government to head a township in Hebi Prefecture in 2003, and detailed his experiences during two years as a township Party Secretary (Gu 2006). Yi Wu, a renowned political sociologist from the central China "*xiangtu*" (indigenous) school of rural governance studies (cf. Day and Hale 2007), spent a year with the cadres of a township in central China from 2003 to 2004 (Wu 2007).

The chapter examines the unintended outcomes on rural livelihoods of two different types of political recentralisation. Following the introduction, the second and third sections examine an overall trend – the merging of townships and villages into larger administrative entities in a wholesale attempt to streamline and centralise government service delivery. The fourth section explores the micro-level processes and consequences of "soft centralisation" (Mertha 2005), whereby individual bureaus at the township level are placed under the supervision of higher-level government agencies, rather than being directly managed by the township government. In the concluding remarks, I summarise the main findings, highlight the unintended outcomes of "political recentralisation" in rural China, and discuss their implications for the livelihoods of rural residents: cadres and farmers alike.

Township amalgamations

The amalgamation of townships and villages is a crucial but under-studied aspect of a national public sector reform programme to simplify and streamline local government in China. However, as previous authors have noted, such reform has been incremental, and the logic of reform has rarely been clearly stated (Wong 2009). Yet, as I will demonstrate below, attempts to bring local government to heel through the shifting of administrative boundaries have a long tradition in rural China (Skinner 1965a, 1965b). While the boundaries of Benghai County have remained unchanged since 1949 (see Table 9.1), the county has experienced a ceaseless change in the administrative boundaries of its districts (*qu*), towns (*zhen*), townships (*xiang*) and administrative villages (*xingzheng cun*).[3] The most significant changes in recent years were the abolition of the district level of government in 1992; further merging of the townships from 24 to 16 in August 2003; and the amalgamation of administrative villages in 2004, which more than halved the number of villages.

The abolition of the seven sub-county districts in 1992 was meant to be part of a countrywide effort to streamline local government bureaucracy. However,

Table 9.1 Changing sub-county administrative divisions in Benghai County

Year	Districts (qu)	Towns (zhen)	Townships* (xiang)	Administrative villages (xingzheng cun)
1949	5	2	31	143
1955	10	1	96	451
1960	–	–	9	79
1965	7	2	56	263
1970	–	1	24	237
1975	7	1	42	270
1980	7	1	42	275
1985	7	10	44	282
1990	7	10	35	282
1995	–	9	15	282
2000	–	14	10	282
2005	–	12	4	130

Sources: *Benghai County Gazetteer*, 1993; Anhui Yearbooks 1991, 1996, 2001 and 2005; unpublished *County Gazetteer*; author's interviews, 2004–2008.

Note: *From 1958 to 1983, townships were renamed People's Communes (*renmin gongshe*) and administrative villages became production brigades (*shengchan dadui*).

this did not lead to leaner local bureaucracy as nearly all district level cadres were shuffled either downwards into the townships or upwards into the county bureaucracy. Conversely, despite the elimination of a tier of government, the overall number of cadres in Benghai County increased dramatically between 1992 and 2004. The other aspect of the administrative reforms of 1992 was to reduce the overall number of towns and townships, from 45 down to 24 (see Table 9.1), which reversed an earlier trend and pattern set in motion during agricultural decollectivisation in the early 1980s. In 1983, when the commune system was abolished, there were 56,331 communes nationwide; while by 1984, town and township governments, which replaced the communes as the lowest level of the formal state, numbered 91,171 (National Bureau of Statistics of China 1985: 94). In this chapter, I refer to "zhen" as "towns" and "xiang" as "townships", because these two jurisdictions are formal and distinct: "zhen" differs from a "xiang" by having a larger overall population and a higher proportion of non-agrarian residents, although political expediency often sees smaller, rural townships reclassified as towns. Table 9.1 indicates that the ratio of towns to townships in Benghai has increased steadily, well beyond actual rates of urbanisation, partly due to such political needs. As a result, by the end of 2004, only four townships remained in the whole county.

Designation as a more urban town (*zhen*) rather than a rural township (*xiang*) government has several benefits, which partly explains the decrease in the number of township governments since 1985. A town government has more authority than a township government, is in a better position to negotiate with the county government for projects and funds, and has been allowed to raise more local revenue through taxation. There is, however, a trade-off. The degree of county government control over town governments is higher. The numbers of county officials "sent down" to work in the town governments are higher, and there is also a larger number of visiting county work teams than in their poorer township cousins. However, the degree of county government control over both *zhen* and *xiang* has increased in recent years.

The percentage of non-agrarian residents is a key criterion in assessing whether an area is a town or a township, and the push to convert townships into towns is, to a large extent, behind the reported rise in the urban population. While increasing levels of industrialisation have led to a greater degree of urbanisation, particularly in the county seat, the official figures claiming that urban residents make up 30 per cent of Benghai's total population are highly inflated. This is evidenced in the fact that between 2002 and 2003 the urban population achieved a Stakhanovite leap from less than 50,000 to more than 100,000,[4] more than doubling after the township mergers in 2003, against the backdrop of a central government urbanisation mandate. One team of researchers found that

> The [urbanisation] plans seem to be rather exaggerated when viewed against a background of the facts. The building commissioner of Sichuan Province, for instance, discovered that when all the target numbers of shi [cities] and

zhen [towns] in the Province were summed, the number of inhabitants was higher than its current total population.

(Fan *et al.* 2006: 298)

The township mergers of 2003, which reduced the number of town and township governments from 24 to 15, further strengthened the position of the county government. All decisions on township boundaries and personnel were taken at the county and prefecture levels, and township personnel said that consultation with the townships was minimal or non-existent. While formal consultation within what might be termed "government structures" was limited, there was informal lobbying by local elites of county Party leaders. As a result, several township governments with strong political representation at the county level were spared amalgamation, while others found themselves saddled with their economically weaker counterparts. The township mergers of 1992 and 2003 were in keeping with national trends that reduced the number of township governments (if not the number of township government employees as indicated above). By 2003, there were 38,028 townships nationwide, a considerable reduction from the 1984 figure of 91,171, and even fewer than the 56,331 people's communes at the end of the collective era. Within the next 10 years, the Ministry of Civil Affairs (MCA) has committed itself to further reducing the number of townships to 17,280.[5] The fact that the mergers were managed by the MCA, a ministry that has traditionally had a relatively low profile at the county level, makes it straightforward for informal intra-Party mechanisms to trump formal government processes. This does not imply nefarious intent *per se*, but is a straightforward consequence of county and township officials being able to "filter" the information flow to their superiors at the provincial level or above, particularly when dealing with a ministry with smaller political coffers, such as the MCA.

The mergers, however, do not mean that township governments have undergone any significant structural or functional changes. The mergers are part of a wider central government strategy for administrative reform, summarised in the eight-character phrase: "Increase the number of provinces, abolish the prefectures, strengthen the counties, and merge the townships." While the main justification for merging townships is administrative cost cutting, improvements in transport and communications are also cited by central government advisers, such as Chenggui Li, head of the Policy Research Centre of the Chinese Academy of Social Sciences (Li 2004). The arrival of paved roads, electricity, and mobile phone coverage in the most remote reaches of Benghai County has made governing easier. The anticipated result of the next round of administrative mergers is that the township boundaries and names of 2010 should roughly correspond to the boundaries and names of the 10 districts and towns that were defined in 1950, and the administrative villages of 2010 correspond closely to the 96 "townships" of 1950.

In general, wealthier and politically influential township governments were able to influence the outcome of the amalgamation decisions, either to bring about advantageous mergers, or to avoid merging altogether. One township, despite having a population of less than 20,000, was exempt from amalgamation reforms. The low population of this relatively urban "township" precluded it from being relabelled as a "town", but many significant figures in the county government – notably the head of the finance bureau and the tourism chief – hail from the township, and they are said to have been pivotal in putting the township off limits to an administrative merger. Also, one of Benghai's largest and most influential industrial conglomerates (a light bulb factory) originated in the township. It should have been merged with an agricultural town to its west, but the argument put to the county government was that the industrialised "township" was unsuited to a marriage with a rural "town" that is widely viewed as weak. The latter town, while not impoverished, was so poorly governed that the county leaders were anxious enough to encourage me not to conduct any research there.[6]

Less influential townships had been forced to undergo amalgamations, however, with unintended consequences for the livelihoods of rural residents. Paradoxically, the more remote and impoverished a township, the more likely it was to be merged with one or more other townships. Thus, the townships with the poorest transport and communication links, and weakest capacity for delivering government services, saw a greater expansion of the area they were expected to govern. In some cases, this meant that some farmers now faced a journey of up to two days to reach their township seat to visit the health clinic or the rural credit cooperative. Such a four-day round trip makes access to such government services very difficult. The abolition of townships is also accompanied by a reduction in health and education services, which are essential components of rural livelihoods (Ellis 2000). Once a township is abolished, generally only a primary school remains, with the junior high school being relocated to the new township seat. Thus, the most disadvantaged rural residents in remote townships face difficulty in seeing their children receive even the nine-year compulsory education, generating new obstacles to the enhancement of human capital, and therefore new stresses for local livelihoods.[7]

Village amalgamations

In Benghai County, village councils are now effectively outposts of township governments, and largely respond to the priorities of their superiors in the township. While the township is the lowest level of formal rural government in the Chinese organisational structure, in practice, village councils should be considered as an integral part of the local state. However, in recent times the rules of the game have changed, and several interrelated developments in village councils have been instrumental to this shift: the merging and amalgamation of administrative villages; the changed employment conditions of village cadres; the further strengthening of the position of the village Party Secretary relative to the village council; the rise in influence of sent-down cadres; and the manipulation of elections by township governments.

Previous research has described the process of shedding local government cadres as a "paradox" (*guaiquan*) where "reductions in bureaucratic staff yield expansion and further reductions result in re-expansion" (Tsao and Worthley 1995: 171), but my research indicates that village cadres have been permanently shed from the government payroll. Recent administrative village amalgamations provided township governments with an opportunity to strengthen their control over village councils. These reforms have proceeded by reducing the number of administrative villages, and by reducing the number of cadres in each village.[8] The rationale for amalgamations was that after the abolition of agricultural taxes, the majority of village councils' work had been eliminated, as tax collection had been the primary task of village cadres in terms of the time and effort required. Compared to township or county cadres, village cadres are soft targets for streamlining, as they are not part of the state staffing system (*bianzhi*), and much of their income previously derived from the now-abolished agricultural taxes. In some parts of China, there have been experiments with amalgamating villager small groups, but township and village cadres in Benghai were united in declaring such an idea as disastrous. As one township head put it to noisy agreement from his colleagues, "It's hard enough managing 10 or 20 households, can you imagine trying to get 60 households to agree on anything?" According to data provided by the county Civil Affairs Bureau, the number of village cadres in Benghai was reduced by 56 per cent in 2005 (the average number of native cadres per village is now four). A stated aim of the village amalgamations was to improve the "quality" (*suzhi*) of village cadres by reducing the average age.[9] The average age is now 44, a reduction of four years.[10] Of the newly-elected (and selected) cadres, more than half are senior high school graduates and 28 per cent are women. However, as men are never selected to fill the role of the women's cadre at the village level, this suggests that only a handful of women now hold the posts of village Party Secretary, village head, or village clerk, a trend that has also been noticed in Shaanxi.[11] In one village that I visited during an election, the acting village head made it clear that there would be only one woman elected to the village council. When asked what would happen if more than one woman received enough votes, he laughed and said that those votes would be thrown away (*reng diaole*). Thus, with greater competition for the smaller pool of village posts, village governments are likely to become even more "masculine" than in the past, even as male out-migration leads to the agricultural sector becoming more "feminised".

In addition to reducing the number of administrative villages and restricting the number of cadres in each village, the county leadership was also promoting a policy called "holding two posts concurrently" (*yi ren jian*), colloquially known as "carrying the load on one shoulder" (*yi jian tiao*). Under this policy, the posts of the village head and the village Party Secretary are held by one person. By the end of 2007, this was the case in 60 per cent of Benghai's administrative villages in keeping with developments elsewhere in China (He 2007). This reform, which critics see as marking a return to the Maoist era of greater Party control, is commonly justified as a means of increasing the "solidarity" of village councils and increasing the effectiveness of the Party in rural areas. It is a response to divisions that have emerged between village committees and village Party branches in recent years, and is also praised for saving on village staff costs. Many local cadres who favoured the reform also saw it as borrowing from the "scientific" management practice, with the new village (or township) supremo having powers similar to the Chief Executive Officer (CEO) of a corporation. It is remarkable that the obscurantist language of business schools has filtered into the language of governance in rural China. While the strained finances of township governments are cited as the main reason for this reform, the result is to effectively emasculate village self-governance and make the village councils an outpost of township governments.

In the words of the head of the Organisational Department of the Shanxi Provincial Party Committee, the reform was a response to the problem that

> In some villages, there are serious problems in the coordination between the "two committees" [the Party branch and the village council] leading to situations where "one cadre's word counts" (*shuole suan*), or "no one's word counts" (*shei shuo dou bu suan*), or even "outright conflict" (*duizhe gan*).

It was hoped the reforms would "guarantee solidarity, reduce infighting (*neihao*), improve cohesion, and strengthen the leadership group" (Guo 2006: 57–58). The downside, from the perspective of village self-administration, is that the village leader must be a Party member, settled upon by an internal Party ballot, not by a ballot of all villagers.

For village cadres who now manage to attain re-election (or re-appointment by the township), remuneration has significantly improved since 2005. In addition to a generous (as much as 100 per cent) pay rise granted to all village cadres, they are guaranteed a form of old-age pension, and better conditions than many township agricultural technicians enjoy. Moreover, village cadres in Benghai are now paid entirely from the township government budget, rather than drawing income from village enterprises, or deriving a percentage of collected taxes. In villages where there are insufficient cadres to carry out key tasks, such as family planning, and the township has sufficient funds, additional village cadres are paid for by the township government.

Those village cadres who lost their jobs in 2005 were assisted by a two-million yuan "poverty alleviation campaign", led by the county Organisation and Poverty Alleviation Bureaus and covering nearly 800 impoverished Party members. The rationale for the campaign was that Party leaders, even at the village level, should never be poor. In the words of one cadre from the Party Organisation Department of the Benghai County Party Committee, poorer village cadres fail to represent the "advanced nature" of the Party and

> are even poorer than ordinary farmers, so there's no way they can help the masses come out of poverty. They can't even help themselves. So when they speak no one listens; if they try to achieve something, the farmers just ignore them.

The campaign combined "thought work" with efforts to retrain such village cadres with marketable skills. However, at least one township Party Secretary noted problems emerging by the end of 2006. He stated on the county Party's website that laid-off village cadres (who identified themselves with ordinary "farmers") were the main leaders (*tiao tou*) of petitions to higher levels of government, and were a source of social instability (*luan yuan*) in stirring up conflicts between cadres and farmers.

A great deal of township government work now involves resolving disputes between amalgamated villages. Some villages that were previously in competition, or outright conflict, are now lumped together. Hard decisions have to be made and accepted, such as which village houses the village council headquarters and the primary school (as at the township level, school amalgamations have accompanied village amalgamations). Different villages come with different resources, as well as different levels and sources of debt. Newly-formed villages may not be recognised by farmers, particularly in areas where there are existing cultural, religious and lineage divisions. This is further exacerbated when the position of village Party Secretary and village head are merged into one post. While in the past the dominant lineage in a village would typically be represented by the village Party Secretary while the minority lineage by the village head, with the merging of these positions, the balance is upset, and inter-lineage conflict becomes more likely. Village mergers will also make it even more difficult to recover township and village government debts, as well as debts generated by collective enterprises (Ouyang 2005). The amalgamations have diminished farmers' regard for the village collective, and reduced the level of state control over rural society (He 2005; Wu 2005).

For village leaders, problems arose when villages with different fiscal situations were merged. For example, one village was involved in a protracted land dispute over an army base. The People's Liberation Army (PLA) had requisitioned over 1,000 mu[12] of (mostly mountainous) land from the village in 1997 and is yet to pay full compensation to the village council. The cadres from the merging partner village were displeased that the merger was going ahead before the matter was resolved by the township government. Other common problems involved debt recovery. Village debts incurred by failed village enterprises were more difficult to recover, and this often affected the prospects of ordinary villagers, who may have put money into a failed business venture with the village or township government. After the village or township ceases to exist, it becomes nearly impossible for these rural residents to recover money owed to them.

At least one administrative village was being run as two separate villages well after it had merged on paper. In this case, the more remote village had been ruled by a particularly rapacious village Party Secretary, who, in the words of one county official, "stole everything that he could" (*shenme dou tanle*). Conversely, the less remote village had access to a steady revenue stream from a large quarry, and had no interest in working with their more remote and troublesome neighbour. In this case, because the village adjoined the county seat there were a steady stream of complainants to the county's Petition Office,[13] and the county government was forced to act, sacking the rapacious Party Secretary and appointing an experienced cadre to improve the governance of the more remote village.

In Benghai County, the primary school consolidations, which have accompanied the village amalgamations, are one of the major sources of farmer discontent, especially for women and elderly men who now spend hours walking their children or grandchildren to the nearest primary school. This, in addition to inconvenience and extra burdens, reduces the amount of time they can spend on agricultural and other income-generating activities. However, a report from a wealthy county in Shandong, where students are bussed to school, found that the amalgamations had been well received (Kipnis 2006). Local conditions and resources differ markedly throughout rural China, even within a single county. A "one size fits all" approach will have a disastrous impact on the livelihoods of rural residents in many places.

Some villagers saw the amalgamation of primary schools as a township government land grab. In one village, the residents were in revolt against the township education office, which wanted to sell off a single-room primary school (*dan ban xuexiao*) that had been closed down the previous year. Single-room schools cater to the youngest children (grades one to three) in the most remote areas, but the County Education Office plan called for all such schools to eventually be closed down. "We built the school with our own hands; the materials were donated by a local enterprise," grumbled one farmer, "Now these township government bastards want to sell it for personal profit? No way." It was, however, a dispute they were never going to win, and the school building was eventually rented out to migrants from elsewhere in the county. Moreover, the larger primary school to which their children were transferred was also closed down in 2006, as the village had been merged with a wealthier village, 3 kilometres by road further down the mountain. For children in remote areas, the risk is that their parents or grandparents would simply find it too difficult to accompany them to school, leading to poor attendance rates, and even non-attendance. The headmaster of the village primary school further down the mountain, after seeing the reported increase in school enrolments following the merger of several schools, said to me, "Do you believe these enrolment figures [indicating that 100 per cent of students in Benghai County from grades one to nine attended school]? I don't. No one does." As primary school education strongly correlates with skills attainment and income prospects, the official school consolidation programme has produced an unintended consequence, which, instead of supporting, could well be detrimental to rural education and local livelihoods (Barrett and Swallow 2005).

"Soft centralisation"

Andrew Mertha described the shifting of township/county agencies to provincial control as "soft centralisation", whereby key bureaucracies are *partially* centralised in order to "regulate and discipline local government agents in their management of the economy and the implementation of policy more generally"

(Mertha 2005: 791). A parallel trend has seen agencies previously controlled by township governments being placed under the control of the county. Table 9.2 presents the current administrative status of the most common township agencies in Benghai County. The crucial distinction to be made is whether the corresponding bureau at the county level has "direct authority" (*lingdao guanxi*) over the township bureau, or whether it only has a "monitoring function" (*yewu zhidao guanxi*). Those that are directly controlled by their line bureau at the county level or above are referred to as "vertical agencies" (*chuizhi danwei*), while those only monitored by their line bureau are effectively controlled by township leaders, and are called "devolved work units" (*xiafang danwei*).

Mertha observed that the first bureaus to undergo "soft centralisation" to the provincial level were those organisations associated with "administrative regulation, financial regulation and commodities management ... because of their vital role in China's economic development" (Mertha 2005: 793–794).

Table 9.2 Administrative status of typical township offices

Management level	Township office
Province	Industry and Commerce Office (*gongshang suo*)
	Tax Agency (*dishui fenju*)
	Telecommunication Agency (*dianxin fenju*)
	China Post (*youzheng fenju*)
	Transformer Substation (*biandian suo*)
	Agricultural Bank (*nonghang yingyesuo*)
	Rural Credit Cooperative (*xinyong she fenshe*)
County	Land Management Office (*tuguan suo*)
	Police Station (*paichusuo*)
	Forestry Station (*linye zhan*)
	Forestry Police Station (*linye paichusuo*)
	Judicial Office (*sifa suo*)
	Hospital (*zhongxin yiyuan*)
	Grain and Oil Trading Co. (*liang you gongmao gongsi*)
	Supply and Marketing Agency (*gongxiao fenshe*)
	Finance Office (*caizheng suo*)
County/township	Family Planning Office (*jisheng ban*)
	Education Office (*jiaoyu ban*)
	Broadcasting Station (*guangbo zhan*)
	Labour and Social Security Office (*laodong shehui baozhang suo*)
Township	Party and Government Office (*dangzheng ban*)
	Agricultural Extension Station (*nongji zhan*)
	Civil Affairs Office (*minzheng ban*)
	Petitions Office (*xinfang ban*)
	Grain Station (*liang zhan*)
	Rural Planning Office (*zhen cun guihua ban*)
	New Socialist Countryside Office (*shehui zhuyi xin nongcun ban*)
	Economic Development Office (*jingji fazhan ban*)
	Industry and Trade Office (*gong mao ban*)
	Ecology Office (*shengtai ban*)

Source: Author's surveys, 2006 (N = 95); author's interviews, 2004–2008.

From the perspective of township leaders, the equation is simpler. Bureaus with "money and power" (*you qian you quan*) are claimed by higher levels of government, while agencies with neither money nor power, known as "clear water agencies" (*qingshui yamen*), are left under the control of township leaders.

As part of the campaign to reduce staff at the township level, certain agencies are being withdrawn altogether. In Benghai, offices of the Agricultural Bank, the Tax Agency, and the Grain and Oil Trading companies have recently been closed in the townships. Other agencies have been reduced in number, so that one agency covers several townships, creating a new, unofficial layer of government between the county and the township, which is usually referred to as a "district management area". Agencies in this category include industry and commerce bureaus, telecommunications, China Post, electric transformer substations, and the supply and marketing agencies. To see whether the management status of an agency influenced its rank in the eyes of ordinary township government staff, respondents were quizzed as to which township administrative and service agencies enjoyed the best working conditions and salaries. Table 9.3 shows the top ten township agencies in Benghai County, and only the one with the lowest ranking, the agricultural extension station, is under full township government control.

The most consistent thread between township service agencies (finance, family planning, land, and education) and administrative agencies (Party and government offices, local tax, police, and industry and commerce) with superior working conditions is the ability to levy and – to varying extents – retain fees and fines to cover salaries, general office expenses and "entertainment". While vertical agencies are physically located in a township, the township Party and government organs in theory have no formal authority to control either the leaders or even the staff of these agencies. In the case of the head of the police station, which is under the line management of the county public security bureau, it is crucial that the township leaders maintain a good relationship with the police chief, as one of the main performance criteria they are judged upon is their success in "maintaining social stability". Along with meeting family

Table 9.3 Relative working conditions of township agencies

Agencies		Best (%)	Good (%)	Management
Finance	*caizheng suo*	70	100	County
Party and Government	*dangzheng ban*	53	71	N/A
Family Planning	*jisheng ban*	11	65	County/township
Local tax	*dishui ban*	21	29	Province
Police	*paichu suo*	18	26	County
Land Management	*tuguan suo*	5	26	County
Industry and Commerce	*gongshang ju*	2	23	Province
Education	*jiaoyu ban*	7	21	County/township
Civil Affairs	*minzheng ban*	2	16	County/township
Agricultural Extension	*nongji zhan*	2	11	Township

Source: Author's surveys, 2006, N = 95; author's interviews, 2004–2008.

planning targets, avoiding "mass incidents" and petitioning to higher levels are a central part of the annual assessments faced by township leaders. Yet, a suite of formal and informal mechanisms are available to bring these staff back into a close working relationship with the township leaders. One technique township Party secretaries often employ is to arrange for the police chief to be granted the title of deputy township Party Secretary, and for them to be brought into the "township leadership group" (cf. Zhao 2007). Thus, the police chief gains access to networks through the Party branch, and has a wider range of responsibilities associated with the deputy Party Secretary portfolio. Similarly, the police station staff are over-represented in more prestigious "township working groups", such as those for attracting investment, which expands their prospects for travel, banqueting, and future business networks.

Thus, the independence of vertical agencies is never absolute. Staff in vertical agencies live and work in the township, and are subject to informal pressures. The head of a township land management agency, which on paper answers to the county, described the relationship as, "I have two wives. I should obey my first wife, but relatively speaking she's far away. My second wife is right here and nags me endlessly, so she usually gets what she wants." As an example, the Rural Credit Cooperatives answer to the province, but township leaders, particularly the township Party Secretary, exercise discretion over who can receive substantial loans (in excess of 10,000 yuan).

Similarly, if the township government opts to improve its revenue base by diverting funds earmarked for flood relief, the finance and civil affairs agencies can be pressed to comply with little danger of anyone blowing the whistle. In return, the heads of these agencies can expect to benefit financially, and the working conditions of these agencies would improve. The lack of funding for township governments has meant that diverting earmarked project funds has gained widespread acceptance among township government leaders and staff as a morally legitimate way to maintain working conditions and benefits (Gu 2006: 151–153). This practice is widely known as "knocking down the east wall to prop up the west wall" (*chai dong qiang bu xi qiang*) (cf. Zhou 2010). Even when earmarked transfers for priority areas such as education are sent down through "designated accounts" to the county government, funds can still be misused by either expanding the number of staff in the target bureau, or by artificially creating a budgetary shortfall by reducing the operating funds received by the target agency, with the funds sometimes diverted away from service-oriented agencies to administrative agencies and personnel (Liu *et al.* 2009; Smith 2009). So while the upper-level intention to support rural education is clear, the power dynamics of local government make it likely that funds intended for hiring teachers to work in remote schools end up being spent on better office facilities, banqueting and other forms of "entertainment", or vehicles.

While wealthy vertical agencies often attempted to separate themselves physically from the township government, creating "separatist regimes" (Mertha 2005: 804–805), devolved agencies were unable to resist the pressure from township leaders. In the course of spending time in different township offices, the blurring of physical boundaries between devolved agencies was striking. In one township, five different agencies shared one small room: the Agricultural Extension Station, the Agricultural Economic Management Station, the Social Security Office, the Poverty Alleviation Office, and the Broadcasting and Culture Station. These five agencies shared three desks. Such an arrangement encouraged a collective approach to township government work. Whether collecting tax arrears or promoting the "new socialist countryside" campaign, township leaders preferred to have "all hands on deck". In the devolved agencies, budget constraints and lack of power often meant that administrative boundaries were frequently blurred, in contrast to more powerful vertical agencies, which managed to maintain at least a separate room, if not a separate building.

Many interviewees felt that they had effectively become an extension of the township Party branch, responding to the priorities of township Party leaders, which tended to change according to the political wind of the day. The head of a township's Urban Construction Office said that he was unable to plan his office's work from day-to-day, let alone over the course of a year. As he explained:

> We don't get a chance to use our skills: the majority of our time is spent on administrative work. We've no time to impart the knowledge that the farmers need, and the work that the leading township cadres assign to us is a mess. One day you'll be hosting a visiting delegation, the next demolishing illegal buildings, tidying up the appearance of the township seat, or clearing rubbish; there's no thought of providing meaningful service to the farmers.

The effect of this chaotic work schedule on ordinary staff was, unsurprisingly, numbness (*mamu*). Thus, unable to work according to "calculable rules and 'without regard for persons'" (Weber 1978: 975), many township staff in devolved agencies, while nominally under the full administrative control of the township leaders, paradoxically become harder to mobilise than staff in vertical agencies. The lack of political and financial power of the organisation where they worked meant there were limited prospects for their promotion or recognition by upper-level authorities. This, combined with the limited autonomy that they enjoyed in their daily work, undermined morale and functioned as disincentive to the local officials in devolved agencies (Zhao 2007).

Not all personnel within devolved agencies were keen to return to higher-level control, however, as past experience had taught them that weak county-level agencies, such as the agriculture bureau, were unable to provide financial security (Liu *et al.* 2009: 989–992; Mertha 2005: 806–808). The township agricultural economy station was rumoured to be returning to vertical line management later in 2009, and many staff were uneasy about this development. As one explained:

> We don't want to return to being a vertical agency, because we don't want to be directly run by the county agricultural committee. At the moment,

the township finance bureau guarantees all of our wages and subsidies [for meals and transport)]. But if we go back to line management [under the county agricultural committee]), there's no way the higher-ups would pay for our subsidies. Nor would the township government pay, because you're no longer managed by them.

Uncertainty was a common theme in many interviews with the staff of devolved agencies, and led these staff to devote a great deal of their energies (and finances) to seeking an escape route, rather than actually doing their jobs. As one county official explained:

Their jobs are insecure. Sooner or later, they'd be out of work. If they don't find a way out, they'd be on the scrapheap. It's not a question of ability; that's no guarantee. They work for the township. No matter how skilful they are, how do they demonstrate this? How do they get the higher-ups to notice their ability? There's no way. Capable or not, they're all in the same boat. So they simply play cards and get drunk.

Another "escape route" was through what Barbara Harriss-White terms the "shadow state", which surrounded township governments, providing goods and services to the formal state, usually at prices above market rates (Harriss-White 2003; Smith 2009: 38–40). A large number of township government staff already had a side business, such as a restaurant, a small construction materials factory, or a printing shop. Over time, this accumulation of (former and current) government officials providing services to the local state is leading to the emergence of a class of "entrepreneurial brokers" (Duara 1988: 73–76) in the county and township seats. The line between state and non-state actors has become increasingly blurred. It is not uncommon for these state entrepreneurs to change their businesses according to the demand for infrastructure and services. One such entrepreneur shifted seamlessly from providing computer hardware (when providing computers for high schools was a government priority) to concrete tiles for canal embankments (when flood prevention became a priority) while holding down his job as a clerk in the Human Resources and Social Security Bureau and as a driver for government officials.

While township staff tended to refer to "township leaders" as a whole, the township leadership group was often divided in terms of which interests it served. Township Party secretaries and township heads, selected by the County Party Standing Committee, were, as a rule, chosen as "a pair", and would generally work together in their daily management and leadership roles. In the event of a falling out, the township heads would usually find themselves isolated. Most interviewees saw the Party Secretary as the most powerful figure in this Party–government leadership partnership, and accordingly sided with the Party Secretary if an internal conflict occurred, as the vast majority of the leadership group were former county bureau chiefs, deputy county heads, or former personal secretaries (*mishu*) to the county leaders.

Personal secretaries exercise power well beyond their official jobs as "secretaries" since they have direct access to power, can exert considerable influence on decision-making processes, which others cannot, and sometimes act as power brokers.[14]

Rather than residing in their township, township Party secretaries commonly live in the county seat, and commute to the township when required. This practice stemmed from both practical considerations, with increasing centralisation meaning that a large number of meetings were held in the county seat, and from personal considerations related to the centralisation of service provision. A frequently expressed sentiment in interviews with township officials was that "everyone wants to live in town", due to the higher quality of health, education, housing and other social services available in the county seat. This attitude permeated all township government staff, and led to township bureaus in or near the county seat being overstaffed, often to quite ludicrous extents. At one stage, the township forestry bureau based in the county seat had more than 30 staff, when at most half that number was required. Within townships, teachers would be expected to "show their appreciation" (monetarily) to avoid being posted to a remote primary school. Depending on the size of the payment, an alternative post at the "key primary school" (*zhongxin xuexiao*) in the township seat could be arranged, or, better yet, a school in the county seat. Younger teachers, in particular, are keen to avoid being posted to a remote village, as it would also reduce their prospects of finding a suitable partner. Aside from providing an additional source of revenue for officials with the power to transfer township staff, from the perspective of rural residents, this phenomenon means that schools and medical facilities in remote villages tend to be understaffed and underfunded, while those in township and county seats have an abundance of staff and resources. This phenomenon is well known to rural residents, and is a major factor driving the migration of rural residents to "urban" county and township seats. For those who cannot afford to "live in town",[15] residing in a village close to the county or township seat will be the goal.

While younger township Party secretaries and township heads generally saw their future in the county seat, and would comply (or at least appear to comply) with the development strategies of the county leadership, older deputy township leaders with little prospect of promotion to the county level owed less fealty to the county leadership, and would often lobby against projects initiated at the county level or above, which they saw as detrimental to local interests. At times, they would come close to the ideal of the Republican era "rural agents" (*xiangbao*), protecting rural communities from vanity projects and land requisitioning (Duara 1988: 48–53). In this sense, the commonly held assumption that younger leaders would necessarily provide a better quality of leadership for rural residents needs some reconsideration. In the case of the most wasteful project recently initiated in Benghai County, the construction of a "government service area" – effectively rebuilding and relocating the entire county government seat because of a perceived problem with the *fengshui* of the present site – the only actors who were able to effectively lobby the provincial government to halt the project were older and retired cadres. It was stymied for more than a year, but eventually the project went ahead, as part of the nationwide stimulus package in response to the global financial crisis implemented in 2008.

Township leaders are frustrated by resistance from staff in vertical agencies which no longer answer to them, by unmotivated staff in devolved agencies, and are pressured from above by county leaders. With township leaders frustrated, focused on their future careers, and spending large amounts of the year outside the township attending meetings or entertaining potential investors, a power vacuum has emerged in many townships. This vacuum is often filled by directors of the general offices of townships (*bangongshi zhuren*), who often control access to the Party Secretary, and thus wield disproportionate influence. These directors coordinate township government staff during the long periods of the year when township leaders are away. While most township government agencies (family planning, finance and police aside) are usually deserted, one director has eight staff working under him, including a driver. Like their counterparts at the county level, their authority derives from their ill-defined powers. Many new township Party secretaries appoint their own directors of the general office, usually a trusted personal friend whom they previously relied upon while working in the county government.

Conclusion

In categorising the outcomes of administrative centralisation in rural China, the consequences for rural livelihoods are unintended in many different respects. The outcome may be unintended, in the sense that policy-makers had not considered all the ramifications of pursuing a uniform strategy across all of China, as with the pursuit of the primary school consolidation programme in areas where transportation is difficult. This unintended consequence may be the most serious impact on the livelihoods of China's rural residents, as attaining a primary school education correlates strongly with income and human capital development. Nor is it likely that policy-makers considered that township and village amalgamations would make it more difficult for local governments and ordinary citizens to recover outstanding debts from the merged townships and villages.

Outcomes may be unintended in the sense that local governments have succeeded in thwarting the original intent of the reform of streamlining local bureaucracy, providing better services for farmers and effectively implementing the New Socialist Countryside Programme, as is the case when increasing centralisation paradoxically encourages township Party leaders to exert informal pressures on government agencies to divert funds to both licit and illicit channels, or when county Party leaders manipulate township amalgamations to suit their interests, to the detriment of poorer, more remote townships. Similarly, it cannot be said that these reforms were intended to disadvantage rural residents in the most remote villages and townships, but reforms which concentrate resources in the county seat have dovetailed with the desire on the part of both rural residents and government officials to "live in town", to produce just such an outcome.

The two types of reform examined in this chapter – "soft centralisation" and the merging of townships and villages – may have succeeded in shifting the locus of power upwards to the county and provincial levels, but they have failed to achieve the originally designed goal of building a more effective bureaucracy at the level of local government. While the abolition of agricultural taxes in 2006 means that the township government has lost much of its traditional extractive function, administrative centralisation has spawned more complicated interactions within the township bureaucracy, and in township cadres' interactions with other institutional actors at the upper and lower levels. The formal dictates of state power are shaped by the informal norms of township politics and by actors embedded in local institutions, interests and power relations. The formal and informal co-evolve, producing outcomes that are both unintended and build on dynamics also witnessed in earlier stages of the reforms.

Notes

1 The extraction of revenue was originally the primary function of township governments (Duara 1988).
2 Due to the need to protect sources, Benghai is a pseudonym.
3 Territory was ceded to a county adjoining Benghai when the county borders were redrawn in 1949.
4 Unpublished Benghai *County Gazetteer*; author's interviews.
5 The change of boundaries, status and mergers of jurisdiction are managed by the MCA through its Department of Administrative Demarcation, which applies unified national rules to changes in the boundaries of jurisdiction and the management of place names.
6 During the course of my time in Benghai, I discovered that there were several reasons for the county leaders' unease about this township, relating to instances of illegal land requisition, a failed township enterprise, and corruption surrounding a national irrigation scheme.
7 This inequality of opportunity within a rural county echoes a nationwide regional disparity in education services. In 2004, Shanghai spent 6,700 yuan per primary school student, while Guizhou spent just 745 yuan per student (Wong 2009: 942).
8 Each village will, at a minimum, have at least three cadres: the village Party Secretary (*cunbu shuji*), who is responsible for overall management of the village, and is appointed by the township. The village may have a village head (*cun zhang* or *cunweihui zhuren*) who is in charge of the elected village committee, though in some villages this position is merged with that of the village Party Secretary. This phenomenon will be discussed later in the chapter. There are also two elected positions: that of the village clerk (*wenshu*), responsible for village finances and submitting reports to higher levels; and the women's cadre (*funü ganbu*), responsible for family planning. In addition, the village may also have several sent-down cadres (*xiapai ganbu*) from the township or county governments. In larger administrative villages, there may also be deputy Party Secretary and deputy village head.
9 It is unclear, however, why younger cadres would make any substantial difference to modes of rural governance, cf. Lü (2000: 255–257).

10 Locally-posted instructions indicated that no one over the age of 45 was allowed to stand for re-election except under "special circumstances". The average age of 44 suggests that quite a few candidates were granted special permission.

11 Tamara Jacka, personal communication, 22 July 2008.

12 One mu is equivalent to 1/15 of a hectare.

13 Rural residents in China can express their grievances with local authorities by lodging formal written complaints with government petition offices at higher levels of government. The petitioning process itself, however, sometimes involves political mobilisation well beyond what the local state can tolerate, and places rural residents in direct confrontation with the state (Li 2008).

14 For a discussion of their influence within Benghai County, see Smith (2009: 37–39).

15 Real estate prices in Benghai County seat commonly reach 3,000 yuan per square metre.

References

Ahmad, Ehtisham and Giorgio Brosio (2009), *Does Decentralization Enhance Service Delivery and Poverty Reduction?* Cheltenham: Edward Elgar.

Barrett, Christopher and Brent M. Swallow (2005), Dynamic poverty traps and rural livelihoods. In Frank Ellis and H. Ade Freeman (eds), *Rural Livelihoods and Poverty Reduction Policies*. London: Routledge, pp. 16–27.

Cross, Sholto and Milton Kutengale (2005), Decentralization and rural livelihoods in Malawi. In Frank Ellis and H. Ade Freeman (eds), *Rural Livelihoods and Poverty Reduction Policies*. London: Routledge, pp. 119–132.

Day, Alexander and Matthew A. Hale (eds) (2007), *Chinese Sociology and Anthropology* 39(4): 3–96.

Duara, Prasenjit (1988), *Culture, Power, and the State: Rural North China, 1900–1942*. Stanford, CA: Stanford University Press.

Ellis, Frank (2000), *Rural Livelihoods and Diversity in Developing Countries*. Oxford: Oxford University Press.

Fan, Jie, Thomas Heberer and Wolfgang Taubmann (2006), *Rural China: Economic and Social Change in the Late Twentieth Century*. Armonk, NY: M.E. Sharpe.

Gu, Wenfeng (2006), *Feichang zishu: Yige xiangzhen shuji de meng yu teng* [Extraordinary accounts: The hopes and troubles of a township Party Secretary]. Beijing: Xinhua chubanshe.

Guo, Xinmin (2006), *Jiaqing nongcun jiceng zuzhi jianshe de xin lu: Changzhi shi tuixing xiangzhen, cun dangzheng "yi jian tiao" de shixian yu sikao* [Strengthening a new path to build grassroots organisations: Analysis and practice in promoting the merging of township and village party-government positions in Changzhi City]. *Qiushi* 21: 57–58.

Harriss-White, Barbara (2003), *India Working: Essays on Society and Economy*. Cambridge: Cambridge University Press.

He, Baogang (2007), *Rural Democracy in China*. New York: Palgrave Macmillan.

He, Xuefeng (2005), *He cun bing zu: Yihuan wuqiong* [Amalgamating villages and merging villager small groups: An on-going calamity]. *Diaoyan Shijie* 11: 30–31.

Kennedy, John J. (2007), From the tax-for-fee reform to the abolition of agricultural taxes: The impact on township governments in north-west China. *China Quarterly* 189: 43–59.

Kipnis, Andrew (2006), School consolidation in rural China. *Development Bulletin* 70: 123–125.

Li, Chenggui (2004), *Zeng sheng, che shi, qiang xian, bing xiang* [Increasing the role of provinces, eliminating the control of cities [over counties], strengthening counties, and merging townships]. Available at: www.chinaelections.org/NewsInfo.asp?NewsID=68868 (accessed 24 May 2010).

Li, Lianjiang (2008), Political trust and petitioning in the Chinese countryside. *Comparative Politics* 40(2): 209–226.

Li, Linda C. (2007), Working for the peasants? Strategic interactions and unintended consequences in China's rural tax reform. *The China Journal* 57: 90–106.

Liu, Mingxing, Juan Wang, Ran Tao, and Rachel Murphy (2009), The political economy of earmarked transfers in a state-designated poor county in western China: Central policies and local responses. *China Quarterly* 200: 973–994.

Lü, Xiaobo (2000), *Cadres and Corruption: The Organizational Involution of the Chinese Communist Party*. Stanford, CA: Stanford University Press.

Mertha, Andrew C. (2005), China's 'soft' centralization: Shifting tiao/kuai authority relations. *China Quarterly* 184: 791–810.

National Bureau of Statistics of China (1985), *Zhongtuo tongji nianjian 1985* [China statistical yearbook 1985]. Beijing: Zhongguo tongji chubanshe.

Ouyang, Zhongqiu (2005), *Xiangzhen gaige, buke qingyan bing cun* [In the course of township reform, villages cannot be merged lightly]. Available at: www.chinaelections.org/NewsInfo.asp?NewsID=3204 (accessed 24 May 2010).

Shue, Vivienne and Christine Wong (eds) (2007), *Paying for Progress in China: Public Finance, Human Welfare and Changing Patterns of Inequality*. London: Routledge.

Skinner, G. William (1965a), Marketing and social structure in rural China: Part II. *The Journal of Asian Studies* 24(2): 195–228.

Skinner, G. William (1965b), Marketing and social structure in rural China: Part III. *The Journal of Asian Studies* 24(3): 363–399.

Smith, Graeme (2009), Political machinations in a rural county. *The China Journal* 62: 29–59.

Tsao, King K. and John A. Worthley (1995), Chinese public administration: Change with continuity during political and economic development. *Public Administration Review* 55(2): 169–174.

Weber, Max (1978), *Economy and Society*, 2 vols, Berkeley, CA: University of California Press.

Wong, Christine (2009), Rebuilding government for the 21st century: Can China incrementally reform the public sector? *China Quarterly* 200: 929–952.

Wu, Licai (2005), *He cun bing zu dui cun zhi de fumian yingxiang* [Negative effects of village and villager small group amalgamations]. *Diaoyan Shijie* 8: 39–40.

Wu, Yi (2007), *Xiaozhen xuanxiao: Yi ge xiangzhen zhengzhi yunzuo de yanyi yu chanshi* [Uproar in a small town: Interpretation of a township's political operation]. Beijing: Sanlian shudian.

Zhao, Shukai (2007), Rural governance in the midst of underfunding, deception, and mistrust. In Andrew Kipnis and Graeme Smith (eds), *Chinese Sociology and Anthropology*, 39(2): 8–93.

Zhou, Xueguang (2010), The institutional logic of collusion among local governments in China. *Modern China* 36(1): 47–78.

10 From taxing to subsidising farmers

Designing and implementing the "four subsidies" in China

Louis Augustin-Jean and Ye Wang

Introduction

The beginning of the 2000s has seen a small revolution in the Chinese country-side. For the first time in Chinese history, farmers did not pay agricultural tax and, in a complete reversal of previous practices, instead started receiving some subsidies. From an international perspective, this policy is not unprecedented: when per capita GDP increases and the number of farmers (in absolute or rela-tive terms) decreases due to livelihood diversification, rural out-migration, and so on, it is not unusual for governments to replace taxes, fully or partially, by subsidies (de Gorter and Swinnen 2002). Indeed, Europe, the United States, and, more recently, Japan and South Korea all share similar experiences. The policy can then be seen either as a transfer of resources from urban centres to the rural sector, aimed at balancing economic development and social equity (as is the case in China), or as a response to the lobbying from farmers, as in many developed industrial countries (Meng 2012).

At the macro-economic level, attention shifts to the question of the efficiency of the subsidies, and the answers vary depending on the definition of "efficiency" and the model adopted by the researcher – the dominant perspective being that agricultural subsidies create distortions and, for that reason, should be elimi-nated. This point regularly surfaces during international negotiations, for exam-ple, at the rounds of the World Trade Organisation (WTO). It is, therefore, hardly surprising that research on the implementation of Chinese subsidies concentrates on this point. For instance, Huang *et al.* conclude that China's subsidy programme "so far, is being accomplished with few distortions to grain sown area or input use" (2011: 69). Despite some differences in assessment, the general consensus among researchers is the acknowledgement that the Chinese agricultural subsidy policy is in line with the WTO's requirements.[1]

From a livelihoods perspective – the core theme of this book, policies related to financial transfers have the potential to deeply affect the livelihoods of farm-ers, and their relationships with the local and central state. The policies, then, should be analysed not only in the light of their economic effects, but also their social and political impact. In China, the subsidy programme is part of the broader policies that target what Veeck and Shui (2011) elegantly called China's agricultural policy "trilemma" – the *san nong wenti*, or the "three rural issues", which encompasses agriculture (*nongye*), farmers (*nongmin*) and the countryside (*nongcun*). These policies mainly aim to curb the imbalance between rural and urban development, stimulate growth in the countryside and boost farmers' income. The Chinese government made it clear that top priority should be given to solve problems facing agriculture, rural areas and farmers (Chinese Communist Party Central Committee, hereafter CCPCC, and State Council 2004).

This broader perspective is helpful to complement the existing research aiming to assess if the new policy of subsidies helps curb revenue imbalance and social inequality. Researchers have started to investigate whether such subsidies have effectively reached the poor, and/or helped equalise revenues (Gale *et al.* 2005; Huang *et al.* 2011; Lin and Wong 2012; Meng 2012); however, the conclusions of these investigations vary. For example, Huang *et al.* (2011) find that the subsidies received do not depend on the level of wealth in a household. Conversely, Lin and Wong (2012) argue that poor farmers as well as people in poorer areas/provinces receive fewer subsidies than others.[2] Finally, based on a survey in Hubei Province, Meng (2012) finds that the subsidies provide some incentives for farmers to work on land rather than migrate to the city, even though their impact on revenues seems to be limited (1.7 per cent, according to Huang *et al.* [2011] and 4.6 per cent according to Lin and Wong [2012]).[3] Yet despite the possible limited direct economic impact of the subsidies, many other benefits can be gained from the policy, including those related to considerations of the Chinese central government's political legitimacy.

Another aspect of the policy affecting its effectiveness is its implementation. Indeed, the design of the policy is an important institutional device that farmers could use to formulate livelihood strategies, and therefore is central to the livelihoods framework (Scoones 2009: 177). The livelihoods of farmers are not only linked to the amount of funds that are distributed, but also to the way they are channelled, i.e. the design and implementation of the policy matter as much as the policy itself. The state is far from being a single, unified monolith, and the implementation of any given policy depends on which governmental body is put in charge, how the policy is interpreted and carried out at the local level, whether it requires cross-sectoral cooperation, and, if so, whether/how this cooperation unfolds on the ground. For example, Augustin-Jean and Xue (2011) show how the meaning of the 2006 law on cooperatives has been distorted during its implementation in Shanxi Province to benefit mainly local elites instead of ordinary farmers, despite the fact that cooperatives have served as an effective tool for development in other locations.

This chapter addresses the implementation and management of four types of agricultural subsidies, or *si butie* in Chinese, as a major component of the *san nong* policy. These include: (1) the direct subsidy to grain farmers; (2) the general subsidy for agricultural input; (3) the quality seeds subsidy; and (4) the agricultural machinery subsidy (see below for details). Rather than directly analysing their effects on living standards, we adopt a complementary approach and focus on the design and implementation of the policy, and their consequences for livelihoods – an under-researched area in the existing literature. This analysis is performed through a detailed case study in Jilin Province[4] focusing on two of these subsidies (the direct subsidy to grain farmers and the quality seeds subsidy).

The chapter is structured as follows. The next section outlines China's agricultural policy development since the late 1970s in order to contextualise the "four subsidies" policy introduced since the mid-2000s. This is followed by a detailed discussion of each of the four subsidies. The fourth section focuses on our case study of Jilin, analysing specifically the implementation and management of the two subsidies (see above), and shows that their design influences their effectiveness in achieving the declared policy goals and thus the impact they have on the livelihoods of farmers. In the final section we draw conclusions based on the analysis.

From taxing to supporting farmers: the evolution of China's agricultural policy since 1978

For decades after the founding of the People's Republic of China (PRC) in 1949, the Chinese government followed the policy of taxing agriculture to support its urban industrialisation efforts. The central government was engaged in a strategy of developing heavy industry in urban areas through extracting agricultural surplus from rural areas. Under the centrally planned economy, agriculture provided the major part of the capital necessary for China's industrialisation. This was achieved through, among other things, agricultural collectivisation, a price scissors mechanism – which artificially set low prices for the main agricultural produce and thus exacerbated the adverse terms of trade for agriculture (vis-à-vis industry) – and the household registration (*hukou*) institution, which prohibited most rural-urban migration. It is estimated that from 1954 to 1978, the agricultural sector provided about 450 billion yuan for China's national industrialisation (Zhang 2008).

With the onset of post-Mao reforms in the late 1970s, a new contractual relationship between the Chinese state and the farming household was introduced through the establishment of the Household Responsibility System, and rural communes were soon abolished. Family farming means that individual households have gained land use rights for collectively-owned land, and land was divided and accessed, by and large, on an equitable basis. Decollectivisation initiated in the late 1970s and early 1980s, combined with other policy measures, in particular, significant price rises for agricultural produce during the first half of the 1980s, led to significant improvement in farmers' income and poverty reduction for the rural population (OECD 2005). However, after a series of price rises for agricultural produce in the early 1980s, the trend started to reverse, and central government policies were swiftly changed to disadvantage agriculture again. As a result, more than 20 trillion yuan were estimated to have been transferred from agriculture to other sectors from 1979 to 2000 (Zhang 2008).

As a consequence, income inequality was severely aggravated in China between 1988 and 1995 with the urban-rural gap being the main contributor

(Khan and Riskin 1998). From 1997 to 2000, farmers' income growth further decreased and rural livelihoods were negatively affected. In 2000, Mr Changping Li, Party Secretary of Qipan Township, Hubei Province, wrote a letter to the then Premier Zhu Rongji, in which he described the rural situation by saying, "farmers' lives are in real hardship, rural areas are very poor and agriculture is very risky" (*nongmin zhen ku, nongcun zhen qiong, nongye zhen weixian*) (Li 2000). In 2002, the 16th National Congress of the Communist Party considered the gap between urban and rural areas to be the main obstacle to further development. In 2003, the term "*san nong wenti*" first appeared in the work report of the CCPCC. In the same year at the Central Rural Work Conference, President Hu Jintao stressed that "the government will give top priority to all its work aimed at solving problems facing agriculture, rural areas and farmers". This was, in his own words, the "focus of the focus" (CCPCC and the State Council 2004). Meanwhile, the central government decided that the policies of increasing farmers' income should target the major grain-producing areas and grain producers.

Generally speaking, this policy change addressed two kinds of concerns. The first is the continued stagnation in farmers' income growth, especially for farmers in major grain-producing areas. From 1997 to 2003, the annual growth rates of farmers' income were only half of those of urban residents. In 2003, the income gap between urban and rural residents was as high as 3.3 to 1. Second, this situation negatively affected grain production and supply (Chen 2004). Grain production had declined for six consecutive years from 1998 to 2004 before starting to increase again (Veeck and Shui 2011: 251). In fact, "in 2000, agriculture contributed negatively to farmers' net income by –112 per cent, of which crop cultivation accounted for –229 per cent" (Bai and He 2002: 73). This is also evidenced in Jilin – while the per capita yield of marketable grain is high, the average net income of farmers was more than 80 yuan lower in 2002 compared with that in 1998. Agriculture in general, and grain cultivation in particular, became so unprofitable that farmers were reluctant to engage in it.

This situation finally caught the attention of China's top leadership and led to a major policy shift. Since 2004, the "No. 1 Document" (*yihao wenjian*) issued by the central government at the beginning of each year has been devoted to rural affairs. The central government's fiscal transfer to the agricultural sector has been increasing rapidly, and agricultural tax was substantially reduced and eventually abolished in 2006. In 2004, the central government's budgetary spending on agriculture, rural areas and farmers totalled 262.6 billion yuan, an increase of 22.5 per cent from that of 2003. In 2008, this spending reached 595.55 billion yuan, showing an annual increase of 163.7 billion yuan or 37.9 per cent (Lin and Wong 2012: 27; Wen 2009). As shown in Table 10.1, the fiscal transfer further increased to 716 and 818 billion yuan in 2009 and 2010, respectively. This amount covers support for agricultural inputs, measures against natural disasters and crop diseases, technological support and development, protection of the crop-growing environment, structural readjustments in the agricultural sector, and so forth (see also Chapter 7 of this book for an analysis of the new agricultural subsidy policy and the official livelihood diversification effort for cotton farmers in Xinjiang).

Table 10.1 Central government's budgetary support for the *san nong* sector in 2009 and 2010 (billion yuan)

Support	2009	2010
Increasing subsidies for farmers	123.08	133.49
Direct subsidy to grain farmers	19	15.1
Input subsidy	75.6	83.5
Quality seeds subsidy	15.48	20.4
Agricultural machinery subsidy	13	14.49
Improving agricultural production conditions	264.22	316.38
Further developing infrastructure and public services in rural areas	269.32	310.85
Supporting agricultural products' reserve and interest expense	57.62	57.62
Other	1.9	-
Total	716.14	818.34*

Source: Ministry of Finance (MOF) figures, Sun (2009).

Note: *The actual spending was higher than budgeted but the details were not transparent, therefore we just looked at the planned budget here to study its structure.

One of the most significant policies in support of the *san nong* sector has been the implementation of agricultural subsidies, especially the "four subsidies", which stand for the direct subsidy to grain farmers, the subsidies for agricultural input, the quality seeds subsidy and the subsidies for the purchase of agricultural machinery. As Table 10.1 shows, while these subsidies are not the main component of the central government's agricultural spending, they are quite significant and have also increased more rapidly than all the other expenditures. In addition, as indicated earlier, since the total amount of agricultural subsidies in China is very much within the limits set by the WTO, it leaves room for further increases in the future. In the following, we analyse the process of managing and implementing these four subsidies within the existing governmental structure.

The introduction of the "four subsidies"

While previously the financial support provided for rural areas was mainly distributed to agricultural institutions, organisations or corporations, the four subsidies have been allocated to farmers directly and distributed to almost every farmer in China (Huang *et al.* 2011). They are designed as an important means to guarantee the supply of major agricultural products and facilitate the increase of farmers' income (*Xinhua News* 2009), even though the effectiveness of the policy for the latter goal is still unclear at this stage. As indicated in the previous section, the introduction of the four subsidies is an institutional response to the *san nong* issue, as the Chinese government attempts to address the problems in rural areas and to improve the livelihoods of farmers. The scope of each subsidy is broader than simply a distribution of money, and positive spillovers are expected in the countryside. In order to understand the scope and aim of the subsidies, we provide an outline of each of them below.

The direct subsidy to grain farmers, or "direct subsidy" (zhongliang nongmin zhijie butie)

In 2002, the Ministry of Finance (MOF) began to conduct trials on the implementation of the direct subsidy in major agricultural provinces such as Anhui and Jilin. In 2004, following a two-year trial period, nationwide implementation started. The central government No.1 Document of the year stated:

> In order to protect the interests of grain producers, the direct subsidy system to farmers should be established. In 2004, the central government should allocate funds from the "grain risk funds"[5] to directly subsidise farmers in major grain-producing provinces. Other provinces (including autonomous regions and municipalities under the direct central administration) should also directly subsidise grain farmers in the grain-producing counties under their jurisdiction.
>
> (CCPCC and State Council 2004)

Accordingly, 11.6 billion yuan were distributed to grain producers in 29 provinces and autonomous regions (*People's Daily* 2004). The policy has been continuously implemented since (Table 10.2).

Generally speaking, farmers can receive this subsidy directly in cash or, more often, paid into a designated bank account. The amount varies according to the location of the farming household and the cultivated grain area. We can see from Table 10.2 that the total amount allocated for the direct subsidy has not increased in recent years. One reason for that is the limited budget of the grain risk funds. Since 2007, the expenditure on the direct subsidy has taken up more than 50 per cent of these funds. The consequences of this phenomenon will be discussed later.

The general subsidy for agricultural input, or "input subsidy" (nong zi zonghe butie)

The main reason for setting up the input subsidy was that the government increased the price of petroleum and petroleum products in 2006. In response to the rising cost of farming inputs such as diesel oil, fertilisers, and so on, the input subsidy was introduced in the same year to compensate for the additional input costs incurred by farmers. It was proposed by the MOF to the State Council with

Table 10.2 The amount of the direct subsidy to grain farmers, 2004–2011 (billion yuan)

Year	2004	2005	2006	2007	2008	2009	2010	2011
Amount*	11.6	13.2	14.2	15.1	15.1	15.1	15.1	15.1

Source: Compiled by the authors from different government reports.

Note: *Planned budget only. The actual spending could be different from these figures (see Table 10.3).

the approval of the Ministry of Agriculture (MOA) and the National Development and Reform Commission (NDRC). The MOF budgeted 12.5 billion yuan in 2006, but the actual expenditure of 12 billion yuan was less than planned (Table 10.3).

The quality seeds subsidy (liangzhong butie)

The quality seeds subsidy was introduced in 2002 for the purpose of revitalising soybean production. That year, the central government allocated 100 million yuan to promote improved soybean varieties. The coverage was 10 million mu[6] of soybean-growing land in Heilongjiang, Jilin, Liaoning and Inner Mongolia. Nowadays, farmers in designated project areas can receive 10 yuan per mu for growing certain promoted strains. It is important to note that not all the farmers in the project areas of those designated provinces are entitled to the subsidy. To be eligible, the farmer is also expected to plant the specific seeds.

The strains and covered areas eligible for the quality seeds subsidy have gradually expanded and the amount has increased. In 2003, the subsidy targeted soybean and wheat growers only, while the following year rice and corn farmers could also receive it. In more recent years, other crops such as cotton and colza have been added. Although this subsidy was introduced in 2002, it is only since 2004 that it has been expanded to cover the four most important crops – soybeans, wheat, rice and corn, which resulted in an enormous increase of the expenditure on the subsidy (Table 10.4, see p. 202). The central government has set clear-cut criteria for its distribution, which is not the case for the other three subsidies. For example, a farmer who is living in the project area can receive 10 yuan per mu for sowing quality soybean, wheat and corn seeds and 15 yuan per mu for quality cotton seeds. Table 10.4 shows the detailed budget related to this subsidy.

The agricultural machinery subsidy (nongye jixie gouzhi butie)

The agricultural machinery subsidy has been jointly managed by MOF and MOA since 2004[7] when the central government allocated 70 million yuan to subsidise farmers and some service organisations, which required the use of

Table 10.3 The amount of the general subsidy for agricultural input, 2006–2011 (billion yuan)

Year	2006	2007	2008	2009	2010	2011
Amount	12	27.6	63.8*	75.6**	83.5	86

Source: Compiled by the authors from different government reports.

Notes
*The amount increased substantially in 2008 because of further price rises for petroleum and petroleum products that year.

**According to the draft budget, the MOF arranged 123.08 billion yuan for the four subsidies in 2009. However, the total real expenditure of the four subsidies was 127.45 billion yuan. The final amount of each subsidy has not been publicly announced except for the direct subsidy to grain farmers, so the amount of the other three subsidies in 2009 is based on the planned budget.

Table 10.4 The amount of the quality seeds subsidy, 2002–2011 (billion yuan)

Year	2002	2003	2004	2005	2006	2007	2008	2009	2010	2011
Amount	0.1	0.3	2.85	3.87	4.15	6.66	12.34[*]	15.48	20.4	22

Source: Compiled by the authors from different government reports.

Note: [*]The amount has increased substantially since 2008.

agricultural machinery and tools. The establishment of this subsidy was to encourage and support farmers to buy advanced and appropriate agricultural machinery, to promote mechanisation, to improve agricultural productivity and to increase farmers' income (MOF and MOA 2005). The central government did not lay down clear and strict guidelines, so provincial governments have to decide how to implement the scheme. The only rule set by the central state is that the money a farmer receives should not exceed 30 per cent of the machinery's price. Table 10.5 shows the budgetary details relating to this subsidy from 2004 to 2011.

As shown above, each subsidy has its own purpose; however, in practice, farmers sometimes have difficulties distinguishing between them (Huang *et al.* 2011). Furthermore, an aspect often neglected in existing research is the way these subsidies are managed. Here we hypothesise that the effectiveness of these subsidies is not only dependent on their purpose, but also on their design and implementation, which can vary considerably according to the governmental bodies that implement the policy at the central and local levels. In other words, and in accordance with Scoones (2009), the way policies are designed and implemented may affect the livelihoods of the rural population. Bearing this in mind, we now turn to examine this aspect of the policy of agricultural subsidies by focusing on two schemes: the "direct subsidy to grain farmers" and the "quality seeds subsidy" in our case study of Jilin Province.

Implementation and management of the "four subsidies"

The four subsidies can be divided into two categories on the basis of the government body administering them. The direct subsidy and the input subsidy are mainly controlled by the MOF and its financial departments at the lower levels of government. In contrast, the quality seeds subsidy and the agricultural machinery subsidy are jointly managed by the MOF and the MOA, and administered by their financial and agricultural departments at the lower levels of government. This division of responsibility has important implications for the implementation and daily management of the different subsidy programmes.

Table 10.5 The amount of the agricultural machinery subsidy, 2004–2011 (billion yuan)

Year	2004	2005	2006	2007	2008	2009	2010	2011
Amount	0.07	0.3	0.6	2	4	13	15.5	17.5

Source: Compiled by the authors from different government reports.

Additionally, the first two subsidies share at least two other characteristics. First, their money flows in a similar way as they are directly paid into the farmers' bank accounts. Second, both are given to grain producers only. In fact, the input subsidy also becomes a kind of direct subsidy to provide incentives for agricultural producers to grow grain. In contrast, the latter two subsidies are more specialised. Both went through a trial period by the MOA before being put into full practice. In addition, farmers do not receive the funds directly in cash. Instead, they are subsidised when they buy designated products and machineries, and the discounts are already included in the purchasing price. The local financial departments then settle the price differentials with the manufacturers after the sale. Because of these characteristics, we can call the first two subsidies "direct subsidies" and the latter two "indirect subsidies" despite the existence of minor discrepancies. For example, the quality seeds subsidy was a direct subsidy when it was first introduced in 2004. However, the situation has become more complicated since 2009 when the subsidy for improved corn and rapeseeds also became a direct subsidy. In addition, the subsidy for improved wheat, soybean and cotton seeds can be direct or indirect, depending on the way it is implemented by provincial governments. Despite these variations, the categorisation remains valid in general. Below we focus on one subsidy in each of the two groups – the direct subsidy to grain farmers and the quality seeds subsidy – taken from our Jilin case study, to analyse their implementation and management and to evaluate the extent to which the policy goals and objectives are achieved.

Management and implementation of the direct subsidy to grain farmers

According to the MOF, the main purposes of this subsidy are to stabilise and develop grain production, enhance its overall capacity, protect grain producers' interests, and provide incentives for farmers to grow grain (MOF 2004). The subsidy is thus an institutional device designed to reshape farmers' livelihood strategies, boost agricultural development, and safeguard national food security. The expected changes may not only be induced by the direct impact of the subsidy on farmers' revenues (since the total amount remains relatively small), but also indirectly, since farmers may also have specific reactions to the new policy environment. The design and implementation of the subsidy are therefore important for the overall success of the policy. However, whether the policy goal of the subsidy can be reached is still a pending question, partly due to its allocation principles.

First, according to the requirements of the MOF, 13 major grain-producing provinces[8] were allocated a total of 10 billion yuan in 2004, 40 per cent of which came from the grain risk fund of the provinces concerned. The participation of the risk fund is significant because it means that the central government considers that the subsidy has been set up to cover, directly or indirectly, the risks faced by farmers in growing grain. The fact that the subsidy is allocated annually suggests two possibilities: that risks are considered permanent, or that the fund is used for an objective other than those determined by design, which can, in turn, affect its effectiveness, e.g. in the case of natural disasters (these two factors are not mutually exclusive, however). In any event, it shows that the design of the subsidy is the result of an imperfect compromise and arbitration – government funding being limited in nature – that can jeopardise its main objective of market stabilisation.[9] It also shows that the notion of risk is at the centre of the decision-making process for implementing this subsidy, with the definition of risk not only encompassing natural disasters, but also including risks of a decreased rice cultivation area, social unrest, and rural protests, to name but a few.

Second, the 13 provinces have to set their own criteria for calculating and distributing the subsidy based on one of the three following factors: the taxed area, the taxed output, or the planting area. Moreover, the planting area can be calculated in two different ways. In practice, the finance offices in townships and villages provide individual farmers with a grain subsidy notice at the beginning of the year. The farmers then go to the finance office with the notice to receive the money (MOF 2004). In 2005, more guidelines were issued by the MOF on the implementation of the subsidy policy. Since then, the major grain-producing provinces have been required to distribute the subsidy based on the actual planting area. If these provinces are to adopt other criteria for distributing the money, they should not take into account non-grain factors but must try to stay close to the planting area principle (MOF 2005).

There have been considerable local variations in allocating and administering the subsidy funds and our fieldwork conducted in only one province may not allow us to provide detailed discussion on how and why such local variations arise and persist. Nevertheless, our analysis is useful for understanding the way in which the institutional framework affects the livelihoods of farmers. We may hypothesise, for example, that when the arrangement seems to be less favourable for some groups of the targeted population or geographical areas, a certain sense of unfairness might arise, in particular among poorer farmers. In other words, our analysis can shed light on the ways in which different distribution principles are selected, as well as the ways that compromises between different agents/agencies (local governments, provincial governments, financial bureaus, etc.) are reached. We now turn to examine existing practices in Jilin.

As indicated earlier, the regulations laid down by the MOF are, to some extent, detailed but complex. As a result, they are subject to local interpretations at the phase of implementation – a point further illustrated by our Jilin case study. In this province, the amount of direct subsidy to grain farmers in 2006 was 1.92 billion yuan (Jilin Provincial People's Government 2006). This amount, however, was decided by a specific office in the MOF in a largely opaque way, which could affect the perception of its legitimacy and induce a sense of unfairness among local populations. At the provincial level, the finance department decided to distribute the total amount based on the proportion of the average marketable farm product of each county. Thus, the total direct subsidy to grain farmers in Dongliao County, for example, was set at 381 million yuan that year. Then, according to the requirements of the provincial government, lower-level authorities should also distribute the subsidy fund based on the same principle. In reality, however, finance offices at the village level decided to allocate the subsidy among the villagers based on the taxed grain-growing area. Further complexities arose when in some other villages the subsidy was distributed according to the grain production output (Jilin Finance Department 2006).

We can draw a few insights from the above discussion. On the one hand, we may hypothesise that universal application of the general principle and rules set by the central government would result in a more equitable distribution of the subsidy fund across the country, and that divergences at the local level could introduce biases and distortions leading to unequal or unfair treatment, and thus be detrimental to local farmers' livelihoods. On the other hand, it can also be argued that the flexibility and discretion allowed to local actors during policy implementation could benefit the local population because village and township officials who better understand the local situation are able to determine the most suitable way of allocating the subsidy, provided, of course, that they do not try to favour their own friends and relatives. Given the vastness of China and the huge differences in local conditions, it is very difficult to judge which of the two implementation methods as stated above would best meet the needs and interests of the farmers in a specific locale. This indeterminacy is confirmed by the diverging conclusions reached by other researchers: based on large sets of quantitative data, Huang *et al.* (2011) argued that the subsidies were distributed equitably without disadvantaging the poor, while Lin and Wong (2012), on the contrary, found that poorer farmers were discriminated against during the allocation of subsidies.

The complexity and huge regional differences in the distribution of the subsidy are only one side of the coin and there are also issues related to the tax base used to distribute the subsidy fund. Two points are worth noting here. First, the finance department in Jilin decided to calculate the "taxed" output based on the average marketable farm product from 1994 to 1998. However, the agricultural tax was abolished in Jilin in 2004, and thus the "taxed" production data became outdated. Therefore, the method selected at the local levels to distribute the subsidy was in clear contradiction to the principles set up by the MOF that are based on the current planting area. The distribution of the funds was decided based on rules and principles that the finance departments found convenient to implement, and which were set according to the data they had to hand without fully considering the designated purpose of the subsidy and the needs of the farmers. The departments involved in the implementation process were unable or unwilling to change their rules of operation to increase the effectiveness of the subsidy. Under such circumstances it was, therefore, questionable whether farmers' enthusiasm to produce grain was really stimulated by this direct subsidy. While this may not be the case everywhere, our analysis shows that even in the absence of discrimination against poorer farmers and/or corruption, equitable and effective distribution of subsidies could be adversely affected by institutional inertia, such as bureaucratic routines, with the decision-making of local cadres complying with these routines regardless of whether they were in alignment with the rules and principles laid down by the higher level of government.

Possibly a better way to deal with the issue would have been to involve the local governments' agricultural departments in the implementation and management of the subsidy, since this would have resulted in officials being more aware of, as well as sympathetic to, the situation of farmers. However, the origin of the subsidy (managed and implemented by the MOF and the finance departments at the provincial and local levels) largely prevents this type of cooperation, at least in Jilin, because it would require both organisations to make compromises, negotiate and even bend their own operating rules. This was evidenced during the fieldwork interviews – when officials in the agricultural departments at the provincial and county level were asked about their knowledge of, and involvement in, allocating the direct subsidy to grain farmers, they said that they had nothing to do with or knew little about it. This indicated that the agricultural departments at the local levels were largely excluded from the process. Without their input, the governments at these levels delivered the subsidy according to outdated data to hand, as shown above, and the finance departments alone issued all the relevant documents and regulations.

However, in other provinces, the situation can be very different and real cooperation between the two administrative bodies may take place. In some locations, the finance bureau informs the agriculture bureau when the subsidy is distributed. In other areas, the finance and agriculture bureaus collaborate, and together they issue documents to guide lower-level authorities on the allocation of the direct subsidy to grain farmers. For example, the agriculture departments of local authorities in Jiangsu Province are responsible for determining the subsidy areas, while the finance departments are in charge of managing and dispersing the funds. The cooperation seems not to have occurred through institutional arrangements, however, but instead is contingent on the personal relations and professional networks (*guanxi*) among the government officials concerned. So far as we are aware, there have not been formal policies explicitly requiring the involvement of the agricultural departments in this respect.

In conclusion, our analysis of the implementation of the direct subsidy to grain farmers reveals certain characteristics that affect its effectiveness. These characteristics are dictated by internal and often unwritten rules and practices at various administrative levels of the Chinese bureaucracy, as well as by constraints that affect the decision-making process. First, the fact that a significant part of the subsidy derives from the grain risk fund implies that the risks that farmers face are considered permanent, and that the subsidy is provided in order to guarantee farmers a certain level of income and protect them against such risks. However, risks are multiple and diverse by nature, e.g. the household-level risks differ from larger issues of social stability or food security. This vagueness and lack of clarity have serious implications not only for the subsidy, but also for the management of the risk funds. Second, the subsidy is directly managed by the MOF and its bureaus at provincial and local levels, and largely excludes the MOA and its local branches. As our analysis demonstrates, this is problematic since it introduces biases and new uncertainties; particularly due to the fact that the local finance bureaus distributed the fund according to the (often outdated) information available to them and on the basis of their own internal mode of operation, leading to variations and divergences from the principles set by the central government. While distortion of national policies at the local level during implementation has been examined by many researchers (cf. Augustin-Jean and Xue 2011), our Jilin case is somewhat different in that the process involves not only personal interests and power relations, but also the mode of operation of the bureaucratic apparatus itself.

It is also interesting to note that some readjustments, or compromises, have been made in certain locales, where agriculture bureaus, which are not officially designated to be part of the management and implementation of the direct subsidy, have been involved in the policy process. This may suggest that personal and professional networks developed among local actors are crucial to smooth the system and allow for flexibility in rules and a suitable course of action to deal with the institutional uncertainties. At the same time, however, this may introduce new uncertainties for the farmers and affect their livelihoods in other ways.

Management and implementation of the quality seeds subsidy

The quality seeds subsidy was introduced in 2004 and was jointly managed and implemented by the MOF and MOA. That year, the two ministries jointly formulated an interim regulation with the aim of providing the subsidy for rice, wheat, corn and soybeans. Its goal was to promote the adoption of improved crop strains locally and then extend it regionally, and to improve the quality of agricultural products. The subsidy was distributed first in the "project zones" that had been established for this purpose. Farmers who lived in these zones could make their own decision on whether to use the improved seeds or not. If they decided to do so, they received 10 yuan per mu for the crops through the seed companies. The size of the subsidy increased year after year in proportion to the expansion of the "project zones". Since 2009, the quality seeds subsidy for improved rice and wheat strains has expanded to cover the whole country. Before we turn to analyse its implementation, we first provide some background information on the evolution of this subsidy policy. It is also important to distinguish between the management of the subsidy for rice strains and for other seeds.

When the subsidy was first initiated, provincial governments were supposed to determine which seeds should be subsidised. In addition, they were also responsible for selecting the enterprises and/or units (e.g. research centres, administrative bodies, etc.) that were to provide the designated seeds through a tendering exercise. It is clear that farmers did not receive the money directly, which was, instead, distributed by reimbursing the seed companies (this is why we consider the subsidy an indirect one). However, the subsidy to rice strains was managed differently since, when it was originally designed in 2004, it was organised as a direct subsidy. That year, the central government decided to subsidise rice farmers in major rice-producing areas as an incentive to expand the planting area and increase the rice supply. The subsidy was set up in seven major rice-producing provinces: Hunan, Jiangxi, Jilin, Hubei, Anhui, Heilongjiang and Liaoning.

Its allocation was determined in accordance with the planting area, based on the taxed area in 2003. One month after sowing, the provincial finance and agricultural departments would jointly apply for the subsidy from the MOF and MOA. The MOA would then verify the sowing area and the MOF would dispatch the subsidy fund to the provincial budget (Jilin Finance Department 2006). As the subsidy for improved rice strains was based on the planting area, farmers received it regardless of whether they made use of the improved rice seeds. To some extent, like the grain subsidy, this also has become a direct subsidy to rice producers.

The reasons for these differences are difficult to grasp, but it may be partially due to the fact that the subsidy initially resulted from a compromise between the MOF, which aimed to increase rice production but may not be so concerned with the technical improvement of seeds, and the MOA, which had a different and broader agenda. Notwithstanding these differences, in 2009, the MOF and MOA adjusted the way they distributed the quality seeds subsidy. A new regulation was introduced allowing for the subsidy for improved rice, corn and rapeseed strains to be provided to farmers in cash and the specific method to allocate the money was to be decided by the provincial governments. This new regulation was intended to simplify the procedure and improve services for farmers. The provincial governments, therefore, were to decide if they should subsidise farmers for other improved strains, such as wheat, soybean and cotton directly in cash or through a differentiated pricing system as happened previously (MOF and MOA 2009). In other words, any provincial government which does not subsidise farmers directly can maintain the existing tender system. According to a 2009 survey, only Shandong, Shanxi, major wheat-producing areas in Anhui, and some areas in Henan continued with the differentiated pricing method to subsidise wheat producers, while most other provinces decided to subsidise farmers directly. At the same time, Shandong, Xinjiang and Hunan also adopted the differentiated pricing method to subsidise cotton producers.

It is worth noting that since 2004 grain production has increased year on year and a report by the MOF and MOA (2006) showed that the quality seeds subsidy achieved "five increases". First, the sown grain acreage increased. Second, grain production grew enormously. In 2004, the average per mu yield of wheat in the project zones was 97 kilograms, or 36.9 per cent higher than that in the rest of the country. The average per mu yields of corn and soybeans in these zones were also 50 kilogrammes and 34.7 kilogrammes higher, respectively, than in other areas. In 2005, the average per mu yields of wheat, silage corn and soybeans in the project zones were 20.9 per cent, 19.3 per cent and 15.1 per cent higher, respectively, than in other areas. Third, the quality of the crops improved. Fourth, the revenue from the sales also increased. Finally, the level of industrialisation of agriculture had been enhanced due to greater concentration of the production belts. It seems that all of the above benefits, apart from the first one, came from the spread of improved seeds and the supporting technology. Nevertheless, the conclusions may be not so clear, as a heated debate about the method of distribution of the quality seeds subsidy has been ongoing for several years with some supporting the original tender system while others argu-ing for direct cash subsidies. The pros and cons of these two positions are presented below.

On the one hand, the aim of the subsidy and the way it was designed seem adequate. If farmers can use the improved seeds along with the support technol-ogy, the production and quality of grain should improve. Since farmers also keep part of their own yield as seeds, using better seeds is expected to lead to increased production. In addition, if the local government promotes trading good strains by means of an open tender, it would not distort the market. If all the designed goals were achieved satisfactorily, the policy would not need to change. We will show, however, that in reality distortions occurred and farmers suffered serious losses. According to the principle and procedure set by the MOF and MOA, provincial governments should select the units that provide the improved seeds through a tender exercise. However, most provincial governments delegated the task to lower-level authorities. This practice often led to local favouritism and unfair competition as the agriculture departments at the county level tended to select their own seed companies. Although the central leadership had decided to sepa-rate local governments from local commercial organisations and activities in 2000, this separation is either ineffective or incomplete, and many enterprises still maintain strong ties with local authorities. When the project zones were small, the business of other seed companies was not seriously affected as they could still sell in areas outside the zones. However, as the subsidy increased, covering even entire regions, those seed companies that were not selected would not be able to survive unless they produce much cheaper seeds. The selected firms, however, could not always produce good quality seeds in sufficient quantity and thus might deliver lower grade ones. Consequently, not only was local protec-tionism frequent, but there was also a general decline in the quality of seeds, which jeopardised both farmers' interests and overall agricultural production.

It is clear, therefore, that not only the policy matters, but also its design and implementation. A rational choice perspective would consider the tender proce-dure the best possible approach, since it would allow the selection of the most competitive firms to distribute the subsidised improved seeds along with the subsidy. Thus, policies would only need to be readjusted in order to disseminate the necessary information on the procedure as widely as possible without distort-ing the market. However, as we have demonstrated above, this perspective fails to take into account the asymmetry of information that exists in the seed business as well as in China's economy in general. After all, to what extent can farmers be confident about the information provided at the local level? In China, as in other developing countries, the answer is not always obvious and may lead to unex-pected choices and distortions. Therefore, many farmers favour the newly adjusted subsidy policy, which directly allocates the funds to them. For instance, one farmer interviewee told Ye Wang that he preferred the new distribution method, as he was not confident in the seeds sold by the firms selected by the government. He considered the subsidised seeds in the county to be inferior because the agri-cultural department did not select the best seeds firms, as he observed: "I know which seed is better. They can't fool me." As we have discussed above, local governments' protectionist practices tend to manipulate and distort the market. Thus, while the tender system seems to meet the objective of the subsidy, i.e. to encourage farmers to use improved seeds, the existing institutional constraints render such a design less effective, and therefore direct subsidies are more suitable, leaving less room for biases and uncertainties for the farmers.

Conclusion

By the early 2000s, the "three rural issues" had become so prominent that the Chinese central government started formulating and implementing a series of policies to address them. Among these policies, the introduction of agricultural subsidies, particularly the four subsidies, could be considered a significant reversal of earlier policies of systematic extraction of rural surplus and a move towards the direction of supporting farmers instead. Given that the subsidy policy is quite new, research on the topic, though emerging, has thus far been insufficient, and there is a general lack of academic effort to evaluate these new initiatives in terms of whether and how they have met (or failed to meet) the policy goals and objectives, and the ways in which they have impacted on rural livelihoods. This chapter, based on an empirical case study, deals with this neglected area by examining the design and implementation of the four subsidies policy, and by interrogating some of the institutional arrangements which have shaped policy outcomes and, as a result, farmers' livelihoods.

We argue that the success of the subsidy policy depends largely on its design and implementation, and that it is important to take into account and prevent the introduction of new risks and uncertainties at all levels of the decision-making process. At the national level, all aspects of the subsidy design should be considered, and not just the policy objectives and fund distribution method. As our analysis shows, the decision to put the MOF alone in charge of the implementation of the direct subsidy for grain farmers and the lack of involvement of, and coordination with, the MOA have resulted in policy outcomes divergent from the originally designed goals, as well as a feeling of unfairness among local farmers regarding the distribution of the fund. However, without more systematic research on the topic, it is difficult to know if later adjustments at the local level have improved the situation. We have also shown that when a policy concerns two government ministries, problems often arise with regard to effective policy implementation because different organisational configurations (e.g. different modes of operation) and existing institutional obstacles (e.g. different objectives conceived by different government bodies) hinder the negotiation process necessary to overcome the bureaucratic rigidity.

At the provincial level, the government has attempted to adjust the method of fund distribution in alignment with policy goals and perceived economic and societal benefits. This explains the flexibility that provinces are granted in respect of how they distribute the subsidy funds, but, at the same time, this introduces new biases. Similarly, the decision to allow more power to the county government in the distribution of funds may be viewed positively, since lower-level authorities are often better aware of the local situation. However, as we have demonstrated in the chapter, this "decentralisation" in decision-making has introduced new uncertainties, which, in the end, may jeopardise farmers' interests and local livelihoods. Such a scenario suggests that local actors pursue their own projects based on their perceived interests intertwined with complex political and social relations, which often leads to unintended policy outcomes. Our case study of the quality seed subsidy illustrates that local institutional actors tend to take advantage of their power and practise local protectionism and personal favouritism, resulting in policy distortions. Moreover, our research suggests that provincial and local governments should take more effective action to disseminate information about the subsidies and their distribution among farmers in order to raise awareness and prevent a situation where farmers are unaware of their existence, as reported by Huang *et al.* (2011), or where the policy is implemented in a way that discriminates against those most in need, as documented by Lin and Wong (2012). Thus, and following Scoones (2009), we argue that appropriate and effective policy-making aimed at strengthening the livelihoods of farmers should take into account the policy's "architecture", and allow for negotiation, flexibility and accommodation of the diversity in the rules of operation of the different government administrative bodies involved.

Finally, the present research analyses and evaluates the new agricultural subsidy policy focusing on its design and implementation. As such, it does not address questions surrounding farmers' own experiences and how they perceive the advantages and disadvantages of the new policy in respect of its impact on their livelihoods, needs and interests. This is an obvious limitation of this research, which is only partly compensated by the wide range of sources collected in the field and incorporated into the analysis. Indeed, a number of scholars have attempted to address some key questions, such as whether the subsidies have effectively reached the targeted population, or reshaped the pattern of rural-urban migration, and so forth. There are signs that, despite the moderate size of the subsidies distributed by the central government relative to the large rural population, the introduction of these schemes has been quite beneficial in terms of boosting agricultural production. That said, more in-depth qualitative research providing perspectives of the farming households is required in order to gain a deeper understanding of the impact of the subsidy policy on the lives and livelihoods of rural people.

Notes

1 In the same vein, despite repeated claims in the Chinese media, it is still unclear if the policy has led to increased grain production. For divergent opinions on this point, see Huang *et al.* (2011), and Veeck and Shui (2011). See also below.
2 However, Lin and Wong (2012) consider all the direct subsidies received by farmers in the context of the *san nong* policy, including transfers for social welfare, while Huang *et al.* (2011) only take into account subsidies linked to agricultural production.

3 Interestingly, Huang *et al.* indicate that a significant number of households in their surveyed sample (11.4 per cent) do not know the amount of subsidies they receive (2011: 58, Table 1). The reasons are uncertain, but an explanation, not provided by the authors, would be that for some farmers, the amount of subsidies is too small to be noticed. This explanation is supported by the fact that the subsidy increases by 32 per cent in the rich province of Zhejiang but only by 1.7 per cent and 1.4 per cent respectively for Liaoning and Sichuan.
4 The fieldwork was conducted by Ye Wang (2010) for her postgraduate dissertation. Due to space constraints, we cannot provide a full justification for our selection of the fieldwork site here. Suffice it to say that the main considerations for selecting Jilin are that it is a major grain producer and one of the few regions in which the policy of subsidies was first piloted. For more details, see Wang (2010: 29–30) and Gale *et al.* (2005).
5 Grain risk funds were set up in 1998 in each province to stabilise markets and cover the costs of the support programmes. Both central and provincial governments have contributed to the fund.
6 One mu is equivalent to 1/15 of a hectare.
7 The MOA had some experimental funds to subsidise farmers before 2004.
8 These are Heilongjiang, Jilin, Liaoning, Hebei, Henan, Shandong, Jiangsu, Anhui, Hunan, Hubei, Sichuan, Jiangxi, and Inner Mongolia Autonomous Region.
9 As Lin and Wong state, "The central government provides for less than one-quarter of all budgetary expenditures, and this share has fallen sharply over the past decade" (2012: 33–34).

References

Augustin-Jean, Louis and Ruining Xue (2011), The nature of cooperatives in China: The implementation and paradoxes of the law on cooperatives in Shanxi Province. In Bejorn Alpermann (ed.), *Politics and Markets in Rural China*. London: Routledge, pp. 187–201.

Bai, Nansheng and Yupeng He (2002), *Huixiang haishi waichu: Anhui Sichuan er sheng nongcun waichu laodongli huiliu yanjiu* [Returning to native place or emigrating to big cities for work: A study in Anhui and Sichuan on the phenomenon of migrant workers returning home from the cities]. *Sociological Research 3*.

CCPCC (Chinese Communist Party Central Committee) and the State Council (2004), *Guanyu chujin nongmin zengjia shouru ruogan zhengce de yijian* [Some proposals on the policy to promote the increase of farmers' income] No. 1 Document, 8 February. Available at: http://news.xinhuanet.com/zhengfu/2004-02/09/content_1304169.htm (accessed 10 April 2010).

Chen, Xiwen (2004), *Jiedu zhongyang nongcun gongzuo huiyi jingshen* [Understanding the spirit of the Central Rural Work Conference], 9 January. Available at: www.glxany.gov.cn/view.asp?articleid=2558 (accessed 10 April 2010).

de Gorter, Harry and Johan Swinnen (2002), Political economy of agricultural policy. In Bruce L. Gardner and Gordon C. Rausser (eds), *Handbook of Agricultural Economics*, vol. 2a. Amsterdam: Elsevier, pp. 1893–1943.

Gale, Fred, Bryan Lomar and Francis Tuan (2005), China's new farm subsidies. *Electronic Outlook Report from the Economic Research Service*, WRS-05-01, USDA, February.

Huang, Jikun, Xiaobing Wang, Huayong Zhi, Zhurong Huang and Scott Rozelle (2011), Subsidies and distortions in China's agriculture: Evidence from producer-level data. *Australian Journal of Agricultural and Resource Economics* 55(1): 53–71.

Jilin Finance Department (2006), *Jinlin sheng 2006 nian dui zhongliang nongmin zhijie butie gongzuo shishi fang'an* [The 2006 implementation scheme on the work of direct subsidies to grain producers in Jilin], 21 March. Available at: www.cccz.gov.cn/wai/pubtemplet/%7B538116AD-AF2A-4978-B786-5A2A1621E91C%7D.asp?infoid=3117& style=%7B538116AD-AF2A-4978-B786-5A2A1621E91C%7D (accessed 10 April 2010).

Jilin Provincial People's Government (2006), *2005 nian yusuan zhixing qingkuang he 2006 nian yusuan cao'an de baogao* [Report on the budget implementation in 2005 and budget draft in 2006]. Available at: www.jl.gov.cn/zwxx/zfgzbg/sjczysjs/200603/t20060309_122116.htm (accessed 20 April 2010).

Khan, Azizur Rahman and Carl Riskin (1998), Income and inequality in China: Composition, distribution and growth of household income, 1988 to 1995. *The China Quarterly* 154: 221–253.

Li, Changping (2000), *Xiang Zhu Rongji zongli xiexin* [Letter to Premier Zhu Rongji], *Xinhua News*, 2 March. Available at: http://news.qq.com/a/20090927/000760.htm (accessed 13 May 2010).

Lin, Wanlong and Christine Wong (2012), Are Beijing's equalisation policies reaching the poor? An analysis of direct subsidies under the "three rurals" (*san nong*). *The China Journal* 67: 23–45.

Meng, Lei (2012), Can grain subsidies impede rural-urban migration in hinterland China? Evidence from fieldwork surveys. *China Economic Review* 23: 729–741.

MOF (Ministry of Finance) (2004), *Shixing dui zhongliang nongmin zhijie butie tiaozheng liangshi fengxian jijin shiyong fanwei de shishi yijian* [The suggestion on implementing direct subsidies to grain producers and adjusting the application scope of grain risk funds], 24 March. Available at: http://ha.mof.gov.cn/gp/jingjijianshesi/200806/t20080624_50340.html (accessed 2 January 2012).

MOF (Ministry of Finance) (2005), *Guanyu jinyibu wanshan dui zhonglian nongmin zhijie butie zhengce de yijian* [The opinion on further improving the direct subsidy policy to grain producers], 3 February. Available at: http://202.123.110.3/ztzl/2005-12/30/content_142985.htm (accessed 15 April 2010).

MOF and Ministry of Agriculture (MOA) (2005), *Nongye jixie gouzhi butie zhuanxiang zijin shiyong guanli zhanxing banfa* [The interim regulations on the use and administration of the subsidy for agricultural machinery], 25 February. Available at: www.agri.gov.cn/cwgk/czzxgl/nyjx/t20070201_767666.htm (accessed 15 April 2010).

MOF and MOA (2006), *Liangzhong butie fahuile lianghao de zhengce xiaoying* [The subsidy for improved crop strains shows good effects], 15 May. Available at: http://nys.mof.gov.cn/zhengfuxinxi/qkfy/200807/t20080717_57858.html (accessed 13 April 2010).

MOF and MOA (2009), *Zhongyang caizheng nongzuowu liangzhong butie zijin guanli banfa* [Regulations on the use and administration of the subsidy for improved crop strains from central finance], 14 December. Available at: http://nys.mof.gov.cn/zhengfuxinxi/czpjZhengCeFaBu_2_2/201001/t20100106_257120.html (accessed 18 March 2010).

OECD (2005), Agricultural policy reform in China. *Policy Brief*, October. Available at: www.oecd.org/dataoecd/3/48/35543482.pdf (accessed 10 April 2010).

People's Daily (2004), *Caizheng buzhang Jin Renqing: Liangshi zhibu, zhengce daowei nongmin manyi* [Finance Minister Jin Renqing: Direct subsidy to grain producers, satisfactory policy for farmers], 13 October. Available at: www.people.com.cn/GB/jingji/1046/2915608.html (accessed 2 May 2010).

Scoones, Ian (2009), Livelihoods perspectives and rural development. *The Journal of Peasant Studies* 36(1): 171–196.

Sun, Yong (2009), *Jinnian zhongyong caizheng jianghui caiqu si cuoshi zhichi sannong* [The central finance will take four measures to support agriculture, the countryside and farmers this year]. *Jingji ribao*, 20 May.

Veeck, Gregory and Wei Shui (2011), China's quiet agricultural revolution: Policy and programs of the new millennium. *Eurasian Geography and Economics* 52(2): 242–263.

Wang, Ye (2010), The management and implementation of agricultural subsidies in China: The case study of the "four subsidies". Master's dissertation, University of Tsukuba, Japan, May.

Wen, Jiabao (2009), *Zhengfu gongzuo baogao* [Report of the government]. The 2nd Session of the 11th National People's Congress, 5 March. Available at: www.china.com.cn/policy/txt/2009-03/14/content_17444081.htm (accessed 10 April 2010).

Xinhua News (2009), *Zhongguo jiang zai WTO kuangjiaxia dafu zengjia nongye butie* [China will substantially raise its agricultural subsidies under the WTO framework], 2 February. Available at: http://news.xinhuanet.com/newscenter/2009-02/02/content_10752205_1.htm (accessed 12 January 2010).

Zhang, Zhongfa (2008), *1949–2007: Zhongguo nongcun gaige yu fazhan 58 nian* [1949–2007: 58 years of reform and development in Chinese rural areas], *China Report*, vol. II. Available at: www.china.com.cn/book/zhuanti/qkjc/txt/2008-02/25/content_10688105.htm (accessed 15 October 2009).

Glossary of Chinese terms

bangongshi   general office (of an organisation)
bianzhi   state staffing system, staff within the formal payroll
bingtuan   state/regiment farms in frontier regions, e.g. Xinjiang, Heilongjiang
changzhu renkou   regular residents with urban local *hukou*
chengshihua   urbanisation
chengshi wailai renkou   population from outside the city without permanent local *hukou*, or rural migrants in the city
chengxiang yitihua or chengxiang tongchou   urban-rural integration
chengzhen zhigong   urban enterprises' employees with local *hukou*
chengzhongcun   village-in-the-city; urban village
chuizhi danwei   vertical agencies (in the government structure)
cunbu shuji or cun zhishu   village Party Secretary
cun fu gan   village women's representative
cun wenshu   village clerk, village accountant
cun zhang or cunhui zhuren   village head
cunzhe   bank account booklet
dabao   big contractors
dagong   go to the city to work, work for others
dai gong   labour-use facilitators or informal labour recruitment agent
dan ban xuexiao   single-room primary school
duizhe gan   outright conflict
gaowei qiye   enterprises engaging in hazardous work
geren zhanghu   an individual account for social insurance contributions
gongdao   justice, fairness
gonggong zhishifenzi   "public intellectuals"
gongqian   work money, wage, pay
gongshang rending   work injury classification certificate
gongzi   work payment, wage
goujian hexie shehui   building a harmonious society
guanxi   social network, social connections
Guojia baqi fupin gongjian jihua   the 8-7 national poverty reduction programme
Guojia fupin tiexi daikuan   national poverty alleviation microloan programme

Guowuyuan xinfang bangongshi the State Council's office for dealing with petitions

heixin the worst conscience

hei zhensuo private medical clinic without formal licence

hukou household registration

jumin residents

kong di unoccupied land

laodong zhongcai labour dispute resolution and arbitration

laoxiang people from one's home region (e.g. village, township, county, province)

laoxiang zhensuo private clinic (without formal licence) run by people from one's home region

liangzhong butie quality seeds subsidy

mamu numbness, apathy, indifference

mishu personal secretary to senior officials

mu Chinese measurement of area, with one mu equivalent to about 1/15 of a hectare

nao make noise and create a disturbance

neihao in-fighting, internal conflict

nongcun rural areas, the countryside

nongmin farmers, rural people

nongmingong migrant workers or migrants

nongye agriculture

nongye butie agricultural subsidy

nongye jixie gouzhi butie agricultural machinery subsidy

nongzi zonghe butie general subsidy for agricultural input

qing bao labour-supply subcontractors

qing shui yamen clear water agencies (local government departments with no money or power)

qu district

renmin gongshe people's communes

san nong wenti the three rural issues

shangfang or xinfang petitioning higher levels of government (by letters and visits)

shehui tongchou common social pool of various pension schemes

shengchan dadui production brigade

shenghuo fei living allowance

shengwu anquan fa biosafety law

shi city

shujie minkun tackling livelihood difficulties of ordinary citizens

si butie the four subsidies

siliao settle privately

suzhi human quality

tao yige shuofa demand an explanation

tongchouqu different local pools for various social insurance schemes' funds

wagong masonry and tiling, semi-skilled labour

weifa   against the law
xiang   township
xiangbao   rural agents (during the pre-1949 Republican era)
xiao bao   labour-supply subcontractors
xiaogong   unskilled labourer
xiapai ganbu   sent-down cadre, dispatched official
xingzheng cun   administrative village
xinshengdai nongmingong   new generation of migrants
yanglao baoxian   old-age insurance or pension schemes
yihao wenjian   central government No. 1 Document
yiliao baoxian ben   medical insurance booklet
yiren weiben   people-centred or people-oriented
you qian you quan   having money and power
zhen   town
Zhongguo renshou   China Life Insurance Company
zhongliang nongmin zhijie butie   direct subsidy to grain farmers
zhuangxiu   internal renovation
zhuren   director
ziju   proof or evidence

Index

Page references for figures are in *italics* and tables are shown in **bold**.